BEHIND
the VEIL
OF VICE

BEHIND the VEIL OF VICE

The Business and Culture of Sex in the Middle East

JOHN R. BRADLEY

palgrave
macmillan

BEHIND THE VEIL OF VICE
Copyright © John R. Bradley, 2010.
All rights reserved.

First published in 2010 by PALGRAVE MACMILLAN® in the U.S.—a
division of St. Martin's Press LLC, 175 Fifth Avenue, New York, NY 10010.

Where this book is distributed in the UK, Europe and the rest of the world,
this is by Palgrave Macmillan, a division of Macmillan Publishers Limited,
registered in England, company number 785998, of Houndmills, Basingstoke,
Hampshire RG21 6XS.

Palgrave Macmillan is the global academic imprint of the above companies and
has companies and representatives throughout the world.

Palgrave® and Macmillan® are registered trademarks in the United States,
the United Kingdom, Europe and other countries.

ISBN: 978-0-230-62054-4

Library of Congress Cataloging-in-Publication Data
Bradley, John R., 1970–
  Behind the veil of vice : the business and culture of sex in the Middle East /
John R. Bradley.
    p. cm.
  ISBN 978-0-230-62054-4 (hardback)
  1. Sex—Middle East. 2. Sex—Religious aspects—Islam. 3. Sex
customs—Middle East. 4. Prostitution—Middle East. I. Title.
HQ18.M628B73   2010
306.70956'09045—dc22

                                                                2010012506

A catalogue record of the book is available from the British Library.

Design by Letra Libre, Inc.

First edition: August 2010

10 9 8 7 6 5 4 3 2 1

Printed in the United States of America.

CONTENTS

INTRODUCTION

The Middle East has long been something of a mystery to Westerners, and the vast literature on the region has oscillated between romanticism and demonization, attraction and repulsion. To paraphrase Freud: What is in the minds of Middle Easterners, or what lies behind the veil, intrigues and mystifies. Rarely has a need to understand the region seemed more important than today. Suicide bombers are so foreign, so different, so inscrutable—after all, if they succeed they cannot be questioned—that they naturally fascinate, and we are compelled to seek explanations.

One popular narrative offers the following explanation for their actions: Repressive Islam rooted in tribal and territorial identity politics shapes the psychology of the region's young men, and as a result some of them launch indiscriminate terror attacks in outbursts of sexual rage and envy. This assessment derives from *The Arab Mind* (1973) by Raphael Patai, an anthropological study that highlighted unique, and by implication inferior, Arab cultural characteristics, personal archetypes, and sexual behavior. The book became a bestseller after the September 11 attacks, and it is used as a kind of training manual for American soldiers, some of whom may have tortured Iraqi prisoners at Abu Ghraib.[1]

"In the Arab view of human nature, no person is supposed to be able to maintain incessant, uninterrupted control over himself," Patai tells us, making one wonder whether a person anywhere in the world has ever existed who could do so, and whether their life would be worth living if they could.[2] "Any event that is outside routine everyday occurrence," he adds, "can trigger such a loss of control and turn the docile, friendly, and courteous Jekyll into a raging, dangerous, and maniacal Hyde, who will return to his former self as soon as the seizure of temper passes."[3] Once aroused, "Arab hostility will vent itself indiscriminately on all outsiders,"[4] and the Arab is thus given to "uncontrolled outbursts of emotionalism."[5] Patai concluded his book by stating that "the challenge facing the Arab world in the 1980s is to digest the overwhelming influx of Western things, techniques, skills, and knowledge. . . . Its successful accomplishment will require total dedication and concentration."[6]

Notwithstanding the alleged association of *The Arab Mind* with the Abu Ghraib scandal, books, articles, and websites continue to explain in Pataiesque terms how the people of the Middle East are inherently repressed and violent, defined by a sense of deprivation and despair. Its young men are hobbled by an overarching obsession with local customs revolving around the need to avoid shame and maintain honor. Arabs continue to reel in a permanent state of Islam-induced sexual anxiety, simultaneously repulsed and seduced by images of Western licentiousness. But now we hear that young Muslims' sexual frustrations are exacerbated by even more direct exposure, through globalization and modern technology, to the civilized, liberated West, which is contrastingly free of sexual inhibitions and conflicts as it romps about in its metaphorical birthday suit. For those who follow Patai, the more advanced West poses a more direct challenge to the benighted Arab male than even the rhetorically resourceful Patai could have envisaged.

The usefulness of this explanation for suicide bombings in a sound-bite culture is obvious, especially for pundits eager to explain away terrorism carried out by Muslims as having to do with sex-charged panic attacks rather than complex foreign policy issues. However, Patai's imitators are now freer to state directly what their mentor only implied: Islamist terrorism stems from an unquestioning adherence to the Qur'an, with its apparent encouragement of violence against infidels, and the severe limitations it places on sexual freedom.

Those targeted by Muslims in attacks, it follows, are random victims of roaming sexual psychopaths.

The American anthropologist Lionel Tiger, in an article entitled "Obama Bin Laden's Man Trouble" in *Slate* in the immediate aftermath of the September 11 attacks, was the first to repackage for the "war on terror" Patai's idea that a permissive and sexualized West provokes a mixture of rage and envy among sexually deprived men living in repressed Arab cultures, who as a consequence express violent urges in the form of terrorist acts. "It is in the crucible of all-male intensity that the bonds of terrorist commitment and self-denial are formed," he wrote. "As they move from Hamburg to Cleveland to Lima to Havana to Jersey City, they are enveloped in tacit camaraderie with their associates who've endured the same training, the same deprivation, the same expectation of enjoying death and heaven in the same shiver."[7]

His idea spread like wildfire, but two essays in *The Second Plane: September 11: Terror and Boredom* (2008) by Martin Amis, originally published in the *New Yorker*, to my mind took it to loftier realms of the absurd. Amis, too, essentially argued that sexual repression and confusion are the root causes of the Islamists' hatred of Western civilization, the key driving forces behind their multiple terrorist attacks. Deeply pious young Muslim Arabs, blindly convinced of their religion's moral superiority but tortured by unrealized sexual fantasies that could only ever be satisfied in the West, privately battle an inferiority complex, specific to their culture and unknown in any other predominantly male environment. It is a neurotic fear that their manhood will forever be found wanting. This envy makes them especially suited to brainwashing by terror outfits. The big idea in *The Second Plane* is that, "when challenged, or affronted, the believer's response is hormonal," and Amis does genuinely seem to believe that the most dramatic result is the attack on the phallic Twin Towers.[8]

Perhaps the most widely read article on the subject of sex and the suicide bomber was written by Ian Buruma in 2006 for the left-leaning *Guardian* newspaper in Britain.[9] Buruma is the author of a book that warns that Europe may one day be governed by strict Islamic law because of unchecked Muslim immigration, as good, polite, and civilized liberals are too blinkered by political correctness or cowed by threats from radical Islamic clerics to take a moral stand in their own backyard.[10] As with Amis, Tiger, and Patai,[11] Buruma has little (if any) direct experience of the Arab world as far as I can tell, and he knows no Arabic. Before the September 11 attacks, he had specialized in the geopolitics of Southeast Asia and Japan, just as Amis had restricted himself to English literature and Tiger had concentrated on writing pop-culture interpretations of Darwin. However, Buruma is among the most explicit and dramatic proponents of this interpretation.

"Sexual deprivation may be a factor in the current wave of suicidal violence, unleashed by the Palestinian cause as well as revolutionary Islamism," Buruma began his article. In this sentence he lumped a historically secular national liberation movement solely dedicated to fighting Israeli occupation (the Palestinian cause) with a broader Islamist movement so diverse as to have taken the form of popular internal revolution (Iran), violent civil war (Algeria), takeovers of countries by minority bands of Western-backed fanatics (Saudi Arabia, Afghanistan, Iraq), and spectacular suicide bombings targeting not only Westerners but innocent Muslim civilians as well. The prospect, Buruma elaborated, of having "one's pick of the loveliest virgins in paradise is deliberately dangled in front of young men trained for violent death" as an appealing incentive to frustrated young males unable to gain relief on earth. And they get to kill two birds with one stone: the first being gaining release, the second being gaining revenge against the licentious and tempting West. In what reads like an update of Patai's conclusion to *The Arab Mind*, Buruma states that access "to MTV, the internet, DVDs and global advertising reinforces the notion that Westerners live in a degenerate garden of sinful delights. This makes the lot of millions of young Arab men even harder to bear, and can provoke a mixture of rage and envy. Once in a while, this rage will explode in carefully orchestrated orgies of violence."

This is intuitively appealing, and reassuring that, well, the fault lies with them, and, gosh, there is really nothing we can do. Notice the trick that is being played: Responsibility is not with us, but with them. Notice, too, the fatalism, usually a trait attributed to the passive Middle East rather than one of the active West. I think such arguments take the "personal is political" to the absurd. Never mind that, if this frustration is a civilization-wide phenomenon, we might reasonably ask why, as Buruma stated, only "once in a while" this rage "will explode in carefully orchestrated orgies of violence." After all, as he also admitted, "even those who are not trained to kill and die live in authoritarian societies in which sex before marriage is strictly forbidden, in which women outside the family home are not only supposed to be untouchable, but invisible."

Buruma and his kind arbitrarily lump several hundred Arabs who have blown themselves up with hundreds of millions who lead nonviolent lives, or engage in occasional fisticuffs, or beat the maid but not the wife, or torture their own countrymen in police cells, or post conspiracy theories on the web, or make a noise at football matches, or weep into their pillow, or write poetry, or dance intoxicated at discos, or express frustrations caused by any number of factors and in myriad ways. The social space those ordinary people inhabit is not, more to the point, a monolith of black-clad women and sexually subdued men, as this book will show.

Worth considering more than Buruma's argument, then, is what it neglected to take account of regarding the reality of the Middle East. For starters, there is the orgy of violence that the United States and its allies unleashed in Iraq in 2003, resulting in the deaths of hundreds of thousands of Iraqi civilians and the sexual torture of Abu Ghraib. Also, the majority of suicide bombings during the twentieth century were not carried out by Muslims but by non-Muslims, and the majority of those carried out by Muslims targeted not Westerners but their fellow Muslims. Robert Pape, the world's foremost researcher into suicide bombings, has shown that the overwhelming majority have been carried out by non-Muslims. In an interview with PBS in 2005 he explained that "what over 95 percent of all suicide terrorist attacks since 1980, all around the world, have in common is a specific strategic goal, to compel modern democracies to withdraw combat forces from territory the terrorists prize greatly."[12]

Then there are the female Muslim suicide bombers in the Middle East. Must we assume that Buruma thinks they had abnormal hormonal surges?

George Orwell wrote in *Nineteen Eighty-Four* (1949) that the sex instinct, more than any other, must be repressed if ruling elites are to maintain control over the masses. Sexual desire is the most basic manifestation of individualism. In societies where ruling elites maintain as tight a hold over both the public and private lives of their populations as political systems and civil societies allow, sexual repression, and the importance of maintaining the façade of sexual normality (however culturally defined), remain insidious forms of repression. However, Orwell further noted: "What was more important was that sexual privation induced hysteria, which was desirable because it could be transformed into war fever and leader worship."[13]

This chimes alarmingly with the fashionable Pataiesque analysis of Islamist terrorism, though for Orwell it was a universal phenomenon. That it is hardly distinctive to foreigners is apparent when we look at the United States and Britain. They have seen their share of lynch mobs, especially in low-income neighborhoods, who call for suspected sex offenders to be put to death or hound them from the local neighborhood, all when multiple wars were being launched in the Greater Middle East by their governments. One could just as easily make a Pataiesque link between sexual panic, a loss of personal control, and violence inflicted in foreign lands. To do so would, of course, be as unconvincing as the parallel argument put forward about the Middle East. Nor should the fact that the man on the Arab street mocks the double lives of some Saudi rulers who preach one rule for their people but themselves practice another, while encouraging state-sponsored Wahhabi preachers to indulge in screaming litanies of condemnation of the dissolute West, strike a discordant chord to Americans, familiar as they are with the hypocrisy of former New York governor Eliot Spitzer who, after a furious crackdown on prostitution, was himself found to have done lively business with a call girl ring. Meanwhile, young British and American men from low-income backgrounds who make up the bulk of the fighting force in Afghanistan and Iraq are not thought to be driven to greater ferocity by being starved of sexual contact in the Middle East or by earlier having been exposed to the unabated sexual hysteria at home.

If the case is nevertheless to be made that one civilization or religion is inherently more violent than the other, and that the root of that violence is to be found in the sexual hang-ups of its people, this must be calibrated to the tiniest fraction. Can we also equate every kick administered by a British or American soldier to an Iraqi with every last pebble thrown by a Palestinian child? Can we establish a direct, causal connection between the fourteen-year-old American girl who was arrested in 2009 and threatened with being placed on the sex offender registry for publishing child pornography *of herself* on MySpace[14] and the Western invaders who killed hundreds of thousands of Iraqis in order to remove one man from power? Again, of course not. Thankfully, no one would think to write a book called *The American Mind* to explain the "war on terror" and its incalculable injustices in the context of the American sexual psyche. The terror of Abu Ghraib and its homoerotic frenzy of sexual abuse is not seen as an American cultural issue. Neither the presence on American soil of almost one million registered "sex offenders" nor the fact that the country is home to the world's largest jail population—a quarter of the globe's total prison inmates— is explained as "hormonal" or having anything to do with an inherently deformed American character.

Given that there is no factual evidence to support the neo-Patais' argument that sexual deprivation causes terrorism, it might be more useful to look at what Arabs and Westerners have in common, rather than what sets them apart. Something Arabs and Westerners certainly do is what one might have thought someone like Amis, considering the kind of fictional world he creates, would take a greater interest in, namely, that they live under rulers who, under different pretexts and with varying degrees of severity, seek to curb the unruly sex urge as a way of maintaining social control. What people in the West and the Middle East have in common, that is to say, is the gap between propaganda and reality, the vast gulf between public and private morality. In other words: hypocrisy.

Drawing on the experience of a decade spent living in the Middle East, I offer in *Behind the Veil of Vice* a more nuanced account than is usually presented of the social world that shapes Arabs' sex lives. The focus is on countries where I have lived and worked or traveled: Syria, Tunisia, Egypt, Iran, Saudi Arabia, Bahrain, Yemen, and Morocco. My sojourn there has the incidental benefit of enabling exploration of the issue of prostitution and other forms of extramarital sex in countries where they have hitherto been least discussed. (In Dubai and Lebanon the sex industries are the stuff of legend but are usually seen as anomalies, and so I omit them.) I show that sexuality in the Middle East I know is every bit as capricious as its Western counterpart, as unruly and multifarious, and occasionally as becalmed, and that it finds expression in ways as various as anywhere.

If prostitution is the oldest profession, it is so because it serves a number of functions, especially in patriarchal societies that seek to regulate sex and limit it to marriage. That sounds paradoxical, and possibly perverse. It is certainly the latter. But it is not paradoxical, because a central element of patriarchal societies is to avoid conflict within the family, which defers, at least in public, to the father, and especially to avoid conflict between families and groups. There are few topics more likely to challenge authority, or risk social conflict, than sex outside approved channels. Historically, approved channels usually meant arranged marriages, as marriage was not about love but rather mutual advantage for the families. A female having sex outside approved channels went against the patriarch's authority and undermined her value, which was based on child bearing and bearing (only) the husband's children. The dangers of attraction outside approved channels is familiar to anyone who has read Shakespeare, especially *Romeo and Juliet*. In the Middle East, the danger of strife, or *fitna*, has long been central, consistent with any patriarchal society. Prostitution's role in such societies, evident also in its prevalence and openness in the United States and Britain for much of their history, is to form an outlet for the fulfillment of sexual desire through a semiapproved channel.

Contrary to the ranting of radical Islamists, who view prostitution and other forms of extramarital sex as evils imported from the West, and in contradiction to the neo-Patai writers' thesis of total prohibition and repression, the Islamic world has known a tug-of-war between the desires of men, the economic needs of women, and laws governing sexual relations outside of marriage since the time of the Prophet. It is a history defined by long periods when prostitution was integrated into society, at times made lawful, but interrupted by crackdowns. In the pre-Islamic Arabian society that Islam sought to impose order on, prostitution was already widespread and was socially accepted to the extent that prostitutes could be recognized by the flags they hung over the doors of their houses.[15] Compared to the endless catalog of thou-shalt-nots of the Judeo-Christian tradition, Islam is relatively tolerant of sexual matters, provided they happen within the comparatively loose bonds of polygamous marriage and concubinage or, if not, do not threaten to disturb the peaceful social order. Islam could therefore have been expected to obviate prostitution altogether, since there were so many other options available.

After all, when the Qur'an came in the seventh century, it did not limit the number of concubines a man could own, although men were warned that married women were out of bounds as concubines unless they were captives, and it forbade forcing any woman, whatever her status, into prostitution.[16] Only two references to prostitution are contained in the Islamic holy book. Both mention that four male witnesses are needed to convict a woman of the crime—and with the crucial proviso that anyone bringing false accusations would himself face severe punishment.[17] The effect seems to have been that, so long as neither the man nor the woman was brazen about the activity, prostitution was more or less given free rein, and despite the range of options available to pious Muslim men, prostitution prospered in the Middle East.

A few years after the death of her husband, the Prophet's widow Ayisha was already grumbling about the shameful conduct of women, and by the thirteenth century Egyptian historians were busy documenting how some women shamelessly sold their depravity to men.[18] Brothels and red light districts were initially kept more or less secret, but the state surrendered to the inevitable and eventually they came out into the open. Egyptian prostitution was officially taxed as early as the tenth century, an example emulated in Andalusia and later in Syria and throughout the rest of the Ottoman Empire.[19] Indeed, prostitution became a key feature of the Ottoman Empire, which legalized it in the second half of the sixteenth century. Although the prostitutes were mostly Christian Armenians or Greeks—in keeping with a tradition whereby the prostitutes themselves (if not the customers) were drawn mainly from non-Muslim minority communities—scholars of the period have discovered that Muslim Turks were also involved in the trade. On the streets or in brothels, indirectly through the slave trade or in places of employment open to women, prostitution was widespread.[20]

Throughout Middle Eastern history, much as in the West, prostitution was tolerated in this way because it served the public interest, whether or not it contributed to the public coffers through taxation. As long as no one complained, as long as it did not get out of hand, the personal was not political. To be sure, an ostensibly pious sovereign would occasionally decide to close the brothels in reaction to popular expressions of indignation, or because he was genuinely appalled at the spectacle. The hanbalites famously organized raids during the tenth century on houses of ill repute in Baghdad,[21] and a century later Caliph Al-Hakim took to the streets himself to demonstrate his displeasure.[22] By and large, though, Islamic rulers tolerated prostitution, or indulged in it themselves. Bouhdiba Abdelwahab, a Tunisian scholar, summed up the broad trends when he wrote, in *Islam and Sexuality* (1971), that "Islam, despite its extreme tolerance with regard to sexuality, which it sees as self-fulfillment and happiness, despite the great case with which it organized sexuality, has utterly failed in preventing Arab societies from having recourse to prostitution." He continued that, though "anti-Islamic par excellence, prostitution was nevertheless profoundly rooted in Arabo-Muslim mores. . . . [T]here is a remarkable continuity."[23]

In the 1970s a number of economic, political, social, and religious factors converged to create a vast expansion in the prostitution industry in the Persian Gulf especially, followed by a more vocal reaction against it. Rapid social and economic changes have since fed into the political discourse surrounding personal choices, including the most fundamental involving sex.

Perhaps most important was the oil boom of the 1970s. It led to a dramatic increase in the middle class, and a new generation of young Gulf Arab men came of age who had money to spend, could travel in search of fun, and grew accustomed to more open social environments while studying in the West. At the same time, an influx into the Persian Gulf of millions of immigrant workers—young, single men from South Asia, the Philippines, or poorer Arab countries like Egypt, Syria, and Yemen—created a greater demand for prostitutes, as did the smaller (but in some ways economically more crucial) groups of Western experts who could not be recruited to the region unless they could expect to live with the same freedoms, including sexual, they were used to at home. Women from as far away as Russia, India, and China—and as near as Morocco and Syria—were willing to satisfy the demand for prostitutes. Endemic local corruption, archaic labor laws (rarely applied anyway), entrenched crime syndicates, a private "visa sponsorship" exploited by dubious middlemen: all combined to bring women to the region in all sorts of superficially legitimate ways to put them to work as freelancers or for a local pimp or madam.

The proliferation of numerous Islamist political outfits, violent and nonviolent, in the wake of the 1979 Iranian revolution, criticizing Arab leaders for their alleged personal decadence and allowing Islamic societies to become so superficially Westernized, put the despotic leaders more on the defensive. The Islamic opposition, like their anti-imperial forebears, highlighted corruption and loose morals as a cause of weakness. But this time the targets were more their own, and thus the charges of hypocrisy all the more wounding. In 2004, a letter to the Iraqi people, purportedly by Osama bin Laden on Al-Jazeera, lambasted Arab leaders as "treacherous" specifically because they "have not followed the right path of Islam but followed their wishes and lusts." Bin Laden further claimed that this "is the reason for the setbacks in the [Islamic] nation's march during the past decades."[24]

By 2008, prostitution had become such a hot issue that it was the subject of a ferocious debate on Al-Jazeera's most popular show, *The Opposite Direction*, which is watched by tens of millions throughout the region.[25] Focused on the pros and cons of mass tourism in the Arab world, it pitted an Islamist against a secular economist, God versus Mammon; gay sex tourism, AIDS, and "cheap meat" (female prostitutes) were discussed with the frankness (and sensationalism) that Westerners are used to seeing on their own television screens.

This book is an attempt to explore the subject with greater depth and subtlety.

CHAPTER *one*

DISSENT IN DAMASCUS

Overloaded with glasses and beer and wine bottles and a vast selection of half-eaten plates of food, my table was vibrating worryingly to the thunderous drums strapped to the young men on stage. They were swirling in tandem to a remixed Syrian classic belted out by the accompanying band and a female singer. Dressed in long, embroidered Levantine shirts, they began encircling each other, then teased their way through the Syrian, Iraqi, and Moroccan belly dancers, all the while pounding away as though to rouse anyone who, despite the racket, might drift off into slumber. Two adolescent boys with pearly white skin and jet-black hair, proudly decked out in leather pants and shiny silk shirts, scurried about the stage on all fours, gathering in wicker baskets the rose petals and money raining down from all directions on the women. The dancers' ripe, ample flesh quivered under figure-hugging gowns. If there was little expertise in the shimmy dances these amateurs attempted to perform, their seductive curvaceousness alone was enough to arouse the hundreds of Syrian men in this downtown Damascus nightclub. When the drummers descended from the stage and approached their tables, the men broke into dancing so wildly expressive that the belly dancers themselves could have learned a thing or two by studying their moves.

I had been brought here by the cleaner at my budget hotel, who subsidized his income by way of showing foreigners, usually Saudis, the ropes, a service for which he charged a $100 flat fee. It was an exorbitant sum, especially for a man who told me he earned $150 a month from his hotel job, though that salary was probably as good an excuse as anyone needed to pay him what he asked for. Because the clubs in Damascus are not advertised they are nearly impossible to locate without a local's help, and this one had cornered the market in the area where I was staying. The table reservation also cost $100, which included the food but not the drinks, which were $20 each, and almost needless to say they were put on my tab as well. Nor did his fee include the company of a woman, which on that evening meant a charming Iraqi in her late twenties. She sat next to us for a charge of yet another $100. Her drinks were on me as well, and a tip seemed expected on top of that, from which I suspected the guide would be taking a cut.

This Iraqi woman he had called over did not, it turned out, work as a prostitute, but rather (as she put it) "an escort." She offered company to men only inside the club whose wish was to chat to her while enjoying the show, eating dinner, and downing a few beers. She was originally from Baghdad, she told me, and had fled to Syria with her family, not as a result of the United States–led invasion but a few months before it had begun and in anticipation of the chaos that would follow it. They were a well-off Sunni family in a majority-Shia neighborhood, and had read the writing on the wall. She started working at the club a few months before I met her, after finishing her education, failing to find a job, and discovering that, after five years in exile, her father's savings were now all but exhausted.

"Do they know you work here?" I asked her.

"God forbid!" she said, with an expression of barely concealed horror. "I tell them I work as a waitress in a restaurant."

"So what would you do if someone from your neighborhood walked in?" I pressed her, rather cruelly I realize in retrospect.

"What would you do if someone from yours did?" she asked me in turn.

"I'd probably dive under the table," I said, not altogether seriously.

"And that's where you'd find me." She laughed, relaxing again.

She told me that, unlike her, some of the women dancing on the stage were available for sex. My guide interjected that no man ever left with any of them, evidently not having believed me when I told him all I was looking for was a drink and a chat, and that I was not going to get into the habit of hitting on prostitutes just because I was researching a book about them. The men and women exchanged cell phone numbers, he added, then met up elsewhere. This way the club owners could claim, in a way accurately, that they were not directly involved in prostitution, but just putting on a show. This setup had the additional advantage that the women could keep whatever money they made from clients outside the club, without having to give a middleman a cut. My Iraqi companion said she received half of the $100 fee paid to the club by the men who chose to spend time in her company, and the tips (hint, hint) were all hers. In the event no customer chose her, the manager gave her $20 for having turned up. I thought it unlikely that she would ever remain alone for a whole evening. She was a stunner, with long, light brown hair, delicate features, impish smile, and a little roll of puppy fat over her jeans—a woman Arab men have such a fetish for. Moreover, even on this weekday night, all of the hundred or more tables were booked, and there were no more than a dozen escorts. I guessed this Iraqi woman could be earning more than $2,000 a month, including tips.

We ordered another round of drinks and I mentally toted up the bill for the evening's entertainment so far. It was a considerable portion of the advance I had received to write this book, and we still had three hours to go until closing time. I looked around and tried to work out how much the owner must be making. Tens of thousands of dollars, even on a slow evening.

"There's no way this kind of club could exist in Egypt unless some cops or officials were taking a monthly kickback," I told the Iraqi woman, Egypt being my comparison because I was living there at the time.

"It's the same here," she said, surprised that I could have thought otherwise. "Only they come every evening, not every month."

"And there's never any problem with the police?" I asked.

"They only come here if we call them, for example, if there's a drunk customer causing some trouble."

"How often does that happen?"

"Never." She shrugged. "At least not since I've been working here."

Damascus became one of the Arab world's leading sex tourism destinations during the 2000s due to a number of related geopolitical developments. The most obvious is the Iraq war and the sudden influx into the country of more than a million Iraqi refugees. Many of them are impoverished, and prostitution offers a means for women living on the margins of any society to earn a living. Two years after the invasion of Iraq, in 2005, Syria also withdrew from Lebanon, following the assassination of the Lebanese prime minister Rafiq Hariri. That, too, led to a mass exodus. However, this time it was Syrians coming home from a country they had effectively been occupying. Many were extraordinarily wealthy, and they brought their cash back with them. Soon, on the outskirts of Damascus, malls, restaurants, and nightclubs were forming entertainment districts where before there had been only sand. Word spread among Iraqi women that there were job opportunities there. This transformation of the suburbs is colloquially referred to as the Beirutization of Damascus.

Israel's assault on southern Lebanon in 2006 had meanwhile led many Persian Gulf governments to issue travel warnings to their nationals to avoid Beirut, although the city was not specifically targeted by Israel in the end. The Lebanese capital has long been the favorite playground for Saudis, who come in multitudes to enjoy the less repressive atmosphere. Whenever Beirut is out of bounds, they usually head to Cairo for the summer. In Egypt, though, Islamic fundamentalism is spreading under the growing influence of the Muslim Brotherhood, and Saudis have plenty of bearded moralizers at home. During the Israel-Hezbollah war, word seems to have spread among Gulf Arabs, too, about Syria's new potential, which in lingering homage to its pan-Arab ideology allows all Arabs to enter the country without a visa. In addition, Syria is only marginally more expensive than Egypt. Not that anyone needs much of an excuse to stay away from Cairo, with its chronic traffic congestion, choking pollution, and legions of touts who have a very well-earned reputation for ripping off all and sundry, but especially Gulf Arabs. These days, many of the cars parked outside the new nightclubs in the suburbs of Damascus have Saudi and Kuwaiti license plates, though the more established clubs downtown, like the one I had visited, still cater almost exclusively to Syrian men.

I wanted to talk to Sami Moubayed, perhaps Syria's best-known liberal intellectual, about the history and more recent proliferation of prostitution. Like other prominent liberals in the Arab world—the novelist Alaa Al-Aswany in Egypt, for example, and the historian Sami Angawi in Saudi Arabia—Moubayed has taken on, quite by accident, the role of cultural bridge builder between his country, which he loves, and the West, which he loves, too. Given his prominence, he is a difficult man to get hold of, and not an easy one to pin down when at last you do find yourself face-to-face with him. A professor, editor, publisher, author, historian, journalist, and political analyst, depending on the day of the week or the time of day, he only found time to chat with me, despite my numerous phone calls and emails, on the morning I was due to leave Damascus. And then we ended up sitting on a bench in a corridor between his endless meetings and a final edit of one of his magazines. In his early thirties, he gives the impression of being borderline hyperactive, which is probably just as well, given all the energy he must require to pursue his various activities. He is also sharp-witted, gentle, and hospitable.

Moubayed is the author of an Arabic-language book, *Damascus between Dictatorship and Democracy*, published in 2000 during what became known as the Damascus Spring. That was a period after Hafiz Al-Assad's death, and the end of his three decades of authoritarian and repressive rule, when there was a brief thawing of the strict limits placed on political participation. When I was in Damascus in mid-2009, though, things were frozen solid again. While there was still enough room for honest reflection on cultural and social topics, I knew that discussing the nitty-gritty of domestic politics would be pointless. Moubayed could never risk speaking critically, and on the record, about the worst features of the Syrian regime. Like so many other liberal Arab thinkers before him, he told me that he placed much of the blame on the West for backtracking on the promises of democracy in the region, because of the backlash against the United States and its "war on terror," the dirtying of the word "democracy" by the Iraq debacle, and the crippling political instability after the numerous wars following the September 11 attacks. These events diverted the attention of reform-minded leaders and provided a convenient excuse for hard-liners to re-assert their control.

Rather than to talk broadly about domestic politics, we stuck to the extraordinary fallout from an opinion piece he wrote in 2007 for the *Washington Post*, "Sexual Repression in Syria," in which he frankly called for prostitution to be legalized in his country.[1] When I brought it up, however, he shifted uncomfortably, telling me that he resented being known as "the guy who wants to legalize prostitution." That was understandable, I said, considering his many other accomplishments, but the fact remained that the article did cause an almighty hoo-ha. Moubayed is the only intellectual in the Arab world to have recently made such a call for state regulation. Both liberal and Islamist groups throughout the Middle East tend to highlight the growth of prostitution and other "deviant" sexual behavior as a symptom of the failures and hypocrisies of their unpopular governments and the resulting moral disintegration of society. Thus Ayman Nour, onetime presidential candidate in Egypt and a supposed liberal alternative to the Mubarak regime there, can use, as evidence of the "dissolving" of the "social texture" of his country, the fact that "the number of crimes for immoral behavior, homosexuality, and whoredom is increasing."[2] This is no different from the bigotry of which the Islamists throughout the Middle East are so fond, as Moubayed was to discover in Syria after his article appeared.

In his own more nuanced commentary, Moubayed had been careful to state at the outset that he by no means endorsed "the act of prostitution." He just did not believe it could be "eliminated," and its illegal status only helped it to "flourish in the Arab underground." Having set the parameters, he drew on his intimate knowledge of Syrian history to offer a sophisticated counterargument to prohibition. "I was always impressed with how open-minded and progressive Syrian leaders were in the early years of the twentieth century, when prostitution was in fact legal," he wrote in the article. "Most of these men, pious men who had been educated at proper Islamic schools in Ottoman Syria, prayed, fasted, and observed the pillars of Islam." Nevertheless, they saw "the need to legalize a profession that, with or without their consent, would happen anyway in Syria." Prostitution was therefore legalized and professionalized, he emphasized, during the Ottoman Empire:

> Back then, there was fear in Damascus that the wandering soldiers would attack or rape young Syrians. That is why affordable prostitution centers were created for them in the Syrian capital, as a form of maintaining public security. This system was maintained when the Ottoman Empire collapsed in 1918. The destruction of World War I, along with the poverty imposed on the Syrians, however, made many young women turn to prostitution for a living, and the years 1914–1918 are considered the worst in the past hundred years of Syrian history. When the French came to Syria in 1920, they professionalized prostitution in major urban cities. . . . Prostitution centers were registered in government records, and guarded by armed men from the colonial troops of France, mostly, from the Senegal. Any woman found to be engaged in illegal sexual conduct more than three times would be arrested and sent to the prostitution center. There she would become an "official" employee. She would pay taxes on

her earnings to the central government and receive checkups twice a week at the Ministry of Health.[3]

Syrians believed that frequenting such places was "wrong, both morally and socially, and during the early years of the [French] Mandate the regular customers were often foreigners and Frenchmen." But by the 1930s Syrian men were regular clients, too. In 1953, the first attempt at combating the trend was undertaken by President Adib Al-Shishakli, "who passed strict laws to prevent prostitutes from entering Syria." A group of religious men approached President Shukri Al-Quwatli and Nazim Al-Qudsi, the speaker of parliament, a few years later, with a request that they close down "cabarets, nightclubs, and all illegal venues for prostitutes." But the Syrian president told them to take a running jump with a suitably religious rebuttal: "If I create heaven for you on earth, what do we leave for God Almighty?"

The government, according to Moubayed, did not consider interfering in the daily life of Syrian citizens a part of its job, but opted instead to make sure things did not get out of hand. "Punishment for immoral action—and reward for piousness—would be given by God in Heaven," he wrote. Prostitution continued to flourish in Syria and was only outlawed by Nasser during the years of the United Arab Republic (1958–1961), when Egypt and Syria were joined in a disastrous union. However, since then, "rather than diminish, the industry has thrived in the black markets." His call for legalization, Moubayed wrote, "far from being a call to promiscuity, or loose sexual mores," is merely an attempt to acknowledge the existence of a problem created (and sustained) by the rigidity of existing traditions and moral standards, and to address a possible, logical, and human solution to it.

"Moral prudes and Islamists might argue against what I just wrote," he concluded, "but it is like trying to brush a problem under the rug instead of exposing it in a civilized manner, with the intention of resolving and humanizing it."

Moubayed strikes all the right notes about the past. Unfortunately, he was spot on, too, in his prediction of how "moral prudes and Islamists" would react to his call for legalization, even if the sheer ferocity and ad hominem nature of their assault caught him off guard. "The article was translated into Arabic without my permission," he told me, "and posted on the most popular Syrian website." It received more attention than any other he had written in the past decade, and according to him within a day almost half a million people had read it, leaving "an unbelievable number of comments." All were negative, he recalled, "containing all kinds of personal insults." One told him bluntly: "Get out of our lives, infidel!" Some accused him of being "an agent of foreigners" who wanted to corrupt the mentality of the Syrian people, while others asked how he could possibly know how prostitution was all those years ago. "The suggestion was," he said, shaking his head as though, two years on, he still could not fully comprehend the response, "there obviously must have been someone in my family working in the profession." The more usual accusation (and expected here) is that the critic, like the restaurant reviewer, must first have tasted the wares. For the historian this is not valid, but that evidently did not matter to the accuser, and one of the most common insults in English, son of a bitch, expresses the criticism of Moubayed's thought succinctly.

In any event, such was the pressure that he was forced to issue a statement in Arabic defending himself, saying that he was not calling for "immoral conduct." But that only provoked six more articles, again all by authors venting their fury. The discussion as a result spread to "just about every online forum in the region." Not a single person, Moubayed said, offered him any kind of support. "Even privately, those who agreed tended to say: 'Why get yourself into this shit?' Until now, whenever anyone wants to write anything negative about me, they use this article as ammunition."

While the reaction to his proposition did not surprise me, that it took on an Islamist slant did. The one saving grace of the Baathist regime in Syria is that it is staunchly secular, and decades ago crushed the Islamists. Few of the women I saw on the streets of Damascus wore head scarves, and the men were as open-minded, at least in their conversations with me, as any I would find in London or New York.

"Syrian society in general is becoming more religious, but not necessarily politically Islamic," Moubayed insisted when I brought this up. "The organization of opposition forces does not exist, but in general religiousness is increasing. The fact is that nobody told the people to write their comments below the article." That one of their kin, a fellow Sunni Muslim, would speak openly about vice threatened and insulted them, he continued. "My best friend—until the moment the article appeared—wrote that I should stick to writing about Syrian history," he said, "and show more respect to our contemporary culture and society, and that basically I'm a disgrace. The fact that he mentioned he was my best friend in his posting gave all the more credibility to what he'd written."

One problem, as Moubayed saw things in retrospect, is that he wrote the article in English and for a Western audience, whereas if he had written it for an Arabic-speaking audience he would have pitched it in a different way. In the Arab world there is, he elaborated, a sense that some things are better left unsaid, even if they are known. Because of the strict censorship from the 1970s of popular culture, there have been many ways of talking about such sensitive issues without discussing them explicitly, in creative and metaphorical ways. "Perhaps that was more challenging, but now people are able to speak about things more bluntly, and they are going for the blunt approach." One consequence is the blunter counterreaction. "At least when you're alluding to a sensitive issue creatively or metaphorically," he reflected, "you can always escape just at the right moment."

Even so, the fact that Moubayed's best friend disowned him publicly suggested that more was at stake here than mere semantics. Had the Damascus Spring really given way to an Islamic resurgence? Were there no liberal countercurrents, however weak, to help keep him afloat as the sole public defender of Syria's tolerant history of sexual freedom? Or was it more a case, as he himself had hinted, of talking about things people would prefer not to, of the washing of dirty laundry in public, which was guaranteed to provoke a backlash because of nationalistic pride? (This thought struck me again as a possibility in November 2009, when in the wake of Egypt's loss in a crucial soccer World Cup qualifying match against Algeria, patriotic rioters took to the streets in both countries, and one of the most popular chants among both groups was that the other's country was "a nation of a million whores!")

"Ten years ago, if I'd invited any young lady my age for coffee at a restaurant or café, this definitely would have meant that she was my wife, my girlfriend, or a very close relative," he said. "The concept of other kinds of open male-female relationships was almost nonexistent, except among the top one percent—the superrich who had studied at Western universities and so on. But such behavior is very normal today, so in that sense things have changed." But many of the changes taking place in Syria, from his vantage point, are only superficially toward greater liberalism.

> Being free or liberal does not mean wearing a short skirt. It does not mean being able to speak a few sentences in English. People here have taken a very crooked interpretation of liberalism. It does not mean going to these posh coffee shops that have mushroomed all over Damascus. Liberalism is what kind of books you read, what kind of ideas you have, what kind of exposure you have to outside influences. So society is radicalizing on both fronts. On the one hand Islamification of society is increasing, but the loosening of society structures is increasing at the same time.

In his conversation with me, Moubayed attributed much of the relaxation in male-female relations to Syria's withdrawal in 2005 from Lebanon and the resulting Beirutization of Damascus. In the past, Syrians lived in ignorance of what happened in other countries and they were more content, he claimed, but now so much was available in the new malls that have been built all over Damascus. "A young Syrian woman who wants these material things will either nag a family member or [her] husband to buy them for her," he said, "or they will sleep with someone to get the money to buy the luxuries themselves." Left unsaid was that this exchange was just another form of prostitution. But there is also poverty, he quickly added, although he had "no idea" what percentage of women worked as prostitutes because of poverty and what percentage did so because "they want material things." Such statistics, he told me with refreshing honesty, "are just not available."

So would he write the same article again today? He paused for a moment, then said as much to himself, it seemed, as to me,

"My argument remains that banning the profession does not help to contain it, and banning it in a society that strictly regulates sexual relations between men and women is especially problematic. The article has still not been completely forgotten, nor has it been completely forgiven. I'm mostly amused by the episode in retrospect. But I'm not sure if I would write it again."

What he did not say, and I would not have expected him to given his circumstances, is what I had realized at the nightclub during my conversation with the Iraqi escort. Because the profits from the sex industry are siphoned off by corrupt officials, the powers that be in Syria could have little incentive to regulate and legalize it anyway, regardless of whether there is public support. The revenue, in the form of taxes, would go into the state's coffers, rather than directly into the corrupt officials' pockets. And for the nightclub owners, there is little difference in paying taxes to the state and handing over a percentage of the profits at the end of each evening in unmarked envelopes.

Syria's sullied international image, because of its support for Hamas and Hezbollah, has tended to frighten Western tourists into avoiding what is in reality one of the safest countries on earth. Tight visa restrictions placed on foreign journalists and human rights activists—there is an extensive, constantly updated blacklist—also contributed to Syria's isolation during the past few decades, meaning it was covered only intermittently by the Western media. However, that situation too began to change after the Iraq war. Western nongovernmental organizations and journalists flooded the country to deal with and cover the refugee crisis, and in their wake came antitrafficking and antiprostitution campaigners. A flood of articles, mostly written by freelancers and activists, started to uncover an apparently dramatic increase in the number of Iraqi women and young girls being trafficked into Syria to feed the country's ever-growing sex industry.

The opponents of sex traffickers are an unlikely ad hoc alliance of evangelical Christian and salvationist feminist groups. Their cause was given a huge boost, both in terms of publicity and funding, by George W. Bush, at the expense of funding for groups fighting AIDS, combating poverty, and promoting women's autonomy. This was in 2003, the year the Iraq invasion was launched. One of the biggest beneficiaries of these faith-based initiatives, receiving tens of millions of dollars, is the International Justice Mission, a militant evangelical outfit that employs hundreds of Christian lawyers and moral cops, and even advocates vigilante raids on brothels.[4] This and other evangelical groups are drawn into a mutual embrace with the salvationist feminist organizations, despite their ideological differences, because they believe that it is primarily prostitution that creates human trafficking, so banning prostitution will largely put an end to it.

Dorchen A. Leidholdt, the coexecutive director of one of the most prominent of the reactionary feminist lobby groups, the Coalition Against Trafficking in Women (CATW), compares prostitution with gang rape, an extreme position that, to my knowledge, not even the most radical evangelical groups openly subscribe to.[5] An international organization, CATW takes an approach to prostitution that allows it to work toward achieving the goal of a global ban under the less contentious mantra of rescuing women and children (grouped together as though women are kids trapped inside adult bodies) from what it refers to as the modern slave trade. A key CATW objective, according to their manifesto, is "to challenge acceptance of the sex industry, normalization of prostitution as work, and to de-romanticize legalization initiatives in various countries."[6] That its definition of trafficking is so broad as to include the Internet, pornography, and sex tourism suggests that it is in fact opposed to the entire lexical scope of the word "traffic," whether used for budget flights or magazine delivery vans, let alone of "sex."[7]

Syria has been targeted by the anti-sex-trafficking lobby like no other country in the Middle East, largely because of the influx of Iraqis seeking refuge from the war. This has resulted in the country being singled out for criticism by the U.S. State Department in its annual reports on global human trafficking. But before we get to the political ramifications in Syria of this campaign, we should first take a little more time to look at the sex-trafficking issue, because it has become central to the way the debate about prostitution in the Middle East more generally is framed. Special reports in the *Washington Post* in 2007 and the *Guardian* in 2009 trashed the belief in the existence of any statistical evidence to support the argument that there is an organized international human trafficking mafia. Although both governments have allocated millions of dollars to unearth victims of trafficking—on the basis of claims by antiprostitution groups—only tiny numbers were discovered. All experts without a vested ideological or financial interest had long before dismissed the statistics that had been provided to the media as fabrications, and the newspapers' two headlines validated their stand: "Human Trafficking Evokes Outrage, Little Evidence" (*Washington Post*) and "Inquiry Fails to Find Single Trafficker Who Forced Anybody Into Prostitution" (*Guardian*).[8] Evidence for the widespread phenomenon internationally, which forms the basis of the annual U.S. State Department reports, is equally questionable. In 2004, UNESCO looked into the issue and concluded that the U.S. State Department "had provided no details on how its 'facts' had been collected or arrived at," and the reports have been criticized elsewhere for their "unsystematic data collection, and a lack of evidence."[9] The annual reports are also alleged to be highly politicized, with countries not hostile to U.S. foreign policy interests far less likely to be singled out for sanctions.[10]

There must be some women forced into prostitution in Syria, since there is no reason to believe the country is different from any other country in the third world. We can likewise take for granted that child prostitution, which the campaigners link to forced trafficking, also occurs, and for the same reason, especially if we define as a child anyone who has yet to reach his or her eighteenth birthday. The problem, as we will see, is that researchers, whether they want to promote the argument or debunk it, find it incredibly difficult to find any kind of hard evidence to back up their arguments, meaning skeptics can justifiably question whether it exists in anything but minuscule numbers. Laura María Agustín is a sociologist who studies sex workers and is the author of the book *Sex at the Margins: Migration, Labour, Markets, and the Rescue Industry* (2007), and a critic of how what she calls the "rescue industry" conflates human trafficking with prostitution. She gives a useful summary of how the inflated figures feed into the mainstream media and form the basis of policy decisions:

> Many of the sources referred to, when investigated, are simply small
> local NGOs, local police and embassy officials, extrapolating from
> their own experience and reports in the media. Most of the writing
> and activism on this issue does not seem to be based on empirical
> research, even when produced by academics. Many authors lean

heavily on media reports and statistics published with little explanation of methodology or clarity about definitions. The "evidence"
is often circular, as officials cite news reports which cite officials. . . .
Sweeping generalizations often feature in such writing.[11]

With this in mind, two sensational dispatches from Damascus can
be taken as representative of the dozens that have appeared on alleged
sex trafficking and child prostitution in Syria since the 2003 war on Iraq.

American freelance writer Joshua E. S. Phillips published what was
presented as an exposé entitled "Unveiling Iraqi's Teenage Prostitutes"
in *Salon* in 2005.[12] His guide and translator was "a young Syrian journalist" who has been "researching Iraqi prostitution in Syria for a year
as a reporter for an online women's magazine." They scoured Damascus for evidence of underage prostitution. However, despite the promise of the salacious headline, it seems to me they found scant evidence
of it. Someone described as a pimp, who was actually not a pimp at all
but a spare-time tout whose main occupation was shining shoes (as the
article also tells us), told them he could find Iraqi girls under fifteen
years of age, but, on my reading of the article, he produced nothing to
back this claim up. A cab driver talked of girls in "furnished apartments" in the suburbs and offered a room "with a sixteen-year-old
maid." You will, he said like some B-movie tag line, "see something
you'll never believe." But Phillips and his guide declined the offer, to
remind us that they are moral, upstanding folk, unlike the locals, who
thus far appear, without exception, to have a gaggle of kids stashed
away somewhere they will pimp out at the drop of a veil.

In the safety of a nightclub, which we are told is so dangerous that
Phillips must not speak English but instead pretend to be from Turkey,
they at last stumbled on Farah, a fifteen-year-old, who was brought to

their table in "camouflage pants and heavy makeup." Clearly in control of her situation, she immediately settled down to negotiate a fee. We have no idea either whether she is bluffing about her age, something prostitutes in their late teens are adept at doing everywhere because they know that youth is a prized commodity. Another woman told them that she was eighteen. Perhaps because that will not titillate sufficiently, we are quickly informed that "she looks much more like fourteen." A last woman, Dana, revealed only that she was from a "jihad neighborhood of Baghdad." We are never even told how old she said she was, or how old the reporters made her out to be.

A nun from the local Good Shepherd Convent claimed that girls under her care had "suddenly disappeared"—most likely "taken out of school, she believes, to earn for their families." There is a dark hint here, but again no clarification is subsequently offered in relation to what the nun was specifically referring to. Perhaps the girls just could not bear to stay another day in the Good Shepherd Nunnery, and had instead decided to sell ducks and chickens with their mothers in the local market? At least there they might get to flirt with the local boys without provoking a lecture on sin from the mother superior.

"Syria Attempts to Combat the Rise in Human Trafficking,"[13] written by an American woman named Charity Tooze, appeared on CNN's website in September 2009. Like the *Salon* article, it was picked up by all the anti-sex-trafficking websites. Tooze majored in women's studies, and was writing a thesis on sex trafficking. Note how the headline casually accepts that there has been a "rise" in human trafficking, although, as we will see, there is little documented evidence available that it has begun.

Then up pop the nuns from the Good Shepherd Convent again. We learn that they now have "several projects that support vulnerable women and children." They include a shelter with twenty-two beds for victims of something Tooze calls "sexual gender-based violence" (SGBV). Given the universal practice of violence against women, we can only be glad that something is being done about it. "One of the new projects the government is supporting is an additional shelter specifically for trafficked women and girls," we are told. However, that seems to indicate that SGBV until now has had nothing "specifically" to do with "trafficked women and girls." One thing that appeared from these and other dispatches was that the sisters must have enviable influence in Damascus, because the International Office of Immigration and the Ministry of Interior are quoted by CNN as supporting their cause. But where was the evidence for sex trafficking in Syria? In November 2008 the United Nations High Commission for Refugees (UNHCR) published a report "outlining the various issues surrounding trafficking." Just as we began to circle the subject, though, we got bogged down in quicksand: The report "did not quantify the issue."

Talking of a lack of quantifying issues: In June 2009 the nuns "reported they've gained access to seventy SGBV cases in the Douma Prison in Syria and intervened with seven Iraqi girls in the Juvenile and Rehabilitation Center in Damascus." The impression I got from this sentence was that these were not the words the nuns were using, but rather a tarpaulin of jargon spread over them. What also remained unclear was whether any of the women were trafficked or even, for that matter, prostitutes. I was equally sure the nuns were only trying to do good. In a piece published by the *New York Times* it was suggested they really just concerned themselves with the welfare of female Iraqi refugees, and had no global agenda except doing the Lord's work as best they knew how.[14]

So nothing thus far in this CNN article about sex trafficking. There was one last faint glimmer of hope: the manager of a "local NGO." This manager "would not reveal her true identity because she fears retribution by both the traffickers and the government." This was baffling, because we had already been told that the government was all on board, in the form of not only the International Office of Immigration but the all-powerful Ministry of the Interior as well. If this manager existed and really was living in fear, we had on our hands a glaring contradiction. This manager said that "there are at least five thousand trafficked girls in Syria" and that "young women are kidnapped from Iraq or sold by family members to traffickers in Syria" who are "mostly" Iraqi. Were they talking here about "girls" or "young women"? How many was "mostly"? Where did the figure of "at least five thousand" come from, regardless of who it might be referring to? It was suspiciously rounded, implying that, say, 3,496 cases would be awfully wide of the mark. The manager concluded that "young women and girls who are virgins are sold for prices ranging from $4,000 to $10,000." Again, this raised more questions than answers. Did "ranging from" mean "respectively"? If not, what accounted for the difference in price? At what age does a girl become a young woman?

The nuns have now taken a vow of silence, and are no longer willing to talk to journalists on any issue. My own request for an interview in 2009, so that I could question them specifically about what they had been quoted as saying about trafficking, was declined. The official reason given for why they no longer talked to the media was that they had been scared as a result of some kind of violence.[15] However, they would also be justified in doing so, I think, as a result of having been roped into media campaigns that interfered with their quiet work of providing some relief to refugees. I was not permitted to speak to the "sex trafficking victims" at other shelters in Damascus, but that was far less surprising, because not a single person ever has managed to interview them. "Though there are no reliable figures," Integrated Regional Information Networks (IRIN), a news agency sponsored by the United Nations, said in a 2008 report, "agencies and activists say hundreds of people from different parts of the world are trafficked to Syria each year for prostitution, domestic work, and even for the sale of body parts."[16] According to this report the victims are in the "hundreds," even though prostitutes form only one of three separate groups cited, as opposed to "at least five thousand" given by the NGO quoted by CNN, although there is no source either for the lower figure. Still, the IRIN reporter had to concede defeat when it came to taking a peek at the actual X-files. "Agencies running the shelters did not allow IRIN to meet any of the trafficked women staying there, citing the sensitive nature of the issue." Of course, the one verifiable fact in the CNN article was that not a single sex-trafficking victim, alleged or otherwise, was interviewed.

What did I find? In addition to the club described at the beginning of this chapter, I visited the two main nightclubs in the city's new entertainment district where prostitution is centered. None of the women I chatted with were under the age of eighteen or knew of any prostitutes who were. The overwhelming majority were, as in the downtown club, in their twenties and thirties. About 40 percent were Iraqis, the rest Syrians, aside from a small number of Moroccans. A Syrian man I spent a lot of time with, who seemed willing to do pretty much anything for a hundred dollars as long as he did not personally get his hands dirty, told me that prostitutes under the age of twenty were to all intents and purposes nonexistent in Damascus, and that tales I had read about fifteen-year-old girls in the suburbs were hard for him to take seriously. Perhaps he was just supercautious. But taxi drivers, too, were visibly irritated when I brought up the subject, even when I hailed them in the seedier downtown part of the city. After we got chatting about the subject, one guy at a downtown coffee shop hinted that he knew of prostitutes who liked meeting foreigners. He must have thought me the most incorrigible pursuer of nymphets ever to have visited his country, so hard did I then try to persuade him to hook me up with an underage one so that I could interview her. My final offer was five hundred dollars. He, too, insisted that he knew nothing about that kind of thing. A few phone calls he made drew a blank.

To put this and so many other Syrian's responses in some kind of context, it is worth mentioning that, despite having a thriving gay prostitution scene, Damascus is unlike just about every other Middle Eastern city I have visited in not having any adolescent rent boys. The local men who cruise with other men told me that everyone understood they were free to do whatever they liked, and without hassle from the authorities, if under-eighteens were not involved, to the extent that those who preferred adolescent rent boys are known to travel to Beirut or Istanbul, where word on the street is that they are available in abundance (for the right price).

Anyhow, the burden of proof surely lies with the proponents of the trafficking narrative, and thus far they clearly have not provided any. The sensational coverage their statements have given rise to has nevertheless helped shift the responsibility for whatever increase in prostitution has occurred in Damascus away from the United States and its allies, whose illegal war slaughtered hundreds of thousands and caused the massive influx of Iraqi refugees in the first place, some of whom then turned to prostitution as a result. Meanwhile, rather than being acknowledged for having welcomed a million refugees from Iraq without complaint as the result of the war the Syrian regime opposed, and despite its limited resources, Damascus was instead singled out by the U.S. State Department in its 2008 annual report on human trafficking for failing to do enough to secure its borders. Syria whispered that the judgment was "based on political considerations" and "not objective,"[17] before promptly becoming the first Arab country to float new legislation specifically targeting traffickers.[18]

It might be that the Syrian regime recognized that there was a problem, denied it for local political consumption, but in reality agreed in private to cooperate. However, since the Syrian regime is even less transparent than the NGOs, we have no way of knowing that, either. Meanwhile, a nonpolitical consequence of the salvationists' antitrafficking agenda, which ultimately seeks to eradicate prostitution rather than regulate it (as Moubayed more sensibly advocates), is that "under the ruse of anti-trafficking interventions, prostitutes' right to work, migrate, receive health care, social benefits, and respect are violated."[19] In other words, the practical effect of this drive to save women from prostitution leaves them far more open to abuse.

If my failure to find underage prostitutes and trafficking victims is a truer reflection of the reality than what is presented in the media, the plight of the (allegedly) fifteen-year-old Iraqi girl described in the *Salon* article could actually point to something positive about the morality of the locals, especially as she is the worst example of child abuse found in Syria despite the sudden influx of one million refugees. After all, there is in more stable, developed countries like the United States and Britain a quantifiably more vicious culture of child abuse. A report released in January 2010 by the U.S. Bureau of Justice Statistics made clear that sexual abuse in juvenile detention is a national crisis. Some 12.1 percent of 26,550 children represented in the survey by a sample of 9,000 who were interviewed said they had been sexually abused at their current facility during the preceding year, and 80 percent of that abuse was perpetrated by staff.[20] The same month, the NSPCC in Britain reported that more than 21,000 child sex offenses were recorded in Britain in 2008, an average of sixty every day.[21]

"There is something familiar about the tide of misinformation which has swept through the subject of sex trafficking," wrote the British journalist Nick Davies in a characteristically dissenting column for the *Guardian*. "[I]t flows through exactly the same channels as the now notorious torrent about Saddam Hussein's weapons."[22] There is indeed a vicious cycle at play. When we get all worked up about an ostensibly but not provably fifteen-year-old Iraqi girl in a club in Damascus, our own collective conscience is appeased regarding the crimes against the Iraqi people done in our name. The 2003 war was preceded by decades of support for Saddam Hussein followed by United Nations sanctions that killed as many as half a million Iraqi children—a mass slaughter that then U.S. Secretary of State Madeleine Albright said was "worth it" to contain Saddam.[23]

In any event, we should deal proportionately with whatever extremes exist, in the Middle East or the West, and treat different issues separately, which is what I will be doing in this book. Prostitution by women who, according to their circumstances, have chosen to work as prostitutes is not the same as by women who have been forced into it.

A woman who willingly pays someone to smuggle her into another country so she can work as a prostitute is not the victim of forced sex trafficking. Twenty-year-old women are not the same as twelve-year-old girls. And a single victim of any kind of abuse should not be exploited by being turned into a poster campaign.

No doubt most of the Iraqi prostitutes in Syria would prefer to be doing a different job. Equally obvious, though, is that they must welcome the work they do have. It allows them to take some measure of control of their lives, helps them to feed their families, and perhaps, for those who earn enough money to put some aside, offers some hope for a better future when they are finally able to return to Iraq.

The ordeal Sami Moubayed faced after publishing his op-ed calling for the legalization of prostitution in Syria tells us something important, not only about his credibility and tenacity, but also about how impossible it has become to have an open debate about the subject in the Arab world. It raises the question, too, of how sensible it is to propose legalization in the present circumstances. If there was such an outburst of threatening hatred in secular Syria, leaving an intellectual so isolated that even his best friend publicly disowned him, what would be the risks in countries where it is the Islamists' dogmatic ideology that dominates the political and the cultural arenas?

Moubayed's admission that he would probably not have written the article if he could have foreseen the reaction to it speaks volumes about who the winners and losers are in this particular battle of the culture wars. At the same time, he also implicitly admitted that, by accepting some things as better left unsaid or expressed only indirectly and subtly, there was a certain kind of freedom. Indifference was the best the prostitutes could wish for. Any publicizing, even of the supportive kind, tended to leave them in a more precarious position. Indeed, if they had read Moubayed's article, what might have struck them most is that they appeared only as a supporting cast, their safety and well-being hardly given a nod to. The thrust of the argument was that prostitution should be accepted because it benefits men. Nor was Moubayed's flip remark to me about the material obsessions of "nagging" women an Oscar-winning moment.

The irony lost on all, though, is that the Syrian regime is quietly keeping alive the traditions that Moubayed lamented had vanished, if not through his preferred method of legalization, then at least by refraining from interfering in the private daily conduct and morality of its citizens. Moubayed told me that the regime, despite the furor caused by his article, had not reacted to it at all, either positively or negatively. Two years on, he still felt free to talk about the subject without inhibition, even boldly restating his call for legalization. In Syria, there are clear red lines when it comes to politics and religion, but people's personal habits are not considered part of the state's domain. However, that still leaves the women vulnerable, because if they report any crimes committed against them, they are also confessing to having broken the law.

Moubayed had made it clear he did not encourage prostitution, and in fact called for it to be legalized precisely because it flourishes in the underground in a way that it could not if it were regulated, as it had been under Ottoman and French rule. He also made clear that his analysis was based on a sober and objective understanding that prostitution has always existed in the country, and always will, and nothing anyone is ever going to do will eradicate it completely. What is equally obvious is that the women who work today as prostitutes in the country will remain marginalized and unprotected as long as they are used as pawns in others' moral games, and viewed by all as passive victims who need to be rescued.

CHAPTER *two*

ISLAMIC FEMINISM

I can think of no more rewarding place in the Middle East to spend a lazy afternoon than Habib Bourguiba Avenue, the mile-long boulevard in the heart of downtown Tunis named after the country's first independence leader. Its palm-tree-shaded cafés and restaurants spill onto the sidewalks, it is home to the country's landmark National Theater and retro cinema, and the spotless side streets are lined with charming, family-run boutiques. Unfailingly polite policemen and -women keep a watchful eye on the street's activities, but from a respectful distance: Crime here is so rare that when something out of the ordinary occurs it makes the front pages. The wide, landscaped central promenade separating the light traffic snailing in both directions is the best place from which to admire the stunning architecture of this Champs-Elysées of the south.

In the mélange of Tunis, nineteenth-century French neoclassical buildings are juxtaposed with others built in the Arab style and 1960s modernist banks and offices. The absence of beggars, aside from a small group of children who have stashed their shoes in a box out of sight to evoke more sympathy from tourists, is extraordinary, as is the manner in which everyone else shows such pride in their appearance that they almost put the Italians to shame. Whenever I return a friendly *salut* to the mixed groups of male and female students on their way home from school, I recall how they are the beneficiaries of an education system ranked globally seventeenth in terms of quality, and seventh in math and science.[1] Few women among the promenaders wear the veil, and most of the women who do are older and married, with children in tow, or visitors from the conservative countryside. Meanwhile, the beautiful women in tight jeans and T-shirts stroll without fear of leers and gropes and insults from the men they encounter, and boys and men cruise each other in full view of coffee-sipping local families. They accept such solicitations as part of the social fabric as casually as they do the reality of the capital's nearby red-light district.

At the end of the main avenue in the French part of the city there is an historic gateway, the Bab Bahr, through which one enters the Arab district called the Medina. Dating back to the seventh century, this magnificently preserved UNESCO World Heritage site is a maze of alleyways, mosques, villas, bathhouses, and cafés. Down a right-hand alleyway from the main square at the Medina's entrance, the crowds thin as one passes a barbershop and a hole-in-the-wall restaurant. Around a corner, there is a woman standing naked but for a slip, leaning against the door of a small, street-level room that contains a dim light and rickety bed. The farther down the alley one ventures, the greater the number of women one encounters. They are as provocatively dressed—or, more precisely, undressed—as those of Amsterdam's red-light district, chatting animatedly and enjoying, between soliciting customers, a snack from one of the vendors who make their way down the lanes. The final alley is a cul-de-sac, meaning that few men other than clients have any reason to come this way.

This red-light district has been around, and for the same purpose, as long as anyone can remember. Generations of women have satisfied the local men in its dingy back rooms. Nor is there any shame induced by frank discussion of the subject. Indeed, Tunisian scholars are given to writing about it without inhibition. In his book *Sexuality in Islam* (1971), Abdelwahab Bouhdiba, a professor at the University of Tunis, writes that "every society has its déclassés, its outcasts or, quite simply, those who live on the fringe of society."[2] The challenge, he adds, is to integrate such marginalized groups as much as possible, and legalizing prostitution is one way of doing so:

> Whatever ability a society has to integrate the individuals who compose it, there will always be deviants and non-conformists. By institutionalizing prostitution society kills two birds with one stone: it controls the deviants as well as giving a status to deviance. In the last resort institutional prostitution forms part of the secret equilibrium of the Arabo-Muslim societies.[3]

The Ottoman Empire and then the French colonial administration were to organize prostitution "as a legal and sometimes official and even military institution," Bouhdiba explains. He traces a tradition in Tunisia along the lines that we saw in Syria. And like Sami Moubayed in Syria, Bouhdiba cautiously approves of this heritage. In his case this is partly because there is "always a marked tendency to aging in legalized prostitution." He gives statistics for the age of registered prostitutes in Tunis in 1967: 2 percent were between twenty and twenty-five; 8 percent between twenty-five and thirty; 40 percent between thirty and forty; 35 percent between forty and fifty; 7 percent between fifty and sixty; and 7 percent over sixty years of age.[4]

That leaves 1 percent unaccounted for. For the sake of all concerned, one hopes that they were between the ages of eighteen and twenty, rather than septuagenarians.

⊗⊗⊗

Tunisia is a tranquil, sun-drenched North African enclave sandwiched between two giant neighbors, Algeria and Libya. Unlike them, it is not blessed with abundant natural resources. Nevertheless, it boasts the highest living standard and most diversified and best-managed economy in the Middle East. On independence in 1956, the country forged a unique identity by embracing the best of the French colonial past while working toward the new elite's singular vision for the future. Now it is an unrivaled champion of women's rights in the Arab world, and a sworn enemy of literalistic, Wahhabi-inspired Islam. Tunisia is also a conscientious investor in the skills and collective well-being of its people, and was ranked the top Arab country in terms of quality of life in 2010 for the second consecutive year by the influential (among expatriates at least) *International Living Magazine*.[5] In a region like the Middle East hopelessly mired in the distant, idealized past and devoid of inspiration for anything but an unattainable utopian future, this autocratic democracy is above all, despite its faults, a reminder of what might have been if it had become the model for developing a socially liberal and economically progressive Arab state.

In Tunisia there are no sex scandals. Nor are there any public slanging matches over the availability of prostitutes and alcohol. The tacky fixtures of the prostitution industry elsewhere in the Middle East (belly-dancing clubs, bars of five-star hotels fronting as brothels) are blissfully nonexistent, too. That means the international media pays the matter scant attention. Where there is no religious drama or social tension, there is no chance of a screaming headline. A 1942 government decree that professionalized prostitution remains on the statute books, and the red-light district of Tunis has its equivalents in all of Tunisia's cities (including Kairouan, Islam's fourth-holiest city), meaning prostitution remains as legal as it is in Hamburg, Zurich, or Auckland. The women who work there enjoy the full protection of the law, pay taxes like everyone else, and undergo regular, compulsory health check-ups, just as prostitutes did during the Ottoman and French periods.[6] Officially the minimum legal age for working as a prostitute, or sleeping with one, is twenty (the age of consent in Tunisia), and old women who serve as security guards can often be seen chasing curious schoolboys from the area. In 1968 the regulations on prostitution were moderated, and thereafter women who offered themselves to men outside of the red-light districts could be sentenced to between six months and two years in prison, and fined between 20 and 200 dinars ($15 to $150 at the 2010 exchange rate).[7]

None of this means that female prostitution does not take place in Tunisia outside of the red-light districts, any more than it has been confined to designated areas in other countries where it is legal and regulated. However, the government has introduced certain laws that do help contain it. For instance, women are allowed to enter any of the popular nightclubs or discos either alone or in the company of other women. But local men are not allowed to enter unless they are in the company of a woman. It does not seem to matter what the relationship between them is, and the point of the rule appears to be to prevent single men from harassing the women inside and, by extension, to discourage prostitutes from frequenting the places, because they are unlikely to find clients there. This rule is enforced throughout Tunisia, and strikes me as quite wonderful, if only in the sense that it is possibly the only instance in the entire Middle East where men, rather than women, are actively discriminated against.

Still, the few hundred officially registered prostitutes could never satisfy the demand created by Libyans, who flood the country during the summer in search of fun. Prostitutes exist in Libya, but they are few in number, and bars and alcohol are completely banned in that country. "In Libya, if a girl sits in a café she's a prostitute, or maybe she's not Libyan," one local man was quoted as saying by the Abu Dhabi-based newspaper *The National* in 2009. "Even in Saudi Arabia women go to cafés. So we're more conservative than the Saudis."[8] The same year, Libyan leader Colonel Muammar Gaddafi let the world know what he thinks of prostitution, with his characteristic flair for eccentric head-line-grabbing behavior, when he invited five hundred female escorts to a party in Rome, gave them copies of the Qur'an, and encouraged them to convert to Islam.[9] Small wonder, then, that so many young Libyan men look forward to their annual vacations in Tunisia. They are loathed with a passion by Tunisians, who view them as Egyptians do Saudi tourists, regardless of their specific intentions in visiting the country: Bedouin imbeciles, bereft of culture and sophistication, but a necessary evil because they pump so much of their oil money into the tourism sector. They are liked for one reason alone, namely, that they are easy to rip off. Aside from holding raucous parties in short-term furnished apartments in Tunis and the resort city of Sousse farther south, where they are not trying to persuade the women they have invited to follow the example of the Prophet, many are given to driving their SUVs in large convoys along the corniche in the early hours of the morning. Eventually they park and form large, drunken crowds to chant pro-Gaddafi slogans, until the Tunisian police arrive and move them on.

Tunisian women are integrated into the local social life, and by and large do not wear the veil, so determining who is a prostitute and who is not is near impossible for an outsider. Local men, though, seem to have developed a kind of "whoredar," the equivalent of the famed "gay-dar" in the West. And the police have certain criteria by which they arrest women they suspect are plying their trade outside the designated zones. There are no sudden raids on nightclubs, still less on private apartments, since that would be considered by the population at large a gross invasion of people's private space. But a Tunisian woman I met in the capital through a friend of a friend, when I decamped to the country to write my last book on Egypt, told me how crackdowns do happen, at least in her experience. She was in her midtwenties, university educated, and from a city south of the capital. A few years earlier she had fallen out with her family, though precisely why I never discovered. Two Libyan men visited her throughout the year, she said, each of whom left her enough money to survive until the other arrived. According to her, the police periodically rounded up women they had been monitoring, and whom they suspected were working as unregistered prostitutes.

Under interrogation, the giveaway was always that the woman was single, living away from her home city, and unable to prove she was employed and therefore in receipt of a regular income. Even the prostitutes in the red-light districts, this woman told me, always hailed from another city, a way of keeping reputations intact; and unless an unmarried woman was a student or employed in the city where she lived, it was highly unusual for her not to be working as a hooker. That struck me as a grossly unfair generalization. But she continued that after being forced to undergo an HIV test, such women were typically sentenced to three months in prison and given a small fine. Court cases are not reported by the media, so statistics regarding the number of arrests are not available.

How did things turn out this way in Tunisia?

The best way to answer that is by comparing the situation in the country to that in Egypt, another popular tourist destination that also had a regulated prostitution industry under the Ottomans and the British, but which outlawed it upon independence. The difference between Egypt after the 1952 military coup and Tunisia after independence in 1956, and specifically the radically different status of women in each country and the governments' attitude toward prostitution, is the difference between the respective leaders who took the helm: Gamal Abdel Nasser and Habib Bourguiba.

Nasser focused almost all his efforts on promoting pan-Arabism, and he led Egypt into multiple disastrous wars abroad and social decay at home. By contrast, Bourguiba emphasized Tunisia's uniqueness, and was the first Arab leader to call for the Palestinians to make peace with Israel. Nasser and his Free Officers movement turned their backs on the West and trashed, like a rock band in a hotel room, every aspect of the British and Ottoman colonial inheritance, good and bad, to create a military dictatorship. The bulk of the Egyptian budget went to the armed forces, therefore into the pockets of Nasser's cronies, and today Egypt is still essentially run by the military establishment. Bourguiba instead recognized the positive aspects of French colonial rule, sidelined the army and gave it minimal funding (and no role at all in politics), and forged security alliances with France and the United States. That diplomacy left him free to create a vibrant society that could face the challenges of the modern world, and to channel whatever wealth his new modern economy created to his people. Perhaps most important to the future of Egypt, Nasser slaughtered the Islamists. This created the resentment and hatred that would cause the blowback of a two-decade-long campaign of Islamist terror, culminating in the massacre of tourists and Egyptians in the city of Luxor in 1997. But pragmatic Bourguiba outwitted the Islamists. He eschewed severe repression, violence, and death camps and convinced his nation, and especially its women, that secularism was in their best interest, while delivering on his promises of a much higher standard of living.

Tunisia settled into its modern, secular identity in the 1990s under Bourguiba's successor, Zine El-Abidine Ben Ali. Appalled by Bourguiba's decision to execute a group of Islamist rebels, he had ousted the by then senile leader in 1987 in a nonviolent coup. Ben Ali thus kept Tunisia free of bloodshed (the rebels were not in the end executed), something the country had managed to do since independence from France was achieved through negotiations, and therefore bloodlessly as well. He adopted more aggressively the form of economic governance Bourguiba had introduced, known now as the Singapore model. This model posits that newly independent nations, often emerging from decades of social and political upheaval, must restrict political participation and freedom of expression during the early years of nation building. It gives priority, that is to say, to the short-term goal of national security and quality-of-life freedoms, above freedom of political expression, and precedence is always given to the collective material good.

This political model has its pros and cons like any other, as we will see. But what no one can deny is that Tunisia is now the Arab world's most prosperous and peaceful country, as Singapore is the wealthiest and most stable in Asia. "Tunisia's economic advance sounds almost too good to be true, in the face of global recession and few natural resources," the Associated Press, not a news organization known to suck up to Arab regimes, could report in 2009. It called the country "a model other autocratic governments have sought but usually fail to achieve."[10] Egypt meanwhile suffers from every conceivable social, political, cultural, and religious ill, and seems constantly to be teetering on the brink of a new popular uprising.

At the heart of Bourguiba's vision, which earned him the moniker the Arab Atatürk (after the Turkish leader who radically modernized and secularized his country after coming to power in 1922), was an undermining of the collective reverence for popular Islamic tradition, especially in the conservative countryside. One of his first moves was to replace the Quranic schools with a modern primary and secondary education system closely modeled on the French one. All educated Tunisians these days are fluent in French and Arabic, and they often speak decent English and a fourth language, too. Bourguiba strongly discouraged his people from performing religious pilgrimages, especially worshiping at local saints' shrines, which he considered a sign of backwardness; and he encouraged in equally strong speeches the study and appreciation of Tunisia's pre-Islamic heritage. A secularist but not an atheist, he used the example of the Prophet, who according to tradition did not fast in Ramadan during wartime, to argue against fasting during Ramadan any time the Tunisian people were engaged in the new collective jihad against economic stagnation, because fasting hindered performance. This led to one of the most extraordinary, but little-known, moments of Arab political theater. In a live television interview aired during the Ramadan fasting hours, Bourguiba paused, turned to the camera, and took a long, symbolic swig from a glass of orange juice. There was, however, nothing symbolic in his promotion of secular virtues. He replaced the *sharia* legal system with civil courts, abolished the independent system of Islamic charity called the *waqf*, brought the mosques and their imams under state control and had their doors locked outside of prayer times, outlawed proselytizing, and in 1981 officially banned the wearing of the veil (he famously called it an "odious rag") in schools and in government institutions in an attempt to phase it out of Tunisian society completely.[11] What is perhaps most remarkable is that he achieved this radical social, cultural, economic, and religious transformation without ever taking the country into any wars, nor executing a single opponent (even in his senile years), or facing down massive uprisings—all the more extraordinary when one recalls the wars and murderous repression that swept so much of the Arab world during the three decades in which he ruled.

Tunisia's pioneering role in women's affairs was achieved with the support of Tahar Haddad, a modernizing Tunisian Islamic reformer who called for freeing women from all of their restricting bonds. A scholar of Tunisia's Great Mosque of the Zitouna, he wrote a hugely influential book entitled *Our Women in the Sharia and Society* (1930), in which he advocated formal education for women and maintained that Islam "had been distorted and misinterpreted to such an extent that women no longer were aware of their duties in life and the legitimate advantages they could expect."[12] In the name of Islam, Haddad denounced abuses against women such as repudiation, whereby a husband could divorce his wife without grounds or explanation, sending her back to her family or leaving her for another wife.

The reformer instead wrote:

Islam is innocent of the oft-made accusations that it is an obstacle in the way of progress. Rather it is the religion of progress par excellence, an endless source of progress. Our decadence is the consequence of the chimera with which we have filled our minds and the scandalous, paralyzing customs within which we have locked ourselves.[13]

✣✣✣

Building upon the positive atmosphere created by Haddad's cautious writing, Tunisian women advanced their own cause significantly by playing active roles in their country's struggle for independence. They joined mainstream demonstrations as people first and women second, in the name of the country's liberation rather than specifically to bring about female emancipation. Like the men, they were arrested, including once for unfurling the main opposition party's banner "in the presence of the visiting French president."[14]

Bourguiba was personally influenced by Haddad's writing and exploited the progressive Islamic atmosphere it had helped to create in Tunisia for the promotion of women's rights. On the bronze door to Bourguiba's mausoleum in Monastir, the town where he was born in 1903 and died in 2000, is written:

THE SUPREME COMBATANT

THE LIBERATOR OF WOMEN

THE BUILDER OF MODERN TUNISIA

It is as the liberator of women that he will always be best remembered, and it is in this context that we should consider Tunisia's decision not to criminalize prostitution. The feminism he championed was not the salvationist kind, but that which encourages women's independence, autonomy, and genuine equality, in light of progressive Islamic thinking that sought to marry Islam with modernity; and it came in conjunction with a kind of sexual revolution unprecedented in the Arab world. His campaign for full female emancipation was launched in the form of a new Personal Status Code, which became law within

months of independence in 1956. It outlawed polygamy, redefined
marriage as a voluntary contract that conferred rights upon the wife as
well as the husband, and set a minimum age for marriage.[15] The consent of the bride was made mandatory, outlawing "the traditional practice of selling young girls, and underscoring the modern concept of
marriage as a bond between two individuals rather than an alliance between two families."[16] Bourguiba simultaneously launched a family
planning campaign, advanced by Western standards of the time, and
focused on advocating birth control. In 1966, Tunisia became the first
(and remains the only) Muslim country to legalize abortion.[17] The aim
of all this, according to a *Wall Street Journal* report in 2003, was "to use
the declining birth rate to gain personally and economically":

> The government spends about $10 million each year to teach citi-
> zens about family planning and dispense birth-control devices to the
> remotest corners of a country nearly the size of Florida. Tunisia has
> gone a long way toward educating its women and bringing them into
> the work force. Men and schoolchildren learn about contraception.
> Mobile clinics offer free pap smears and breast exams. Tunisia has
> even persuaded its religious leaders to loosen their interpretation of
> the Qur'an to fit the cause.[18]

The result: a fertility rate of 2.08 today, compared to 7.2 in the 1960s.
Life expectancy in Tunisia is above seventy-four years, schooling and
health care are free, the poverty rate is less than 4 percent, and high lit-
eracy rates have helped a third of Tunisian youths to enter university,
where women make up 60 percent of the students.[19] Since The
Change, as the transition of power in 1987 from Bourguiba to the current head of state Ben Ali is known, per capita income has increased

more than five-fold, from $725 to $3,800.[20] The *Wall Street Journal* further reported on how evidence for the campaign which led to the reduced birth rate "is everywhere."

> Condoms are distributed free in all clinics and sold for a nominal price in shops. Birth-control pills and the morning-after pill are available free to almost anyone who needs them. The construction of primary schools stopped a decade ago as the average number of students in a primary-school class dropped to twenty-eight in 2000 from thirty-eight in 1985.[21]

While discussion of AIDS, or at least the reality of the sexual behavior that results in its spread, was taboo throughout much of the Middle East in the early years of the pandemic, Tunisia in 1985 was the first country in the region to implement AIDS awareness and information campaigns, when the first Tunisian cases of HIV infection were detected. Such national strategies against AIDS, as well as providing free medical treatment for infected persons, has resulted in Tunisia being one of the least infected countries on the African continent.[22] During 2008, when just forty-seven people were officially known to have become infected, the Tunisian government nevertheless opened eleven new specialized AIDS clinics, guaranteeing anonymity for everyone who volunteered to be tested.[23]

That Tunisia has one of the lowest AIDS rates in Africa and the Middle East is even more remarkable when one considers the broader context. It is one of the region's most popular tourist destinations, with seven million visitors a year (Tunisia's native population is 10 million)—a country where a casual mixing of the sexes is the norm in all strata of urban society; where the hijab is severely discouraged; and where religion plays no overt role in public life. One reason for the containment of the disease is clearly the government's progressive attitude to sex-related health issues. Another is surely Tunisia's requirement that registered prostitutes undergo regular health check-ups.

Following Napoleon's 1798 expedition to Egypt, Western travelers flooded there, and by 1834 belly dancers working as prostitutes in Cairo had grown so numerous that the ruler Mohammed Ali banished them to Upper Egypt. That had what must have been, for some, the decidedly more stimulating consequence of Turkish boys in drag replacing them. In 1866 Mohammed Ali's successor, Ismail Pasha, brought the women back to boost the national economy, and as a result he earned the nickname Pimp Pasha from expatriates;[24] but the Westerners themselves began taking Eastern dancing women to Europe and America, culminating in Chicago at the World's Columbian Exposition of 1893, where the performances of Little Egypt were the biggest draw.

Pimp Pasha instituted state regulatory measures that required prostitutes to obtain health certificates and undergo routine medical examinations.[25] However, the continued influx into Egypt of foreign women created global newspaper headlines, and the "white slave trade" panic was born. It was led by Western feminists, and by the mid-1920s upper-class Egyptian feminists had formed an alliance with the international women's movement.[26] They marched under a banner that not only called for women to have equal rights in the workplace but also denounced prostitution and called for the protection of women's honor and virtue. Prostitution—and sexuality generally—thus became more politicized as local anti-imperial movements (nationalists, feminists, Islamists) used it as a symbol of decadence and foreign influence. Such movements sought to reject the Egyptian past, which was seen as a period of weakness defined by lack of autonomy, and project an image of strength for the present and future, which meant independence. Restoring the nation's honor was central to their agenda, and the concomitant was protecting women from exploitation. Indeed, it is no accident that the situation of prostitutes these days is worse in those countries that are most radically opposed to Western influence. Such movements, again at first glance paradoxically, became implicit allies with emerging international organizations, especially Western, championing women's rights and fighting prostitution to protect fallen women. What united these strange bedfellows is that each, in its own way, was driven by salvationist impulses, or the drive to save—whether in religious or secular terms—those who, as a nation or as individuals, had fallen from grace. In Egyptian political discourse, the Violated Prostitute became a metaphor for the Raped Colonial State, and the Call to Save Her became a metaphor for the Anti-Colonial Struggle.

Never mind that this distinctively Christian way of looking at things has nothing fully analogous to it in Islam. Indeed, until 1922, when the government undertook a review of the prostitution laws in Egypt, prostitution had almost never come under attack, and there was by no means a consensus on the issue. An article in a local newspaper in 1893 on "The European Contagion in Oriental Countries," which called for "the removal of prostitutes and clandestine houses from respectable neighborhoods," is the only example of its kind before the twentieth century that historians can find.[27] However, in 1923, just as the feminist campaign and the legal review got under way, a series of articles was published in the main daily newspaper, *Al-Ahram*, under the headline "Slaughterhouses of Virtue," and another series, "Official Prostitution in Egypt," followed in 1926.[28]

The author of both series was Sheikh Mahmoud Abul-Uyun, a well-known Al-Azhar scholar and fervent nationalist. In one article he wrote: "Yes, Islam prohibits adultery and ordains that adulterers be lashed and put to death by stoning. . . . Nothing could be more heinous and more devastating to the prestige of a government, and an Islamic government in particular, than for it to legislate and organize adultery."[29]

Note here the difference in tone and emphasis to that of Tahar Haddad, who was writing on women's issues in Tunisia during the same decade. More remarkable than what Abul-Uyun wrote, however, was the response in Egypt. Abul-Uyun certainly had his supporters, but he also had many detractors. *Al-Siyasa*, the mouthpiece of the Liberal Constitutionalist Party, accused Abul-Uyun of meddling in affairs that "were none of his business," and argued instead that prostitution was "a necessary evil" and that all that could be done to counter it was

> to contain its ills within certain bounds and consider creating new social factors to replace the material means that religious strictures have devised to counter the spread of prostitution. Such factors can be brought about by strengthening the moral fabric of the young in a manner that channels their material and moral energies towards noble endeavors, thereby diverting them from the many inducements to corruption they will encounter in adulthood.[30]

Moreover, the Ministry of Interior vetoed a decision to close down brothels in the wake of the legal review, since prohibition, they said, "would render it impossible to enforce the regulations governing prostitution. Under such circumstances the police would be unable to take the legal procedures against prostitutes who take up residence in respectable neighborhoods and open their premises for prostitution," a ministry communiqué stated, adding: "A thorough study of the question is essential if the results of actions taken are not to conflict with the ultimate objectives of reformers."[31]

Nevertheless, the powerful International Woman Suffrage Alliance, founded in Berlin in 1904, called in a resolution passed during its 1923 congress for an "end to state regulated prostitution and a suppression of the international traffic in women and children."[32] Feminists back then, too, were exploiting the panic surrounding human trafficking in the form of the "white slave trade,"[33] and Egyptian feminists, aligned with the international feminists and also opposed to prostitution, entered into a marriage of convenience with the Islamists. In 1928 the Muslim Brotherhood was founded and its influence, along with that of the establishment clerics and international women's movements, grew exponentially during the following decades. Initially, the Egyptian feminists had earned the Islamists' wrath as a result of their calls for women's liberation, and especially the shedding of the veil, leaving them vulnerable to charges they were promoting licentiousness and that they, too, were loose women. Their campaign against prostitution was partly a response to the fear of being labeled pro-vice.[34]

The head of the Egyptian Feminist Union (EFU), the first nationwide feminist movement in Egypt, founded in 1923, wrote to the sheikh of Al-Azhar, Egypt's preeminent Islamic institution, to enlist his support on religious and moral grounds in the campaign against prostitution: "The EFU would also like to request Your Eminence to draw the attention of the government to the houses of prostitution that have spread throughout the country posing a danger to morals and virtues. Recognizing prostitution and licensing it is a great shame for a government of an Islamic country whose constitution states that the official religion is Islam."[35]

Scandal followed scandal, it always being easier to whip up a moral panic than to provide a rational opinion, and by 1949 there was such intense debate surrounding the issue of prostitution, both at home and abroad, that the unpopular King Farouk, himself a notorious womanizer, closed state-licensed prostitution houses. In 1952 a military coup sent Farouk into exile, and power went to Gamal Abdel Nasser. A year later, Nasser dealt the death blow to legalized prostitution by outlawing prostitution entirely.

Nasser was secular-minded, though, and later he would crush the Muslim Brotherhood by executing and torturing their leaders in death camps and sending thousands of their members into exile. But he had worked with the Brothers in the years leading up to the 1952 coup, and his outlawing of prostitution was likely aimed partly at pacifying them. It was also a result of his obsessive purging of all foreign influence on Egyptian political and cultural life. Egypt nevertheless remained socially liberal until the 1970s, when Nasser's successor, Anwar Al-Sadat, brought the rank-and-file of the Muslim Brotherhood back from exile (they had mostly decamped to Saudi Arabia) and used them to counter the influence of the leftists, who had organized in protest at Nasser's increasingly despotic rule. During that decade, and throughout the 1980s, Islamic fundamentalism therefore grew in influence in Egypt, and "belly-dancing nightclubs were torched and dancers were barred from television."[36] Today, dancers are free to perform in Cairo's city center, but they must cover their navels or risk fines or arrest.

Five decades after prostitution was banned in Egypt, in the name of Islam and the feminism that protects women's virtue and honor, how does the situation of women in the country compare to that of Tunisia's women?

While Tunisian women basically walk the streets free of hassle, Egyptian women suffer more abuse and harassment than women in any other Arab country, indeed, perhaps in the world. According to the Egyptian Center for Women's Rights, in 2009 some 98 percent of foreign women, and 83 percent of Egyptian women, said they had experienced sexual harassment.[37] The Egyptian media, free to cover social issues in the sensational manner that is the only way it knows how, thrives on an endless series of sex scandals, which are nowhere to be found in Tunisia. Unlike in Tunis, prostitutes can be found in all middle-class districts of Cairo, but especially those that are home to the Egyptian elite and holidaying Gulf Arabs, and I know from my years of living in Egypt that they are given to wearing the *niqab* (a garment covering the whole face with two eyeholes and severely discouraged in Tunisia). Whereas the Tunisian authorities have taken measures in nightclubs and discos to contain soliciting for sex, one is never more than a few hundred meters from an East European hooker in the Egyptian Red Sea resorts of Sharm El-Sheikh, Taba, and Hurghada, and the Egyptian authorities are reduced to rounding them up and announcing their mass deportation.[38] And whereas Tunisia has tackled the AIDS issue so successfully that it is statistically minuscule in the country, in 2010 Egypt reported a sixfold increase in the number of cases, and yet is still, after more than two decades, dithering about whether it should treat seriously the threat the virus poses.[39]

Back in 1926, at the height of the debate about the legal status of prostitution in Egypt, *Al-Ahram* published a letter charging that the attempts by Abul-Uyun and others to secure the support of government ministers for his prohibition cause were demeaning to their status and prestige. The anonymous author of the letter, in words that now seem extraordinarily prescient, also suggested that Abul-Uyun's approach to prostitution was ultimately detrimental:

> Have you given any serious thought at all to the consequences of prohibiting prostitution? If indeed you have, are you of the opinion that prohibition will be conducive to the spread of virtue? I, for one, do not believe it will. On the contrary, good sir, I fear it will allow this practice to evade government control entirely and spread epidemically.[40]

A report on child prostitution in Tunisia was published in 2003 by one of the most influential of the West's antiprostitution groups: End Child Prostitution, Child Pornography and Trafficking of Children for Sexual Purposes, or ECPAT.[41]

The report starts with the dry pronouncement that "we must analyze this phenomenon [the commercial exploitation of children] in a scientific manner and, most of all, address the topic with due caution and consideration." We are told in the report's opening pages that "the statistics contained in the report *do not* highlight information specifically related to commercial sexual exploitation of children" (my emphasis), which is presumably why it is entitled "A Situational Analysis of Commercial Sexual Exploitation of Children in Tunisia."[42] What, in my view, the report discovers, or more accurately does not, based on the unavailable statistics, makes one wonder why it was published at all.

The first thing we learn is that in Tunisia seventeen girls and nine boys have recently been represented in legal cases as "victims of sexual exploitation" and that the crimes committed against this small group were "of no specified nature." That means they could have had nothing at all to do with prostitution. Such statistics "are important because they give us an idea of the overall state of the children and the relevant legal framework," the authors explain.[43] They do indeed, namely, that thus far Tunisia's children appear to be admirably well represented in court and certainly not the mass victims of any kind of unwanted sexual advances. We are even told by ECPAT again that the statistics "don't give us a clear idea of commercial child sexual exploitation in Tunisia."[44]

Here the report might sensibly end, the laptop be shut, and the scientific investigator decamp for more fertile pastures. Instead, consider the key evidence provided, aside from a small number of victim narratives based on interviews that do not indicate a trend, to prove the "considerable" numbers of underage female prostitutes said to exist in Tunisia in 2003: "The existence of underage prostitution is confirmed by the considerable number of girls who resort to illegal sex work and who are imprisoned. A study conducted by psychologists and doctors in the 1990s revealed that prostitution is the main offense for which adolescents are sentenced (78 percent)."[45]

By "in the 1990s" they actually mean, as a footnote points out, a frustratingly untraceable study published in 1991, which in turn reveals this 2003 ECPAT study was likely based largely on information gathered as far back as the 1980s, given the time it takes to research, write, referee, and publish academic papers (even provided they are not themselves based on earlier studies). Relying on such outdated research is especially problematic in a country like Tunisia, which has witnessed dramatic economic and social changes, all of them positive, over the past two decades, resulting in the eradication of social inequalities and the emergence of an affluent middle class that today comprises some 80 percent of the population (measured by home ownership, schooling levels, and income).[46] Child prostitution in any country is inextricably linked to poverty, homelessness, and a lack of education, and in the 2000s Tunisia suffers on a grand scale from none of these ills.

In any event, the report cites no absolute numbers. We do not know how many adolescent girls were sentenced to prison terms in total, so the 78 percent figure tells us nothing. In the developing world, there persists among scholars a quaint belief in the power of percentages, and it is no rare thing to find a portion of four in eight apples referred to as "50 percent." But if twenty girls in total were imprisoned, it would mean only about fifteen underage female prostitutes found in the whole of Tunisia during that period, and the figure would therefore point to a positive situation. Also: does "adolescents" include girls who are three days short of their eighteenth birthday? I suspect it does, because the term is used interchangeably in the report with "underage," and ECPAT and other child salvationist groups have been singled out not only for offering impossibly high figures about the prevalence of child prostitution in the countries they seek to colonize and plunder but for conflating children, adolescents, and young men and women into a single demographic.[47]

Why in this study are we anyway conflating "adolescents" and the "underaged" with "children"? Defining as a "child" anyone under the age of eighteen is to my mind pointless in any context, but especially so in this one: since "adolescents" are singled out as a different group, the "children" referred to in the study's title should properly be referred to as "pre-pubescents." But in that case there would probably remain, at a generous guesstimate, two cases to whip up a panic about.

What distinction, more to the point, did the researchers of this 1991 study themselves draw between these radically different groups of young people?

We have no way of knowing, because all the relevant footnote says is: "Dr. Samira Mahjoub Negra, Souad Rejeb, Dr. Mohammed Chafik Landoulsi, Dr. Rached Mahjoub. Study on Juvenile Delinquency, Tunis 1991." If you Google "Study on Juvenile Delinquency, Tunis 1991," you get one hit: the ECPAT report you were desperately trying to escape from. Searching for "Etude sur la délinquance juvénile" is equally fruitless. Some of the research listed in the ECPAT bibliography, included to give it an air of scholarly authority and depth, dates back even farther, to the mid-1970s.

In 2005, two years after the ECPAT study appeared, the U.S. State Department concluded that "child labor and child prostitution" are "not significant problems" in Tunisia.[48]

I think such studies by ECPAT and other similar organizations risk diverting attention away from the very real problems so many of the world's children face: hunger, poverty, violence at the hands of their peers and parents in brutalized inner-city environments, and a lack of access to health care, education, and clean water. The studies also, more troublingly, encourage us to view the subject of prostitution through the lens of child sexual exploitation instead of treating them as distinct and separate issues. That way, anyone who argues in favor of legalizing prostitution can be bombarded with the stories of how two girls were drugged and raped and sold into slavery: If you support the former, you condone the latter. Yet the same argument is never used in relation to anything else. Not since the heady 1960s has anyone dared to suggest that marriage and the nuclear family should be outlawed because of the large numbers of men who rape their wives and sexually abuse their children. No one has yet proposed a blanket ban on all retail because many workers are underpaid and exploited in the discount outlets of our shopping malls.

As far as one can tell, given its barely comprehensible English, the message of the ECPAT Tunisia report was not anti–child prostitution, since it found scant evidence of it, but antiprostitution in general, and was in particular critical of Tunisia's refusal to criminalize it:

> [The Tunisian] Penal Code addresses only one type of sexual ex-
> ploitation in general and of commercial sexual exploitation of chil-
> dren: prostitution. This is why Tunisia did not ratify the U.N.
> Convention for the Suppression of the Traffic in Persons and of the
> Exploitation of the Prostitution of Others of December 2, 1949. All
> other forms of commercial sexual exploitation are not explicitly sup-
> pressed or forbidden by normal legislation.[49]

What gets the salvationists in a tizzy, then, is Tunisia's refusal to classify all prostitutes as trafficked victims, casting grown women and children together in the same leaky boat on the imaginary seas where the slave trade continues to flourish. A year before the ECPAT report appeared, the U.N. Committee on Elimination of Discrimination Against Women issued a report on a meeting that focused on Tunisia. It stated explicitly the ambiguously worded antiprostitution agenda of the ECPAT research. After listing the numerous advances in the status of Tunisian women, it was noted that members of the U.N.

committee and Tunisian representatives did not see eye to eye on certain issues:

> The report notes that prostitution has declined as Tunisian women have become more emancipated, and several establishments have closed. In 1998, the number of authorized prostitutes came to 422 in a total of fifteen establishments. The remaining brothels are subject to strict medical and health controls by the Ministry of Public Health. The report states, however, that Tunisian society is tolerant of prostitution, and the practice can be only gradually reduced as relationships between men and women based on equality and reciprocity are strengthened.[50]

The key word here is "however," implying as it does that state regulation of prostitution, legal protection of prostitutes, social tolerance of the profession, and official monitoring of sex workers' health and well-being is somehow in contradiction with a progressive society and the advancement of women's rights. It is classic salvationist feminism. Here the U.N. report implicitly espouses that the ideal universal goal is the social marginalization of prostitution through prohibition. However, the Tunisian position was articulated by Bouhdiba in the quote above from his book *Sexuality in Islam*, where he points to how regulation "controls the deviants as well as giving a status to deviance." The Tunisian government's no-nonsense approach to sex and personal morality, including prostitution, has, as we have seen, in fact brought countless practical benefits to its people, whereas the Egyptian salvationist attitude has had nothing but negative consequences. Legalization and regulation, then, are not separate from, but an integral part of, the most advanced women's rights campaign ever seen in Africa and the Middle East.

While the Islamists' view of women across the Middle East is especially egregious, it is not all that different from their strange bedfellows in neopuritanism. Salvationist feminists like those on U.N. committees preach women's rights but their desire to protect women is little different, at base, from the Islamic fundamentalists who also seek to prevent women from driving or going to elementary school. The desire of both sides to control people, and intolerance toward deviation, has the effect of increasing vice, by definition. If deviation from accepted behavior is wrong, in addition to being illegal, then anyone rejecting the stated norms is engaging in vice. As the American novelist Tom Robbins once famously put it: When freedom is outlawed, only outlaws will be free. The neopuritans, whether Islamic or feminist, seem to fear most women's independence and their right to control their own fates, or at least their own bodies. The goal of any self-respecting human being tolerant of others is to favor anything that increases a person's ability to control her own fate, and at the very least maintain sovereignty over her own body. So rather than condemn prostitution tout court, it is far better, as in the Tunisian model, to condemn exploitation and loss of freedom of choice. Any sane person condemns coercion and violation of privacy, and any good person would like to see conditions improve so that trading sex for money is not the best of a set of bad options. But the obsessive focus of neopuritans on the regulated sex market, especially when arbitrarily linked to child abuse and sex trafficking, diverts attention from more important and difficult problems.

Once we remove moralism from the equation, once we recognize that exchange between consenting people is the foundation of any liberal society, then we realize that accepting sexual variety to flourish is a sign of a healthy, not a corrupt, society. When sex outside of controlled channels is defined as deviance, it is the most exposed, the least powerful, who suffer. Behind the veil of vice lies the sanctimony of those who would impose their way—be it *sharia* or evangelicalism of a Christian or feminist hue—on people who are defined as sinners, the fallen, and so requiring protection and salvation. The vice lies in the exploitation, in the coercion, that result from driving natural human drives and needs into the shadows.

That is the ultimate perversity.

Dostoyevsky famously said one can tell something about a society by entering its prisons. So, too, can one gain insight into a society based on how it treats those on the margins. The degree of respect given to prostitutes in any society is a measure of its progressiveness, freedom, and modernity. The prostitute's status and the respect society has for her is a reflection of our own status and self-respect.

Tunisia has clearly done well by its people, and by its women in particular. However, there is one crucial problem with the Singapore model of governance: The ruling elites who steer countries through the postindependence turmoil toward modernity and greater equality seem to be of the opinion that the process is endless. Those who hold power, in other words, are never willingly going to give it up. Gradual change is in principle, of course, a good idea, certainly in countries where a blatant disregard for civil liberties go hand in hand with outright brutality and a plundering of the nation's resources. In such instances—and in the Arab world Egypt is an obvious example—any long reign of extreme censorship especially tends to hamper not only cultural expression, but the capacity for it as well. The most extreme example, Saudi Arabia, is a country now devoid of art or culture of any value whatsoever, Islamic or otherwise, official or clandestine. Under such circumstances, censorship, like any prohibition, strangles the soul, not only of the censored but of the censor, too, so that over time the authorities find themselves turning in an ever tighter circle as the perimeter of the permissible draws in.

The situation is complicated, though, in a country like Tunisia, where sudden and dramatic change in favor of Western-style democracy at this juncture does still risk undoing what good work has been done. Freer and fairer elections risk bringing to power a small band of rabid Islamists who can be guaranteed to whip up populist campaigns against Western influence, women's liberation, alcohol, and prostitution. As we shall see, that is what has happened in countries like Bahrain, Yemen, and Morocco, where a push toward democracy has brought radical Islamists to power. And it is not that Tunisia is suppressing its bubbling underground of multifarious ideas and manifold creative expression. For sure, the press is censored, but then the nation's excellent schools and universities teach evolution, Marxism, and even Nietzsche's theory that God is dead, all as part of the history of ideas. And the government monitors and revises textbooks to ensure they do not promote stereotypical role models for women. I know from my own conversations with Tunisian friends that students are encouraged to debate any topic in the classroom so long as discussion does not turn into a political rally. One told me that when he had raised concerns that they were discussing the death of God in his philosophy course at the university, the professor had told him: "Learning is learning, and religion is religion. Don't confuse the two." If only that advice were echoed in classrooms throughout the Middle East. The country, moreover, has a thriving, state-sponsored literary scene and the best art house cinema industry in the region, where again no subject but the private lives of the rulers is taboo.

What the Tunisian government does suppress is straightforward political opposition that organizes outside of the official perimeters, which, of course, it sets, and that seeks to overthrow the existing order. That constriction of discourse cannot be unconditionally accepted, but the problem in condemning it at the present time is that the group most determined to bring about change is also the one it is most difficult to have any sympathy with: the Islamists. A few hundred of them languish in prison, having attempted to overthrow the secular order, and the threat they pose even in this staunchly secular country cannot be overestimated. As in Turkey, Tunisia's nearest equivalent in the Middle East, a decade of George W. Bush's wars and Israel's assaults on the Palestinians have so much incensed the population that hatred of American foreign policy is near universal. Increasing numbers of younger women are starting to wear the veil, and the government has even had to make concessions on the Islam front by setting up a new radio station dedicated to (nonpolitical) religious themes.[51] In 2002, a suicide bomb attack on a synagogue in the southern resort of Djerba that killed twenty-one people had a dramatic impact on the economy because it led to a large drop in tourism. Suspected Islamists have been killed in shootouts with security forces in and around the capital as recently as 2007. Ordinary Tunisians only have to look to neighboring

Algeria, where 150,000 people have been killed in a brutal and ongoing civil war between Islamists and the secular government, to know that the threat of widespread chaos and carnage is not concocted.

In light of the above, the best place for Islamists who want to overthrow the Tunisian state is indeed the prison cell, where they might be persuaded to modify their ideas, and not least because the first thing they would do if they gained power is deprive everyone else (and especially women) of their treasured liberties faster than they can scream "Allahu akbar."

CHAPTER *three*

TEMPORARY MARRIAGES

"She can't take her eyes off you."

It was the third time since setting off from the hotel fifteen minutes earlier that my Iranian fixer had felt compelled to point out I was being solicited by a local woman. I momentarily glanced at her, as I had the others, from the back window: about thirty years old, colored head scarf pulled high to reveal curls dangling next to a face plastered with makeup.

"You're supposed to be fixing me up with government officials, not hookers," I reminded him.

The driver said something in Farsi, and the fixer looked over his shoulder and asked me: "Are you giving him the green light?"

"The green light?" I repeated.

"Yes, the green light," the fixer said again. "That's what you do here in Tehran. If you want to pick up a prostitute on the way to where you're going, you say to the driver that you're giving him the green light."

"Isn't that a bit risky?" I asked. "Wouldn't some drivers refuse to play along or be offended?"

The taxi driver demanded a translation. He burst out laughing when the fixer finished, and again told the latter to relay something.

"He says the only people taxi drivers in Tehran refuse to pick up are the mullahs," the fixer said, giggling himself now. "They have to take their robes and turbans off and pretend to be normal people, or they'll wait in the street forever."

Under normal circumstances I might have prolonged the chitchat, but this elderly man I had hired to work as my translator and guide seemed determined to do anything but the task he was being paid $150 a day to fulfill. In the hotel lobby that morning, he had returned the sheet of paper I had given him, on which were listed the subjects I wanted to write articles about and people I needed to interview, with barely concealed contempt.

"Yes, yes," he had mumbled, lighting a cigarette. "You want to go to a Friday sermon, meet a government spokesman to talk about the nuclear issue, and talk to an oppressed Jew. And yes, you can quote anything I say, as long as it's off the record. I'm thinking of changing my name to An Iranian Who Spoke on Condition of Anonymity."

It was not that I failed to see the point of his humor, and was in fact so in agreement with the object of his scorn—what is sometimes called hotel or parachute journalism—that this trip to Iran in 2006 would be the first and last time I would engage in it myself. The Singapore-based newspaper I was working for at the time had made me an offer I could hardly refuse: a month traveling around Iran, all expenses paid, including return flight, domestic transport, hotel bills, food, daily payment for a fixer, and even $80 or so a day spending money for myself, all in addition to my normal monthly salary.

It was an opportunity to see the country, and I had already decided that later that year I would be giving up journalism to concentrate on writing books. This would be my only chance to get a journalism visa for Iran, which does not see Singapore as a hostile entity; and I could at least travel to the southwestern Khuzestan region bordering Iraq, where Iran's oil fields are and where half the local Iranian population are ethnic Arabs and therefore Arabic speakers. I did make it down there, the only Western journalist to have done so in years.[1]

But on that first day in Tehran, I was seriously concerned that the fixer's contempt for the folly of the intrepid Western foreign correspondent was going to scupper any chance I might have of at least producing the copy required to meet the standards of parachute journalism.

"Tell the driver I'm giving him the red light," I said. "The last thing I need is being arrested by the vice squad."

"Oh no, you just get married," he said.

"I didn't come all this way to get laid," I insisted. "And certainly not to get married."

"No, not married," he continued. "You just do it by saying you're married to one another."

"Yes, I've heard of that," I said, thinking it might be a good idea for an article, not least because it was a subject I would have no problem getting this fixer to concentrate on. "It's called a *mutaa*."

He grimaced as he contradicted me: "It's called a *sigeh*."

I thought at the time we were referring to two different versions of the same thing, temporary marriages. Later I discovered the confusion arose because I was using the Arabic word, whereas he was using the Farsi.

The taxi driver butted in again.

"He says don't worry about the vice squad," the fixer said. "Just bribe them. A few dollars. They'll go away."

"You're forgetting one important thing," I finally declared. "I'm not a Muslim."

The fixer solemnly gave the driver the news and confessed to me that he had assumed I was a Muslim when I told the officials in the Ministry of Information I spoke Arabic and had lived in Saudi Arabia.

"You can convert," he said unconvincingly, as a way, it seemed, of closing the subject.

⊗⊗⊗

My guide made it all sound so simple.

Yet to say that the Islamic Republic is conflicted about sex would be the understatement of the millennium. In fact, Iran seems to be performing effortless stunts of conflictedness at a height that most younger, less troubled cultures would be quite incapable of reaching. The sex debate provides plenty of fodder for the Islamic Republic's many enemies, and so turbulent is Iran's recent history, and so extreme the contradictions, that wherever you turn you are never more than ten feet away from a scapegoat.

To begin with, there are two ways of prostitution in the Islamic Republic.

One of them is illegal and remains a dangerous calling with severe penalties for both prostitute and client. Inevitably, these penalties are more severe for the woman than the man, usually a number of lashes with the cane, though executions also happen. All the same, this form of prostitution is a huge and burgeoning industry, and its center is the holy city of Qom, known colloquially among Iranians as a destination for both pilgrimage and pleasure. Qom appears to have become a prostitution hot spot due to the abundance of shrines where female runaways with no shelter can take refuge by sleeping in rooms intended for pilgrims. Since they have no way of making a living, after a while many reportedly get involved with the sex trade.[2]

But prostitutes can be found on the streets of any city in Iran.

In 2002, it was estimated that there were 85,000 of them in Tehran alone,[3] though one more recent official estimate is as high as 300,000 for this city of 12 million.[4] There are both streetwalkers like the ones I had encountered, who pace the roadside and nip furtively into customers' cars, and women who work in brothels. Streetwalkers everywhere are always at the bottom of the pile. A documentary by Iranian filmmaker Moslem Mansouri on YouTube that looks recent—it is on digital video—suggests that many of the women who turn to this kind of prostitution, walking the streets and soliciting and serving a number of customers a day, do so because they come from broken homes, either running from their parents or because they are divorced.[5] Regular jobs are hard to come by for most Iranians and especially destitute women, some of the women interviewed in the documentary say, and they are in any case often a kind of glorified prostitution in the sense that those jobs that are available to such women make them vulnerable to sexual harassment from their employers. Instead, one of them explains, it makes more sense to turn straight to prostitution, where the income is better, even given the risk of arrest.

Iranian prostitutes are also becoming increasingly visible abroad.

"'Fatima' from Persia has become as familiar as 'Natasha' from Belarus. Iranian whores long have been a scandal in the Arab states of the Persian Gulf, which periodically round up and expel them," as a cranky columnist for *Asia Times* by the pseudonym of Spengler puts it.[6] Iranian women made up 10 to 15 percent of the prostitutes working in Belgium, the Netherlands, and Italy, according to a European study.[7] That is perhaps unsurprising, with an official Iranian unemployment rate of 12.5 percent (it is probably much higher) in a culture that overwhelmingly still favors men for such jobs as there are to be had, while the economy is shot as a result of the 1980–88 war with Iraq, corruption, and international sanctions.

A female Iranian member of parliament, Jamileh Kadivar, who is the wife of a former culture minister, has said:

> If we had adopted a proper management in various economic fields, we would never have been faced with the phenomenon of special women. A needy woman who has no support while officials have not fulfilled their responsibilities toward her has to give in to corruption in order to make a sustenance.[8]

It is also true that the vice squad is not the cleanest outfit in town.

In March 2008, a sting operation led to the arrest of Tehran's chief of police and head of the vice squad.[9] General Reza Zarei, it turned out, was something of a French-farce character. Once a humble provincial police chief, Zarei had risen to eminence, reportedly thanks in part to patronage from the notoriously humble president Mahmoud Ahmadinejad. He had become famous in his three years at the top of the vice squad for his harsh TV sermons. In his heyday in the 2000s, Zarei's office was naturally obsessed with head scarves and other pious trivia, giving out some 35,000 warnings for offenses like unmarried couples holding hands. Thankfully, his fall was swift. Zarei was arrested in 2008 in a brothel in flagrante delicto in the presence of several women whom he had asked to take their clothes off and stand in a row in front of him and pray naked.

The arrest had been ordered by Iran's justice minister, Ayatollah Hashemi Shahrudi, whose office had been watching him for weeks. According to *Der Spiegel* magazine,

> With his remark that a "high police official" could exploit his position for "material" as well as "private" gain, the prosecutor hinted that Zarei may also be suspected of pimping. Iranian police as well as the nation's Revolutionary Guard have, in fact, long stood under suspicion of taking kickbacks from Iran's various red-light districts.[10]

So far, however, there is nothing in the story that could not have happened in any number of countries where prostitution is illegal, and for the corrupt therefore provides a source of income for cash-strapped police officers, or an easy way to bolster the arrest quota through an end-of-term roundup. That a tug-of-war between various factions of a regime may lead to the sacrifice of a bent senior official is also a feature of politics the world over.

What makes the situation noteworthy in Iran is the second option for prostitution, namely the temporary marriage my guide had recommended when he saw me quail at his suggestion of picking up a woman off the street.

Sigeh, as it is called in Farsi, is said to date back to pre-Islamic Persia. It is a marriage contract for a predetermined period, anything from an hour to six months, at a predetermined price. The price may be in name only, or cash, or any sort of consideration paid out over the term of the sigeh. In the days before Islam, the woman and any children that resulted from such arrangements remained in the woman's family, but under Islam the children are the legitimate wards and heirs of the man. In principle, sigeh can be notarized, but this is not necessary, as the couple can simply confirm the contract between themselves verbally and without witnesses.

While a man is limited to four wives under a full marriage contract, there is no limit to how many temporary wives he may have, though, as ever, the unmarried women allowed to enter into sigeh partnerships are limited to one temporary husband at a time. The man can also divorce his temporary wife at any time during the contract, whereas the woman cannot. At the same time, the woman is not obliged to obey a temporary husband in everything, as she is under the full marriage contract, and a man in principle has to specify the time of day when he is going to visit the wife, who is under no obligation to move in with him.

In reality, the whole idea is that she does not move in with him. Once the agreed term is over, the woman is supposed to observe a waiting period of two menstrual cycles, known as *idda*, to ensure that no children have resulted from the marriage, and then she is free again.[11]

The usefulness of sigeh in facilitating street prostitution is limited, if all the niceties are observed. No streetwalker who, as it were, religiously observes two menstrual cycles worth of *idda* after every temporary marriage is going to make much of a living. But that is a big if, and in other ways it ties the hands of police seeking to crack down on prostitution. For one thing, no would-be arresting officer has any way of knowing when the woman was last married unless he has been shadowing her; indeed, since the institution can, if entailing only a verbal agreement, leave no paper trail, he has no way of knowing whether a couple are joined in sigeh or not. My guide was quite correct to say that all a man would need to claim was that such a temporary marriage contract had been talked about, and it was then up to the officers to prove otherwise.

At the same time, women caught several times in quick succession with different men are unlikely to be abiding by the rules, so this still makes the business dangerous unless the arresting officer is bribable. (In the case of the chief of the vice squad, there seems to have been no doubt what sort of establishment he was visiting at the time of his arrest.) Police officers, moreover, can be vindictive. Hell hath no fury like a little man with a little frustrated power.

Where sigeh really comes into its own is in more leisurely arrangements, since it amounts essentially to a kind of legitimized fling, whether for money or pleasure (or both). One writer on the subject, Shahla Haeri, a professor of cultural anthropology at Boston University and the author of *Law of Desire: Temporary Marriage in Shi'i Iran* (1989), interviewed women who participated in sigeh, and found that many of them used it to their own advantage. They would use it for economic security or as a way to satiate their sexual desires. Women have also often used sigeh as a way to either resist permanent marriage or to resist being fully possessed by a man.[12]

Haeri cites a woman called Mavashah, who said on the sexual aspects of sigeh, "I want to get married [her euphemism for sex] all the time, every night." Mavashah said she resents the idda period because this gets in the way of her combining business with pleasure.[13] In this respect, sigeh is a particularly useful way for widows and divorced women, who are considered more or less dead to the marriage market, to have a sex life. In purely practical terms, a nonsexual sigeh can also be performed between an adult male and one or more adolescent girls for the purpose of making him their *mahram* (male social guide) so they are more flexible in socializing and associating with boys their own age.[14]

This arrangement would also seem the natural option for pre-marital sex. The age of marriage is rising in Iran, chiefly because the cost of setting up house is becoming more prohibitive, as are dowries and expected cash gifts from the groom and the price of the festivities if there is to be any hope of keeping up with the Joneses. According to one survey, the average age of marriage is now an astonishing forty years for men and thirty-five years for women.[15] That figure seems un-likely, but even shaving off a decade, as other estimates do, would make the age high for the region, and it is improbable that members of ei-ther sex preserve themselves until then.

In the same survey, by a national youth organization, more than a quarter of the men between nineteen and twenty-nine admitted they had premarital sex,[16] which suggests to me that the other three-quar-ters may have been economical with the truth. (It is especially unclear, in this survey, whether men who had sex in temporary marriages con-sidered that to be premarital intercourse, and homosexual experience, very common among the young in Iran, is not touched on at all.) Still, even if the findings raise as many questions as they provide answers, there is no reason to dismiss the broad trend that prompted the ques-tions in the first place. President Ahmadinejad, for one, takes the late marriage issue seriously and has introduced a "Reza love fund," named after one of Shia Islam's twelve imams, to provide marriage loans, and plans have been announced to establish marriage bureaus to help peo-ple find full marriage partners.[17]

In recent years, there has also been a heavy push in another direction.

Clerics and senior government officials are promoting temporary marriage as a way to deal with the undeniable realities and to stem the social chaos they fear if fornication were to go totally unregulated. None other than former president Ali Akbar Hashemi Rafsanjani, often portrayed as a "pragmatic conservative," first broached the matter in a sermon in 1990, eleven years after the revolution. "Don't be promiscuous like the Westerners," he told his flock, and then, in one of the familiar somersaults of the pious, he recommended sigeh as the solution.[18] The sermon, alas, did not go down well, and brought thousands of protestors into the streets. But in those days, what did not? It sometimes seemed there was precious little on Iranian TV except locals, preferably women in all-over black sacks, protesting against one thing or another, burning the American flag one day and an effigy of Salman Rushdie the next.

The movement in favor of sigeh continues and has nothing to do, it appears, with the divide between "reformists" and "hard-liners" that is often being played up in the Western press. For a start, some feminists are all for it.

"First, relations between young men and women will become a little bit freer," Shahla Sherkat, editor of *Zanan* (Women), a feminist monthly, told the *New York Times* in 2000. "Second, they can satisfy their sexual needs. Third, sex will become depoliticized. Fourth, they will use up some of the energy they are putting into street demonstrations. Finally, our society's obsession with virginity will disappear."[19] Hard-line officials, too, remain overwhelmingly in favor of sigeh. Some have recommended it as a kind of trial marriage, because gender segregation, which severely restricts opportunities for unrelated men and women to mix in public (and in theory private, too), makes it difficult for teenagers to get to know each other, or simply as a way to satisfy sexual urges.[20] In 2007, Mostafa Pour Mohammadi, then minister of the interior, reportedly called temporary marriages "God's decree for the young people." Temporary marriages, he elaborated, "must be bravely promoted. Islam is in no way indifferent to the needs of a fifteen-year-old youth in whom God has placed the sex drive."[21]

If he made this statement, it is by any standards extraordinary, and not least because it sounds so sensible.

Before we get too excited, though, it is worth bearing in mind that what is meant by a hard-liner is really a reactionary advocate of the old-time religion. That includes all the practices a strict interpretation of the religion permits, as well as the ones it prohibits. In other words, a hard-liner is not necessarily a puritan in the same way that, say, a feminist in the salvationist Anglo-Saxon tradition is a puritan. He is not against sex: The question is in an odd way quite beside the point. The obsession is with rules, and more specifically with forestalling contingency. Similar contradictory tendencies can be seen in countries like Britain, where some traditional conservatives are resisting the prohibitionist surveillance state instituted by what were once considered liberals, while some traditionally right-wing newspapers speak out for greater individual freedoms even as others remain blithely committed to banning everything in sight.

There is no denying, then, that the lines are messily drawn, and that the potential for confusion is immense, even within any one of the camps that have been joined in temporary marriage on the issue. The same feminist magazine, *Zanan*, whose editor used to be all in favor of sigeh, is these days against it, having finally it seems concluded that a negative aspect of its duration is that the woman has no right to divorce her temporary husband.[22] Some so-called reformists have used the same argument *Zanan's* editor had previously used to welcome it—that sigeh is the thin end of the wedge—to condemn it, and this time for undermining the institution of the family. Conservative women have been pointing out that temporary marriage is still overwhelmingly used by married men for concubinage, and that the woman can get an unspecified raw deal as a result. Presumably, that means because the man does not have to make an honest woman out of her.

The conservative, but not extremist, website Islam Online, meanwhile, describes sigeh as "one of the glorious laws of Islam,"[23] yet a newspaper identified as hard-line by the BBC thought the end of the world was nigh because a travel agent in Tehran was advertising trips to the Caspian Sea for temporarily married couples. Shahla Haeri summed it up when she told the *New York Times* that neither the clerics nor leading thinkers had begun to analyze its implications in a coherent way. "If they are really serious," she said, "they should study the matter in the context of sexuality, birth control, sexually transmitted diseases, morality, religion, and gender relations."[24]

A tall order, perhaps.

What is certain is that sigeh remains an emotive issue among ordinary Iranians, and a chief reason is the high premium placed on a bride's virginity. If it is known that a woman has been in one or more temporary marriages, she may be seen as tainted and thus no longer eligible, quite apart from the bad light it may cast on her family. One conservative female member of parliament asked Interior Minister Mohammadi the fair question whether he would be willing to tell a prospective groom how many temporary marriages his daughter had been in.[25]

A twenty-six-year-old woman, identified as Elnaz, made a broader point:

Many families, including mine, are now quite tolerant of their daughters having boyfriends if there are any prospects of marriage later,
but temporary marriage is another story. My father would rather die
than let me enter into a temporary marriage, even with my boyfriend
of three years, because it clearly speaks of the intention to have sex.
He won't even allow my brother to do this, because he considers any
girl or woman who accepts to be temporarily married a prostitute.[26]

Another woman, who had been in a frequently renewed temporary marriage with a man for five years, told the *New York Times*, "I
think sigeh is good, very good," but added she would not do it again.
"I want to get married permanently now, as soon as possible."[27]

Socially, then, sigeh seems to occupy a strange twilight where it
bumps up against all kinds of prejudices and convictions and may as a
result be treated very differently from one house to another, even in the
same street. Ordinary people in societies where strict taboos are said to
exist are often quite pragmatic about them, and a "don't ask, don't tell"
policy is the preferred way of dealing with what to an outsider may
seem glaringly obvious violations. This is especially true in places that
have not yet been impressed with the latter-day duty to Come Out.
There is no way of knowing to what extent people blind themselves to
things they have decided not to notice, but in my experience they can
go for years doing so.

Whatever the theory may say, the promotion of sigeh has in practical terms been a runaway success. In November 2003, Tehran's no-
tary office said temporary marriages registered there had surged 122
percent in the previous six months alone. The office blamed poverty
and economic problems.[28] At the end of 2009, the U.S.-financed
propaganda outlet, Radio Farda, reported an increase of 28 percent for

the year, though the source of its data was unclear.[29] It seems true enough, however, that there is a growing practical acceptance of the institution, for whatever reasons.

What facilitates it is that technical virginity can be restored, if it needs to be, by an affordable surgical procedure and that the means of birth control are widely available.[30] Together with the official sanction, they make an irresistible combination, whatever one's views about the ethical ins and outs of the question may be.

The increase in temporary marriages has been triumphantly seized upon by yet another odd coalition, this time of right-wing U.S. bloggers, Zionist mouthpieces, and Iranian feminists in exile, also usually based in Israel or the United States.[31] Their equation is simple: Sigeh equals prostitution equals evil. In any case, it does not matter, so long as an emotive topic can be used as a stick with which to beat the Islamic Republic. For the sake of balance, it is therefore perhaps worth citing Monique Girgis, a learned Iranian scholar who favors the regime and favors sigeh:

> Sigeh is . . . beneficial to women in several ways. For one thing it is less restrictive; women do not have to be as obedient during a sigeh marriage as opposed to a permanent one. Sigeh marriage is a way in which women can be with many men legally in the same way that man can take other wives. She is able to be with different people under the blessings of Islam.[32]

That seems a powerful argument for the institution, whichever way you look at it. Girgis has an agenda, as does everyone else here, and her defense of the Islamic Republic on the grounds that it did not make matters significantly worse for women than they were under the shah is not exactly a glowing recommendation.

However, I am more interested in one particular point she made:

> Many people have compared sigeh to prostitution, but it is different in the eyes of Muslims for two reasons. First, any children that come of a sigeh marriage are considered legitimate. Second, sigeh is thought to combat immorality. Sigeh is a spiritual and religious state, whereas prostitution is disorder.[33]

For many, and most of all for nonbelievers, the mind of a believer is difficult to imagine at the best of times, but this odd statement should not be dismissed out of hand. One of Graham Greene's favorite anecdotes, from a low point in British literary life, concerns his fellow Catholic convert Evelyn Waugh, at dinner with the film directors Alexander Korda and Carol Reed:

> Suddenly at table Evelyn developed an extreme anti-Semite rudeness towards Korda. The next day I was with him in a taxi and I said, "Why did you insult poor Alex like that?" He said: "He had no right to bring his mistress to Carol Reed's house for dinner." I said, "But I had my mistress with me." Evelyn's reply was: "That is quite different. She is a married woman."[34]

For people who are persnickety about their religion, little things like that can make all the difference. Still, I would venture that many ordinary Muslims, like many ordinary Christians, have no sense of the transcendental at all. They are no more "spiritual," in Girgis's shopworn expression, than a street lamp. Religion for them is a set of customs and traditions, essentially of habits, which they are admittedly capable of getting rather heated about, but they do not perceive themselves as, say, sleeping on a cushion of angels, or existing in any state other than the strictly physical.

Few people experience a constant state of grace when they have sex with their spouse, whatever that may feel like, even if their marriage is blessed with bells and whistles by their respective churches, or experience guilt when they commit adultery, if they experience any at all, as a yawning absence of the divine from sexual congress (and indeed they may enjoy it as much or more because of the guilt). That is perhaps especially so in Islam, which except among the Sufis is a this-worldly, nonmystical, practical religion. If you cannot actually feel it, what is the difference between a blessed state and an unblessed one? It is essentially the word of one side against the other. The argument from transcendence "in the eyes of Muslims," therefore, has only a limited resonance, at least to my mind.

What really matters to most people, I would argue, is whether sex is permitted, and what the neighbors will think of it.

Nothing gives your average bored Sunni bigot surfing the web more instant gratification than zooming in on sigeh to condemn the Shia as debauched heretics, but there could be few more vulnerable moral high grounds where he might pitch his flag of religious superiority than this particular spot in cyberspace. The Sunnis, after all, have their own versions of this arrangement, called in Saudi Arabia a *misyar* (or visitor's marriage) and in Egypt an *urfi* (or customary marriage). It is true that both misyar and urfi differ from sigeh, primarily in that they are not supposed to last for a predetermined period of time (which in most cases they nevertheless do);[35] and, again unlike sigeh, they are theoretically required to satisfy all four main conditions for marriage of the Sunni canon: mutual consent, two male witnesses (or two female and one male), some form of public announcement, and the payment of a dowry (although the latter can be symbolic and thus take the form, say, of the reading of a verse from the Qur'an).

However, scholars point out that there is little agreement on what the Prophet had to say about whether he expected any of these unconventional marriages to outlive his own lifespan:

> Scholars say the Prophet Mohammed sanctioned these marriages for his companions during their wars and campaigns to spread Islam in present-day Saudi Arabia. It was also deemed a practical solution for travelers who came to strange towns and needed a woman to look after them and their belongings while they were there. Other historians argue that the practice existed in pre-Islamic societies and was initially permitted by the Prophet Mohammed, but that he forbade it at a later stage.[36]

Some 1,400 years later, and the Sunnis are no nearer to forging a consensus about the religious legitimacy and social desirability of either misyar or urfi, not least because the rules, insofar as anyone knows what they are, are evidently flouted on all sides. Indeed, the raging debate in Saudi Arabia and Egypt about whether such marriages are ethical and religiously permitted, or just a cover for prostitution and casual sex, can at times make the corresponding discussion in the Shia world seem crystal clear. Sunni critics who call misyar and urfi marriages glorified prostitution or, at the very least, a cover for illicit sexual relations between men and women, do so because such arrangements avoid the full responsibility of a conventional marriage, which is undertaken as a lifelong commitment and focused on raising children. Others argue that, while misyar and urfi are not in principle un-Islamic, the way they are practiced often is.

When it comes to laying down the law on misyar in Egypt, the late grand sheikh of Al-Azhar, Muhammad Sayyid Tantawi, strikes me as a classic ditherer.

When the bill proposing the decriminalization of urfi marriages was making its way through the Egyptian parliament in 1999, he reportedly said that they "entail the loss of the wife's rights, and are incompatible with the way the state functions." However, he did not say categorically that they were un-Islamic. Instead, he is reported to have explained that an urfi marriage could in fact be acceptable if it complied with "all the conditions of legitimate matrimony." At the same time, he insisted that he "personally" did not "recognize it, like it or even heed it because it entails the loss of the wife's rights and is hateful to God." Therefore women who accept this type of marriage have made the wrong decision, he reportedly concluded, and a law should "be drafted to impose certain penalties on unofficial marriages in order to protect women."[37] If this circular argument is the plainest advice the country's leading Sunni authority has to offer, it is small wonder Egyptians were, and by and large remain, confused on the question. When Tantawi spoke at a conference in Cairo on the same topic a decade later, in 2009, according to reports, he confessed that he was still in a pickle, but while his advice was no less ambiguous, he did this time around stop short of calling for urfi marriages to be banned.[38] Nor did he restate his belief that they are "incompatible with the way the state functions."[39]

That was no great surprise: By that time, the Egyptian regime, which had long since legalized urfi and which continued to pay Tantawi his salary, had made it clear that the debate was to be considered dead and buried.

From a religious perspective, everything nevertheless does hinge on whether urfi marriages "comply with all the conditions of legitimate matrimony," as Tantawi put it. Alleged deviations highlighted by opponents include secrecy (sometimes not even relatives are told), indifference to establishing a family (the last thing either party wants is more kids), the woman's agreement to give up her right to a dowry or an alimony in the event of divorce, and the lack of a role for the bride's father in the actual marriage ceremony, provided one even takes place (sometimes the father may not be called on to give his daughter away).[40] However, for many the absence of long-term commitment and laborious interfamilial negotiations are precisely what makes misyar and urfi so attractive, and in a broad sense the debate between the supporters and detractors is akin to that which took place in the West between traditionalists and liberals during the sexual revolution of the 1960s.

However, in the Islamic world the roles have been reversed: The conservative Sunni scholars who make up the religious establishments in Saudi Arabia and Egypt are generally cautious supporters of the liberalizing trend, whereas the reactionary feminists who have spoken out publicly on the topic are invariably antisex and therefore aghast at the mere thought of its taking place outside of a conventional marriage. In 2006, the Mecca-based Islamic Jurisprudence Assembly, a constituent body of the Muslim World League, announced that misyar marriage was permitted, and in doing so gave the custom the all-important Wahhabi seal of approval. This fatwa stated in part that "a marriage contract in which the woman relinquishes [her right to] housing and support money . . . and accepts that the man visits her in her family house whenever he likes, day or night . . . is valid."[41] An amendment to the Egyptian Personal Status Law in 2000 had already legalized urfi marriages for the first time since they were banned in 1930 in an effort to discourage marriages that were "registered" only by word of mouth and therefore unknown to the authorities.[42] In 2000, the Egyptian government had moved in response to what newspaper reports claimed was an extraordinary growth in such marriages among Egyptian university students during the economic crisis of the 1990s, when conventional marriage became impossibly expensive for a new generation of Egyptian men in their late teens and twenties.[43]

Marriage officials in Saudi Arabia, meanwhile, were quoted as saying that about 70 percent of marriage contracts they vouch for are of the misyar variety.[44] Because urfi, unlike misyar in Saudi Arabia, is still not registered in Egypt, statistics about how popular it is are unavailable. But a lack of statistics has never stopped researchers in any area from hazarding a guess, and some claim that these days it is more common among the young than conventional marriage. Moreover, because urfi falls outside the remit of civil law, the official minimum age for marriage in Egypt (which is eighteen) does not seem to apply, or at least might conveniently be thought not to; and some forms of urfi (there are dozens) have reportedly become common among Egyptian high school kids, who have created "strange names" for their marriages, including blood marriage, Adam-and-Eve marriage, postage-stamp marriage, and even tattoo marriage.[45]

An internet search conducted by a women's magazine turned up at least six online misyar matchmakers. One called www.msyaronline .com is the largest in terms of members, and so popular in terms of the number of hits it receives that it ranked among the top 11,000 sites on the web in any language.[46] It offered, according to the magazine, four reasons why it was promoting this type of marriage, aside from the obvious one of making a killing: an increase in the number of spinsters and widows and those of "special circumstances"; the refusal of women to have a cowife, leading men to marry the misyar way so the first wife doesn't find out; the desire of unmarried men to get halal pleasure reconcilable with their circumstances; and the escape from some of the responsibilities of marriage and its costs.[47] On another such website, www.zojah.com, a girl wrote, "I'm 18, from Jeddah and I want a romantic man for misyar marriage."[48] The bottom line is that misyar allows for a man and women to have extramarital sex without falling foul of strict adultery or prostitution laws. This cleverly nips in the bud any possible social ramifications that could result from mass arrests, and thus helps to maintain the crucial veneer of Islamic piety and social cohesion.

As is usually the case when it comes to the minutiae of sharia law, once the rule has been laid down by the clerics, the onus then falls on the human actors to behave according to the spirit, as well as the letter, of the law. But as ever when such customs generate intense public discussion, they also attract the attention of the media, and once they are out in the open the authorities can no longer ignore them and are forced instead to pronounce some sort of position they expect people to obey under threat of punishment. That is why the fatwa issued by the Islamic Jurisprudence Assembly, quoted above, expressly spoke out against marriages with intent to divorce.

Misyar allows women to live in their own homes and be visited by their husbands for sex and intimate companionship. While women opting for misyar are usually divorced, widowed, or beyond the customary marriage age, many of the men are already married. The latter, though, do not have to provide a home and financial support, or alimony in the event of divorce, as they would for a wife under the full marriage contract. This setup, Sunni supporters agree with their Shia cousins, provides a framework in which divorcées and widows can find companionship when they would not otherwise be considered eligible.

Saudi men, especially students abroad, often advertise for widows and divorcees who are prepared to enter into such an arrangement, which allows them to appease the religious conscience while living a life that is similar to that of their Western counterparts who have a girlfriend. But in Saudi Arabia, misyar has also become popularly known as "holiday marriage." Wealthy men from the kingdom's tribal interior who spend their summer break in the Western port city of Jeddah or the mountain resort of Taif, both in the more cosmopolitan Hijaz region, have used the arrangement to find themselves a woman for the duration of their stay there, and can also travel with the woman on a holiday abroad. Sheikh Ahmed Abdulqader, an Islamic consultant and a legal marriage officer in Saudi Arabia, told the Saudi-funded Al-Arabiya news channel that such summer holiday marriage "is important so that men do not fall into prostitution during their travel abroad."[49]

One way misyar is facilitated in Saudi Arabia is through a clandestine marriage brokerage, where callers reportedly dial phone numbers and get through to a taped message in which a woman with an alluring voice tells them to punch in a secret code to learn more. The answerphone message finally says: "My dear brother. May God help you find a wife to compensate you for your troubled life. Know that the broker charges these prices. $1,350 for a virgin or $800 for a non-virgin."[50]

But a misyar marriage, others argue, seemingly strips women of even more rights than conventional marriage, because rather than getting money from a short-term marriage, the wife gets nothing in terms of finances. Thus she gives up her right to live with her husband, to housing, and *nafaqa*, a woman's Islamic right to have her husband pay for her living and maintenance costs.[51] That is not what always happens, and it paints women too easily as hapless victims who are unable to take control of, let alone exploit to their advantage, the numerous opportunities for financial gain a misyar marriage in particular has to offer.

In Saudi Arabia the woman usually agrees in a binding Islamic marriage contract to be set up with certain material provisions (an apartment, a car with a driver, etc.) in exchange for living with a married man. She may also forgo any prenuptial demands, but since she does not get a dowry or access to other material support, she usually asks for something. The more attractive and younger the woman, the more leverage she has in getting material positions. A woman agreeing to a "pleasure marriage" that involves a one-time encounter, according to one survey in 2007 published in the Saudi-based *Arab News*, might be able to count on $100 to $270 a month for a misyar marriage that is properly entered into, as should be the reality, not as a one-time encounter, though the amounts vary widely and can depend on whether she has children.

Sometimes the marriage is conducted in an official capacity "in the presence of a state official or imam, sometimes two witnesses to the agreement are required, and in other cases an oral agreement between the two parties will do just fine."[52] An oral agreement will do just fine only if all the players are honest and trustworthy, which is where the whole enterprise often collapses. Newspaper reports about deliberate deception abound: In 2007 a Saudi woman was sentenced who "took advantage of the high demand for misyar brides" by duping three men out of more than $20,000.[53] Two years behind bars and three hundred lashes were given in 2009 to a married woman who cheated several men by posing as unmarried, agreeing with the men to have misyar marriage, and then fleeing after receiving the "dowries."[54] Two more women were arrested during the same year for allegedly cheating men seeking misyar marriage by receiving part of the dowry money upfront and then disappearing before signing the marriage contract.[55]

There can also be no doubt that men sometimes, or even often, dodge their responsibilities, from the trailer parks of California to the housing estates of Great Britain, from the slums of the Philippines to the coastal resorts of the Arabian Gulf. Pointing that out is only fair. But like some of their sisters among the exiled Iranian community, throughout the Middle East it is the leaders of women's organizations—often identified as feminist but really archconservative across the board—who have come out most vocally against misyar, on the grounds that it undermines the institution of the family. Bahraini activist Ghada Jamshir, who lobbies for a reduction of clerical influence in family affairs, told Middle East Online that liberals should "rise up" to combat misyar marriage:

> I don't encourage misyar marriage, nor mutaa [sigeh] marriage, because they deny women and children their rights. I believe in a normal marriage which is based on the couple living together for their lifetime. . . . The women's rights movement, liberals and the intelligentsia, as well as all those who believe in liberty, should move to defend freedom in general, and women's freedoms in particular.[56]

Well, people will learn to live without her encouragement.

Always bear in mind that the freedom she is so boldly defending is that of middle-class women who expect to be settled, or are already settled, in financially secure, monogamous marriages. And it takes a mighty stretch of the imagination even to describe the situation of such women in the heartland of neighboring Saudi Arabia as "free." The freedom of a girl who does not wish to spend the rest of her miserable life with the first ape who offers a price to her father does not seem to come into the equation. Nor does the freedom of women who, unlike Jamshir, cannot rely on a convenient liberal background to skirt the strict requirements of segregation. Least of all the freedom of women who simply wish to have a fling, without being tied down for life with what might turn out to be a horrible, abusive man.

By speaking out so boldly for "freedom" as she understands it, Jamshir is in fact devaluing the term, much as George W. Bush and his cohort did when they meant instituting illegal detention and torture centers on foreign soil, plus extraordinary rendition of "free" citizens to the dungeons of Egypt and other countries where torture is essentially a pastime for the bloated security forces. Hoda Badran, of the Alliance for Arab Women, chimed in, saying, "Social values are derived from principles given to children through their families. The negative consequences of urfi marriages are clear for all to see," and she cites "mothers abandoning their children due to the secrecy of the marriage, court cases, and, most dangerous of all, the degradation of the sanctity of marriage."[57]

By which, again, she means the sanctity of my marriage.

The point about abandoned children is true in some cases, but it conveniently ignores the masses of divorced women who are tossed on the scrap heap because no man will ever marry them again under the full Islamic marriage, and who would, and do, drift about in a sort of living suttee, and are also often forced to abandon their children. There are a million street kids in Cairo alone, and in parts of Saudi Arabia divorcées literally creep about the streets and duck into doorways for fear of harassment by the religious police, who will demand to know where their *mahram* may be, and are often essentially confined to the tiny apartments they can afford after their husband has thrice uttered the magical phrase "You are divorced."

There are too many such comments to cite, invariably from these leaders of women's organizations who, given the endemic nepotism in Egypt and Saudi Arabia, are usually the wives of wealthy and influential public figures, often of a half-understood Westernized bent—meaning slightly to the right of Fox News on family matters—and almost always on the wrong side of menopause. They are never from rural backgrounds, they are never and were never poor, they are never young, and they are usually talking through their metaphorical hat.

In a more sensible vein, Salama Al-Khafaji, a Saudi Shia lawmaker who supports the concept of sharia law but advocates women's rights, "calls the re-emergence of misyar an 'unhealthy phenomenon' and says too many men are using temporary marriages to exploit women for sex." However, "with the right intentions," she has said, "misyar can serve the noble purpose of helping divorced and widowed women financially."[58] Zeinab Shahine, a professor of sociology at Egypt's Ain Shams University, agrees. According to *Al-Ahram Weekly*, there are certain conditions, Shahine believes, when urfi marriage is a good compromise:

Shahine mentioned examples of a man whose wife is ill and who wants to get married without causing her any more pain; a widow with married children who would like to remarry but does not want to embarrass her children; or a woman who needs the pension of her deceased husband but wants to marry again. "It would be unfair to ban urfi marriage," Shahine said. "What is happening today, on the other hand, is a kind of deviation that should be addressed by social scientists. Legal awareness should be raised through university seminars and media campaigns.[59]

That, too, is only fair, because what is sauce for the goose should in an ideal world be sauce for the gander. But to close up, for the sake of some half-baked principle, one of the few byways strictly religious societies allow both men and women to make their own choices and enjoy themselves is surely the wrong way of bringing a freer world about.

The Prophet Mohammed seems to have been an eminently reasonable and practical man. The Qur'an came out as matchless poetry, or so we are told, but it was fundamentally a rudimentary code of laws and guide to practical living, with a smattering of half-remembered biblical tales retold by travelers or adapted to suit his purposes or both. If he had a fault, it was his lack of imagination, or, if you like, his impatience with the mess of ambiguous stories that we now feel are vital to a civilization's development. He thought, to put it crudely, that a few plain founding myths would do. This makes the Qur'an, even for the respectful nonbeliever, a rather unexciting read, somewhat like Buddha's sermons. Imagine that the Bible was seven parts Leviticus plus a few pedestrian bits of Genesis, all camels and sheep in highly ambiguous verse. "The hoopoe I almost forgot," as Thomas Mann wrote, parodying Moses, "Thou shalt not eat him either."[60]

The advantage is that the Qur'an is short. But that is also the disadvantage, since the Prophet, as far as I can see, did not anticipate that his own death would seal it in amber. While he was alive, that is to say, he could always have another vision if fresh matters came up, but such was his stature that none of his successors could have had the gumption, even if the opportunity had arisen, to claim the prophetic mantle and expand the founding texts, which were never written down in the Prophet's own lifetime, but became instead mere custodians or librarians, at best providing dubious glosses on the rump material he left.

Great leaders often think they are the last important man on earth. It is surely among the Prophet's many admirable qualities that he did not. Nor could a man as dedicated to breaking new ground and conquering new territory have anticipated the fundamentalists. Making that point may sound odd in our time, familiar as we are with the death sentences issued to any Muslim who might dare to suggest that the Qur'an is anything but the revealed Word of God for all time. But it was actually only in the ninth century that rabble-rousing hadith scholars completely rejected what had remained until then the widespread belief that the Qur'an was created in temporal time and therefore open to interpretation according to historical context.[61] Their constipated purpose, of paring everything back to the bare essentials and then reducing those to a single immutable meaning that represented exactly what God intended, is to my mind the exact opposite of everything Islam stands for, but alas they won the argument.

So what of sigeh, misyar, or urfi?

Dodging the question of terminology—though we should perhaps get used to thinking of sigeh especially as "a sort of temporary marriage in a manner of speaking," as opposed to simply "temporary marriage"—what the Prophet seems to have done is to regulate it so that children born as a result are legitimate to the father and the institution fits into the patriarchal system of custody and inheritance as a whole. It was a question of consistency. If concubinage is a fact of life—soldiers get lonely, boys will be boys—then he was going to tidy it up a little so the world did not end up crawling with unwanted, abandoned, and despised bastards as a result, making sure that men took some responsibility and treated the women with a modicum of respect and consideration.

That seems to be the spirit of the law. The spirit giveth life, St. Paul tells us, but the letter killeth. Oh, the global wailing and gnashing of teeth at the notion that a marriage should be "temporary"! Well, where anyway does it say marriage? It was only the second ruler after the death of the Prophet in 632, Caliph Umar (an instinctive despot, archbureaucrat, and late convert to boot, with all the concomitant tendencies to spy on his own people and meddle in their business), who felt things had Gone Too Far. That essentially is where the difficulty for Sunnis begins, because they revere Umar as the second of the four "rightly guided" caliphs. As he had a massive empire to bring under control, he can perhaps be forgiven for his celebrated iron fist. That, though, is also what apologists used to say about Stalin, and Umar is even said by some to have beaten his son to death for drinking alcohol. At any rate, Umar decided that misyar was "no better than fornication" and outlawed it.[62] Instead of ending the practice, however, this merely led to a catalog of bylaws under which the Sunni world groans to this day. The result is that misyar is now overwhelmingly perceived by Sunnis as a temporary or lesser form of marriage, instead of the eminently sensible attempt to regulate legal prostitution that it once was, or is seen as the latter only by those who wish to condemn it.

Umar was assassinated in 644—many Shia say not a moment too soon—by a Persian. As the Jews killed Our Lord, so the Persians killed Our Umar, and thanks to the long memories of the region, relations with the Arabian heartland never really recovered. Luckily for the Persians, who became Shia, they still consider the caliph quite wrongly guided, so sigeh remains in Iran more or less what it was at the time of the Prophet. Unluckily for them, however, the Muslim community does exist to some extent across the Sunni-Shia divide, and certain movements and ideas have a tendency to spill over, none more so than the hysteria of cultures dominated and ruled by men, and old men at that, about untrammeled sex. (Not that matters would be any different, as we have seen, if they were ruled by middle-aged women.) The splitting of hairs and the quest to turn guiding principles into immutable laws are also common to both Sunni and Shia religious scholarship. By now, therefore, Sunni and Shia scholars really do see sigeh or misyar or urfi as fundamentally different from a casual arrangement for sex, which would amount to the capital crime of adultery—a concept now stretched well beyond any sane definition in both Shia and Sunni cultures to include any sex out of wedlock.

In some ways, it does not matter what you call it. The important point is that the religion has found in itself a back door permitting what it ostensibly forbids, which is what every functioning religion, or for that matter ideology, needs to do. And here, as in many other aspects of life that often baffle Western observers with their inconsistency, Middle Eastern sexuality has proven itself solidly resistant to dogma.

The fact that 70 percent of all marriages in Saudi Arabia these days are misyar is a wonderfully uplifting statistic. There is a kind of higher hypocrisy at work that allows many people, if not nearly everyone, to have their cake and eat it, too. Ordinary Sunnis and Shia are perfectly capable, that is to say, of tuning out the background hum of clerics and so-called feminists and God knows who else arguing about the finer points of doctrine and ethics, and concentrate instead on the simple fact that here is something they are permitted to do if they wish, and that it can make their lives a little bit easier and more enjoyable.

That the solution is not ideal is undeniable, but then solutions rarely are. The only real problem arises when the issue of age comes in, since temporary marriages are also used as a cover for child prostitution, and on a global scale.

CHAPTER *four*

CHILD BRIDES

At first glance, Songkhla in southern Thailand, near the border with Malaysia, is indistinguishable from hundreds of other provincial towns in Southeast Asia. The endless rows of nondescript shop houses that make up what there is of a commercial downtown betray little traces of local tradition, still less of civic pride. The old governor's mansion is a good enough example of a Sino-Portuguese villa, but not much different from such buildings dotted throughout the Malay Peninsula. The town is lined by a wide, deserted beach, where a few concrete shacks double as convenience stores and seafood restaurants. An old wooden fishing village, clinging to the embankment wall, completes the local attractions.

Although Songkhla remains the provincial capital, the money has long gone to the nearby boom town of Hat Yai, where there are hundreds of gold shops, department stores selling knockoff goods, and a teeming red-light district. All thrive on an endless stream of Malaysians hopping across the border to seek brief respite from the strict Muslim norms, and higher prices, of their country's northernmost provinces, which have been governed by Malaysia's hard-line Islamist party for the past decade. The majority of the Songkhla's population is Thai Buddhist, with an admixture of Malay or ethnic Chinese. But the town also has a small expatriate community, drawn by the offshore oil operations for which it serves as a convenient base, or by a dribbling demand for native English teachers from the provincial universities. Sadao Road, at the northern end of town, is home to a string of sleepy bars where women of no great beauty or liveliness make themselves available to keep the expatriates and occasional tourists company.

I visited Songkhla in 2004 during a research trip to report on the ongoing insurgency in Thailand's Muslim-majority southern provinces,[1] and it was in one of those bars, when I stopped for a beer, that I met Na. I found myself unusually eager for a chat with the woman who seemed to come with my order. The women in the place had washed up there from Isan, the poor region in the northeast of Thailand that supplies the rest of the country with menial labor and prostitutes. But not Na, it turned out, who was born in Songkhla and came from a relatively well-off ethnic Chinese fishing family. Thin and with a long graceful neck and delicate Chinese features, she had a feline stillness that allowed her to sit on her haunches for hours and observe the goings-on. Her voice was like fingernails on a blackboard, but she spoke remarkably good English. She was twenty years old, she told me, and had a four-year-old son, a dark-skinned boy who sat beside us (it is not unusual for Thai prostitutes to bring their kids to the bars where they work), and who seemed to have inherited his mother's impassive watchfulness. One reason Na interested me is that, after I told her that I was based in the Middle East, she managed to say a few sentences in broken Arabic. That is not unusual among Muslim Thais, but is highly so for someone from the Chinese Buddhist community. Over the next few days—while waiting for a meeting with a radical, Saudi-educated Thai Muslim cleric in a neighboring province, whom I was going to interview about his new local Arabic-language university—I winkled Na's story out of her.

I most wanted to know how she had learned to speak Arabic. She said a middle-aged man from the United Arab Emirates, who worked for one of the oil companies, had once lived on her street. He would walk by the house, day after day, to fix his gaze on the fifteen-year-old Na in her blue-and-white school uniform, who no doubt was motionlessly observing his passage. This went on for some weeks, until one day he stopped and asked for a word with her mother. He offered the marriage terms quite frankly, and without embarrassment. So much gold, so much ready money. Na's mother, she said, put the offer to her, but made it clear that the choice was hers. Na thought about it, in her deliberate way, for a day or two. Finally she concluded—as she told me—"Yes, can do."

Na did not say whether the arrangement had raised eyebrows among the neighbors. But Chinese people, especially in the diaspora, are often distrustful of others, most of all of other Chinese; and they would consider it the height of absurdity to poke their nose into each other's personal lives. Their eyes and ears reach exactly as far as their neighbor's front door. In any case, in Thailand's ingrained culture of polygamy a large age gap between partners is not uncommon, it being universally acknowledged that a mature gentleman of good fortune must be in need of a minor wife. The Thai age of consent is fifteen, and the minimum age for marriage officially seventeen, but common-law marriages are widespread throughout all strata of society. So long as some kind of informal event has been held, like a handing over of the dowry or a blessing given by a local monk, the couple are to all intents and purposes considered married. The registration requirement can be put aside until some other kind of legal necessity makes it unavoidable. Nevertheless, the marriage between Na and the Emirati was not a success. Hers was not a sweet temper, and neither was his. Soon they were fighting daily. She said he often hit her when they argued. However, a bigger bone of contention was the Arab's first wife, whom Na discovered he had left behind in the Emirates and to whom, she feared, he would eventually return, thus leaving her and their son to fend for themselves. When the boy was three years old, that is what the man did, and he has not been seen or heard from since.

I never figured out any particular reason why Na subsequently turned to prostitution. She was not driven to it for cultural reasons: working-class Thai men usually do not object to "shop-soiled" women. Moreover, coming from an industrious Chinese family, she also had a laundry shop, where she employed one of her older fellow prostitutes as help for a daily pittance of three dollars. She had been able to buy the shop and the washing machines by cashing in the gold that was part of her dowry, which her mother had kept safely hidden away for her. Perhaps she considered working in the bar a source of easy income, or felt that brief liaisons with itinerant but solvent foreigners would prove easier to manage than a relationship with a local, whom she would probably have to keep.

At the time the story struck me as improbable, despite the credence given it by Na's smattering of Arabic and the fact that her son, while not Arab-looking exactly, did not resemble any of the other ethnic Chinese kids running around the town. I did not like the brutal Arab in the story, nor the cold bargain he was said to have proposed to Na's mother. I appreciated still less the dubious globalized flavor of the tale. In southern Thailand, the Arabs I encountered were not sex tourists. They were hard-line Wahhabi preachers, usually from Saudi Arabia, who had smelled fertile ground where their unkind version of Islam might take root. There was a clear historic purpose to their presence.

After I left southern Thailand I forgot all about Na. However, in the course of my research for this book, her story came flooding back, as I realized that such bargains are indeed struck all the time throughout Asia. They are invariably initiated by older Gulf Arabs who already have a wife or two at home. Often they involve girls even younger, and certainly more vulnerable, than Na.

Thailand forms only the outer fringe of this phenomenon of older Arab men taking much younger foreign wives, chiefly because the country has a lively conventional sex industry catering to Arab visitors. In Bangkok and the tourist resorts of Pattaya and Phuket, for instance, the wails of Arabic pop music waft through substantial parts of the entertainment districts. Often they are conveniently located near private hospitals that appeal to Arab women. Such is the stifling monotony of the Persian Gulf states, they even jump at the opportunity provided by health treatment to escape it. Let the wife have her obesity-related health problems seen to, the unspoken reasoning seems to go, and the men of the family can amuse themselves in the nearby discos and cafés—nipping, when the need arises, into a short-time hotel around the corner.

It is in poorer, more densely populated countries like Indonesia (with its overwhelming Muslim majority) and India (with its large Muslim minority) that such arrangements thrive most conspicuously. Indonesia, in particular, is a popular holiday destination for Gulf Arabs, partly because it is the largest Muslim nation in the world, home to almost as many Muslims as there are in the whole of the Arab world. Saudis, especially, are suckers for the Islam brand; but once on vacation they—like tourists everywhere—want their fun.

Indonesia has relatively little to offer in the way of outright prostitution when compared to Thailand, but it does have the next best thing: a large population of women and girls willing to enter into temporary marriages for a reasonable price. Strictly speaking, these arrangements are illegal under Indonesia's civil code, but local Islamic judges are often only too willing to solemnize them. Once the religious aspect has been dealt with, which allows the visiting Gulf Arabs to wrap themselves in the cloak of respectability, the legal side is of no great significance. Indeed, some in the Indonesian government, rather than discouraging the practice, seem to be all in favor. The country's vice president, Jusuf Kalla, has stated that he sees nothing at all wrong with Arab men paying local women to marry, and then divorcing them days later, even going so far as to suggest that it could be a fine way to boost tourism. In 2006, during a travel industry seminar, he acknowledged that many Arab tourists travel to the hill town of Puncak, near the capital, Jakarta, to enter into short-term marriage contracts with Indonesian women. "We need different kinds of marketing campaigns, more targeted. At the moment most Arabs go to Puncak. If they go there looking for widows or divorcées that is not our business, it is not a problem. So what if the man goes home, the lady gets a small house, that is good, isn't it?"[2]

Faced with unexpected international press coverage, Kalla was later to claim he had been joking. His remarks, though, have the casual, folksy flavor of a widespread attitude. The more extreme example of temporary marriages with minor girls—the context, however unfairly, in which Kalla's remarks gained brief international attention—is a centuries-old local tradition, and is vigorously defended by Indonesian clerics. One of these clerics is a wealthy man in Java who in 2008, at the age of forty-three, married a twelve-year-old girl in a ceremony attended by thousands of guests. When the news broke, he gave short shrift to the barrage of complaints. "I know the limitations," he reportedly said. "If she hasn't menstruated, I won't have intercourse with her."[3] More surprising, perhaps, than this cleric's cold assessment of his own ethical standards is that among many Indonesian girls and women there is a great deal of support for these more traditional-minded community leaders.

Take, for instance, Ayisha Noor.

From a town east of Jakarta, she was sixteen when she married a Saudi visitor. "We in Indonesia consider the people of Mecca and Medina the blessed ones," she told *Arab News*, which published an exposé on the subject derived from articles in the kingdom's Arabic-language dailies.[4] The Saudi gave Ayisha a dowry of six hundred dollars, according to the report, saying he would pay half up front and half a few days later. The girl insisted that her family did not know the man was intending to have only a temporary marriage. It is difficult to put too much weight on that assertion, since those who marry Arabs on a temporary basis are unlikely to admit the fact in public, because it means they are owning up not only to breaking the law but also, perhaps more crucially, to having agreed to be treated as glorified prostitutes. Anyway, undeterred by her first experience, Ayisha said that she later married yet another Saudi, and according to the same principles. She finally wound up, according to the newspaper, as a singer and dancer in a local nightclub.

One of the more obvious problems arising from this kind of situation is that a dowry of a few hundred dollars cannot be expected to help in taking care of any children born to such sham marriages. Adding insult to injury, the amount quoted is barely what a Saudi tourist would pay for a one-night stand with a high-class hooker in Lebanon. The Saudi Arabian embassy in Jakarta claims that it helps such women track down the fathers of their children, presumably with a view to making them provide some kind of child support.[5] Often, though, the Saudi men refuse to acknowledge these children. The Indonesian consul in Jeddah has said that Jakarta is now "taking appropriate measures to curb the practice," pointing out the not very useful (or for that matter relevant) background information that it is often elderly and disabled Saudis who find a young bride that way. The Indonesian government, stung by the criticism in the international media, also undertook what appears to have been a one-off crackdown, expelling a group of Saudis who "married" local women because they were of the temporary kind, and therefore against the law.[6] In reality, though, the legal formalities are rarely observed on the ground once the Islamic conscience has been appeased, nor is the law of the land generally used to stop the temporary marriages in the first place. More uxorious Saudi grooms tend to take their brides back home on a visa for domestic staff. Some of the girls "later come to the consulate to seek advice," as the Jeddah consul delicately put it.[7]

In India, too, the practice of temporary marriages seems to have taken on all the trappings of a thriving prostitution industry:

> Rich, middle-aged Arabs increasingly stalk the deprived streets of Hyderabad like medieval monarchs would stalk their harems in days that we wrongly think of as distant history. These Viagra-enabled Arabs are perpetrating a blatant crime under the veneer of nikaah, the Islamic rules of marriage. Misusing the sanctioned provision which allows a Muslim man to have four wives at a time, but under strict conditions, many old Arabs are not just marrying minors in Hyderabad, but purchasing more than one minor for sex under the guise of marrying them in a single sitting.[8]

Thus the *Times of India*, in its inimitable style.

The paper quotes an Indian activist, Jameela Nishat, who counsels such girls, as saying, "The Arabs prefer teenage, virgin brides." Often the transactions have a straightforward, industrial aspect, with half a dozen prospective brides gathered at a home that, Nishat said, resembles a brothel, where they are "paraded before an Arab who would lift the girls' burqas, run his fingers through their hair, gaze at their figures, and converse through an interpreter." Most of the girls there, she added, were minors, which presumably meant under the age of eighteen. The paper claimed such temporary marriages were, as a matter of course (and as in Indonesia), abetted by local Islamic clerics, who prepare both marriage and divorce formalities together, or agree in advance to solemnize the divorce formalities by email, telephone, or even text message. In one instance a forty-five-year-old Emirati married two girls "aged between thirteen and fifteen" for about four hundred dollars, but disappeared after the wedding night. How common such marriages are is indicated by the fact that the only reason this particular case made the newspapers was that the shameless Emirati failed to pay up, forcing the girls to turn to the media for redress.[9]

Closer to home, poor and populous Egypt—where many wealthy Gulf Arabs have second homes—offers what the newspapers like to call "rich hunting grounds" for young brides. There the prices range from $500 to $1,500, with the girls often ending up as domestic servants in the groom's home back in Saudi Arabia or some other repressive Persian Gulf state, where the abuse of domestic servants has been extensively documented by human rights groups. Under Egyptian law, the new wives, if they are still in the country, are permitted to file for divorce a few months down the line. However, the grooms then often insist on unrealistically high compensation from the girl's family, roughly $10,000.[10] That undermines the whole point of the initial dowry, which is supposed to guarantee a period of financial security in the event that the girl's husband either dies, does a runner, or just proves impossible to live with.

If such cases make headlines and spark legislation in a country like Egypt, where the tendency is to maintain the public image through denial, the horses must be seriously frightened. A new law, enacted expressly to curb such unions with minors, stipulates a maximum twenty-five-year age gap between partners if one of them is a foreigner. Rolled out among much fanfare, it was principally aimed at preventing the much-publicized case of a ninety-two-year-old Gulf Arab planning on marrying a seventeen-year-old Egyptian.[11] The government-owned *Al-Akhbar* daily reported in 2007 that one hundred and thirty-seven couples who married that year where the husband was a foreigner broke the law regarding a maximum twenty-five-year age gap.[12] That figure represents only those that have come to light, or where the girl's real age is put on the marriage certificate. So it seems reasonable to conclude that the real number was higher.

Who would try to sell off a child in this way?

It may seem difficult to imagine that those doing so often have the best interests of their young daughters at heart, that they love their children as much as any other parents do. But, I would posit, that is often the case. Since I have spent much of the last decade in Egypt, it was there that I, too, found myself the object of such a proposal, as a potential groom. No thunder rent the stormy skies: The offer was casually made and soon forgotten (at least by me). However, the incident, although providing no great drama, does shed some further light on the subject, and in particular the way that even a loving father might see the arrangement as a way, perhaps the only way, of lifting his daughter out of poverty.

I got to know this particular Egyptian family in the late 1990s. At the coffee shop where I spent my afternoons a rather sickly kid, Ali, then about seven years old, plunked himself down on a chair near mine. He said nothing, and neither did I. But he barely blinked during the time he stayed there, did not leave until after I did, and the next day returned to fix me with his mysterious gaze. On the third day, I told the waiter to give him a drink. Ali brought it over to my table and sat next to me, but maintained his baffling silence—responding to my questions about school and family with only a nod or shake of the head. We settled into this routine, to the point that if I arrived at the coffee shop and he was not already waiting for me, cries of "Ya Ali! Ya Ali!" would ring through the street, our friendship having become famous among the locals, and a few minutes later I would see him come running round the corner. By that stage I did not have to order him anything: The waiter automatically brought him a soft drink and a sandwich. His elder brother, Mohammed, who was nine years old, one day tried to get in on the act, but Ali was possessive and rudely pushed him away. A week or so later, Ali's father arrived on the scene.

"Are you John?" he asked, extending a hand.

"Yes," I told him. "Your son has become my best friend in the coffee shop."

"I know," he laughed. "He doesn't stop talking about you at home."

"I'm glad to hear he can speak," I said. "He's never said a word to me."

"He's just shy," the father explained. "In the house he's like another boy."

He invited me to dinner that night, and that, as they say, was the start of a beautiful friendship, which is as important to me today as ever.

In addition to Ali and Mohammed, there were two daughters in the family: Fatima (two years younger than Ali) and Maha (two years older than Mohammed). The apartment was as spotless as one would expect in the Arab world, where personal and domestic cleanliness are so important, but tiny, with just two rooms and a poky shower and kitchen. This meant the family of six was living on top of one another. I mentioned how Ali and Fatima looked much more fragile than the older boy and girl, prompting the mother to explain that she thought this was because they had been born shortly before the terrorist attacks in Luxor in 1997, which decimated the Egyptian tourism industry for a year. As a result, the father lost his job as a waiter at a five-star hotel, and as a consequence the two younger kids grew up on a less nutritious diet.

Soon afterward, we made a deal: I would give the family a monthly allowance if the mother would cook for me every day at their house (the food that first evening had been fantastic). Since I do not know how to boil an egg, this setup would cost me less than eating in dodgy restaurants, and it had the added benefit that the whole family got to eat well since the mother could make enough for all of us. I would also get to practice my Arabic with a lively Egyptian family for a few hours every day, worth a thousand hours of expensive private tuition.

After I returned to Egypt in 2004 from my stint in Saudi Arabia, I paid for Ali and Fatima to attend a private school, since in the intervening years they seemed to have learned nothing in the rundown, overcrowded state school at the end of their street. (The two older kids had spent their first years in a private school and could at least read and write well and, with the help of private classes, were able to sail through the annual examinations.) The fees for the private school were not extortionate, and I was able to cover it by using the money I was making—in those days before the financial crisis—from currency speculation.

Fast forward to my thirty-seventh birthday in 2007.

The mother had baked me a cake, with icing and candles, as she did every year when I was in town, although ordinary Egyptians do not usually celebrate birthdays. The father, who had found another job at a hotel, in addition to his morning job as a civil servant, took the evening off to join us. Now Fatima was a twelve-year-old tomboy, albeit one who cried annoyingly whenever she could not get her way; Ali was a strong and happy fourteen-year-old, as permanently by my side as he had been on that first day, and given to reminisce that he had instinctively known on that first day that I would wind up taking care of him and his family; his older brother Mohammed was a taciturn sixteen-year-old, frustrated at the lack of privacy in the home, and spending his time on the computer playing games and chatting with friends; while Maha, a plump eighteen-year-old, was studying for a diploma in finance.

I rarely saw the father, and when he was around between shifts he was a man of few words. That night, though, he was especially friendly, and kept bringing up that it was shameful for a man to reach his thirty-seventh year and still be unmarried. The usual exclamations ensued, until the father said, with such seriousness that a deafening silence ensued:

"Wait for Fatima."

I glanced at her: a boyish girl on the brink of her teenage years, in jeans and T-shirt, hair tied up in a ponytail, her beautiful little face quite still and unemotional. Everyone else was staring at me.

Clearly, this suggestion had not come out of the blue, but had been discussed beforehand.

"Wait for her until when?" I asked, not sure if this was a joke.

"Until she finishes school," the father said, adding in a more casual tone. "You get engaged now."

I started to search for polite excuses, finally mumbling: "I'm not a Muslim. I'd have to change my religion."

"It's just a piece of paper," he laughed. "You always say there's no difference between Christians and Muslims."

"But she's twelve," I finally spat out.

"It's normal, normal," he said reassuringly.

"Maybe for you," I replied. "But for us, it's a scandal."

He thought about this for a moment, then said, "You told us you weren't famous."

A few months earlier Mohammed had found on YouTube an interview with me on CNN. After the excitement of his discovery had died down, I explained that large numbers of people appeared occasionally in the media, and even had their books reviewed quite widely, but were still (like me) unknown to anyone but a small circle of experts writing in the same field, and probably known only to a minority of them.

"It's true I'm not famous now," I said. "But if word gets out that I'm engaged to a twelve-year-old girl in Egypt I'll be the most famous person in the world."

It occurs to me now that the law banning foreigners to marry locals if the age gap is greater than twenty-five years had just been proposed in the Egyptian parliament, or raised in the media after campaigners complained about the child-bride phenomenon, and since the age gap between me and Fatima was twenty-five years I should have used that fact to end the discussion. Then again, it might not have bothered anyone in that household: Female circumcision, too, is officially banned, but is still widely carried out. They finally dropped the subject, correctly concluding that I had declined the offer. When I left, Fatima stuck her tongue out at me, and told me she would marry a Western tour-guide who would be "younger and more handsome" than I. Even in a well-educated and not desperately poor household, then, the idea of marrying off a young daughter, however symbolically, to a relatively wealthy foreigner was not considered strange.

The family had accepted without complaint their son's friendship with an adult foreigner for what it was, innocent and accidental, but Western parents in such a setup would I guess be sent into paroxysms of anguish. However, I later discovered that the father had spent the first week asking the locals about me, to make sure that I was not up to anything suspect. So these were neither evil nor careless people, and they had a great deal of affection for, and were very protective of, their children. I think Fatima had in fact been consulted about, and as best she could had consented to, the arrangement, because Maha had been given complete freedom to choose her own husband-to-be during the previous six months when she was looking for someone to marry after she graduated. Maha, I suppose, would have been a more logical offer, but we were so close that we called each other "brother" and "sister." What brother marries his sister? Or perhaps at eighteen she was not considered much of a prize. What is also clear in retrospect is that the parents were mainly trying to ensure a steady kind of support for their youngest daughter.

If these kind parents could consider marrying off their twelve-year-old to a six-foot-two white man knocking on forty years of age, it can be imagined how such matters are treated by much larger and less educated families in, say, the dirt-poor countryside, where there is not even enough money to feed the brood from day to day, and where a wealthy Gulf Arab may suddenly arrive on the scene bearing gifts.

Reports about child brides, especially when the "marriage" lasts only for the time it takes for the man to have his way with the girl, are apt to provoke, in wholly understandable ways, a veritable Saint Vitus' dance of knee-jerk reactions. Old men lusting after young girls, complicit fathers, the wealthy preying on the poor, religion abused to unholy ends—these are rich pickings for those eager to find fault with the Islamic world. Yet consider for a moment the story of Gary Glitter, the former British glam rock star convicted of sharing a bed with prepubescent girls in Vietnam. He is the most prominent example of Western men who trawl Southeast Asia's tourist resorts in search of prepubescent girl prostitutes. The Glitter case overturned a stone with a multitude of creepy-crawlies at the bottom, but it was not said to reveal any inherently evil tendencies in the Christian cultural sphere to which Glitter must be thought, in the very widest sense, to belong. Instead he was treated—in the shrill way that he was—as an individual pervert who had gone to a place where he heard he could indulge his predilections, mostly because he could afford to pay for them, and who was found out and punished for it. In that he is probably the moral, or if we prefer the immoral, equivalent to an Arab man arrested in India because he has failed to pay the dowry for his overnight "marriage" to a young girl.

❦

Nevertheless, it is interesting to look more closely at the question of young girls getting married to older Arab men before they can, by reasonable standards, be considered ready for it, or with whom they are unlikely to have anything in common. It is likewise interesting to look at the means by which Islam as practiced in many places—as opposed to the never-never Islam of theoretical conception—can enable such arrangements, if only to put the issue into some sort of rational context.

Aside from the question of free choice, the most basic issue is health. Early childbirth and the quick succession of pregnancies common among girls married very young carries a high risk of obstetric fistula, a hole in the genital-urinary tract that usually develops when a prolonged labor presses the unborn child so tight against the birth canal that blood flow is cut off to the surrounding tissue, which necrotizes and eventually rots away. This leads to chronic incontinence and odor, and often to ostracism as a result. Left untreated, fistula can cause chronic medical problems, including ulcerations, kidney disease, and nerve damage in the legs, quite apart from the mental suffering associated with this deeply embarrassing disease. Inevitably, this disease is associated with the poverty and poor medical care one would expect to find in the environments where girls are most often married off very young, and has mostly been eradicated in the West (where if it occurs it can be treated with reconstructive surgery). In Africa, Asia, and the

Arab region, an organization called the Campaign to End Fistula estimates that some two million are living with the condition, and up to one hundred thousand new cases develop each year. Girls younger than fifteen are also an estimated five times more likely to die during childbirth or pregnancy than older women, the organization says, adding that pregnancy-related deaths are the leading cause of mortality for girls aged fifteen to nineteen worldwide.[13]

These figures reflect medical facts that must come even before any consideration of the fear and psychological damage young girls can experience when placed in a sexual relationship with an adult, let alone with a much older man from a strange and distant culture. If you are a child, to put the matter simply, marriage is, on a fundamental physiological and physical level, bad for you. That the practice is common regardless of religion—one study claims that in South Asia some 49 percent of the girls are said to marry as children—is neither here nor there.[14] As a rule of thumb, the practices civilizations are quickest to abandon when they reach a level of prosperity can be assumed never to have been very welcome or wholesome, the odds and ends of local herbal lore aside. Marrying prepubescent children, like defecating into the groundwater, is one of them.

At the same time men and women in all parts of the world tend to maintain an attraction to the objects of their desire from the time of sexual awakening, and who are usually roughly the same age. Common sense suggests that desires intense enough to shape our preferences wane with advancing age, to the point where geriatrophilia is a rare condition even among the old. But the pertinent question is whether we are permitted—or should allow ourselves—to act on any lingering desires for the young, and, if so, how young, and in what context. And this is where Islam can justifiably come in for a bit of close scrutiny.

⌘

The Qur'an offers some instruction to the effect that a marriage should be between equal partners and that the woman's informed consent is required. However, Muslims the world over believe that the Prophet Muhammad married his favorite wife Ayisha when she was six years old and that the marriage was consummated when she entered the Prophet's house at the age of nine. Many reform-minded scholars now think she was, in fact, anything up to twenty years old when the marriage was consummated. They say this because, according to the hadith in which Ayisha is reported to have given the account, Ayisha counted her age backward from the beginning of Islam, which is assumed to be the year one in the Islamic Hegira calendar. Like the year one A.D. this is, however, an agreed upon but by no means historically accurate date.

Worth bearing in mind, too, is that the Prophet had no children who are known to have survived by any of his spouses after his first, much older wife, Khadija, and that he was in the habit of marrying for the sake of strategic alliances. It is therefore at least a possibility that the marriage with Ayisha was never consummated at all. That would break with custom, but the Prophet, being who he was, seems to have been pretty much a law unto himself, and in particular when it came to those governing marriage. Still, the historical Muhammad, like Jesus the Man, is of little or no relevance to what the faithful masses overwhelmingly believe, since they prefer to follow whatever facts constitute the canon legal scholars have established over the centuries. Theological niceties are of little interest to the adherents of any religion, who wish to see such big questions settled so they can get on with the more interesting (for most of us, vastly more interesting) business of living.

Such subtleties are, though, of interest to theologians.

Islam is a didactic, political religion, bereft as it is of the conven-ient salvation mechanism of the Christian faith, and sets as among the duties of the believer the encouragement of what is right and preven-tion of what is wrong. It is this insistence on yes or no answers that ac-counts for the enormous tedium of some Islamic scholarship. This tendency to obsess about trivial detail is often rightly mocked—no one who has ever read Ayatollah Khomeini's remarks on the consequences of sex with camels and sheep could ever forget them—but that does not mean it never gets around to matters of importance or that it never arrives at perfectly sensible answers to the larger questions. In the case of child marriage, what is interesting is that scholarship has, from the early days of Islam, been reluctant to take the tradition about Ayisha's age at marriage as carte blanche for anyone wishing to emulate the Prophet in that regard.

In an outstanding academic thesis on the subject, Anjum Ashraf Ali, a lawyer born in the United States of Pakistani parents who grew up in Saudi Arabia, has concluded that the understanding of commu-nities in the Muslim world where child marriage is still widely practiced "is mostly informed by local religious leaders . . . who base their justi-fications on medieval perspectives and interpretations of what consti-tutes divine law."[15] Her own fine analysis of just those medieval perspectives reveals that early Islamic thinkers had a far more complex approach, and a much greater anxiety on the subject, even though they had barely emancipated themselves from thinking of girls as chattel. The question was the precise time when it might be wise, according to Islam, to give a girl away in marriage.

Child marriage was widely practiced in the Middle Ages in East and West, but there can be little doubt that even ancient Greece and early Islamic Arabia saw only the onset of puberty as the end of child-hood in biological terms. There was simply no point to an earlier con-summation if the purpose of marriage, as it has been for most of human history, is procreation. Thus, Ali writes, in one collection of early rul-ings, "a few different opinions on child marriage are mentioned," one of them holding, in the face of what one might have thought was the sacrosanct tradition of the Prophet's own life, that marriage was not permissible until the girl had reached puberty. Indeed, the majority claim that age is not an issue, but rather that the validity of the mar-riage depends on the physical capacity of the girl. If there are no ill ef-fects that can result from consummation, then marriage is allowed even if the child is under the age of nine. If, however, the girl is sickly and thin, then contracting a marriage for her is not permitted even if she is much older. For others the age of nine was seen as the watershed; but if the man consummated the marriage before she had reached that age, they "must be separated." While a number of traditions discuss the benefits of marrying children off young (usually to other younger chil-dren, in a kind of symbolic ceremony) to "protect their chastity"—in other words, to prevent the abomination of sex outside marriage—an-other, headlined "distaste for the marriage of small children," simply advises believers that it will lead to trouble.[16]

An overview of the various opinions within the stricter Hanbali school demonstrates a similar hesitance among some to accept child marriage wholesale. One report Ali has unearthed says that Ahmad Ibn Hanbal, who founded the strictest school of Islam in the ninth century, stated that there should be no marriage of a female minor under any circumstances. Certain other scholars argue against this from within the same school, but Ali also reports an opinion that if a minor boy is to be married it should only be for "absolute necessity"—

defined by some as the need for sexual relations. "Clearly," she writes, "this limits the acceptability of marrying a minor."[17]

In medieval scholarship, the question is usually considered on the margins of other matters, such as property or guardianship; but underlying it there is a sense, however occluded by legalistic nitpicking, that most reasonable people who have their ward's best interest at heart and feel affection toward her would naturally wait to marry her off until she is ready. In other words, medieval scholarship leaves much to the discretion of the individual father or guardian, who is assumed to be a reasonable person unless and until erratic behavior proves him otherwise. However, Ali adds a caveat: "When examining the scholarly opinions surrounding the issue of child marriage, one cannot help but note the lack of acknowledgment of psychological factors that may be involved in potentially abusive situations." Although there seems to have been some debate over when a girl can be said to have reached "the age of desire," concern for honor and family financial welfare, she concludes, "loomed much larger."[18]

It was only in the modern era that child marriage became a big issue in itself. In the Ottoman Empire of the seventeenth and eighteenth centuries, many girls were married off before puberty, often to older men, and this happened across all classes, with the nobility even showing a particular preference for such unions—perhaps unsurprisingly, given that marriages of convenience to consolidate power and extend influence have been the bread and butter of the powerful since Adam delved and Eve span. However, some legal scholars of the era showed the same reluctance as their medieval forbears to pronounce a blanket age of consent. Overall, a boy was considered ready for marriage when he could care for his basic needs, and a girl when she became *mushtahah*, or desirable in a sexual sense, with one of the questions that determined this being, "Is she buxom?"[19] Whether the girl had any desires of her own was still not part of the considerations. This remained the pattern until the nineteenth century, when laws were for various reasons codified by the Ottoman Empire, or when reform movements sought to bring sharia law into some sort of conformity with the modern situation of Muslims. The Salafi movement in Sunni Islam tried to do this by going back to basics, calling for a return to the Qur'an and, especially, the Sunnah, the tradition of the lives of the Prophet and his earliest followers. But in the case of child marriage, Ali believes, the strategy "backfired."[20] In its progressive desire to move believers away from blind adherence to the divergent schools of legal thought, which was then common, it saddled them instead with an often fanatically literal commitment to the early traditions, and there, inevitably, you come up against Ayisha again, "entering the Prophet's house" at the age of nine.

For a snapshot of what reformers campaigning against child marriage today are up against we can briefly go to Yemen, a country explored in more detail and in a different context later in this book but where tribal tradition is particularly deep-rooted and where in rural areas especially it combines with conservative Islam and abject poverty to erect stout ramparts against the influx of modernity.

The country is the unlikely home of the 2008 *Glamour* magazine's Woman of the Year. Nujood Ali, one of sixteen children living in an impoverished suburb of the capital Sanaa, was ten when her father decided to marry her off in 2008 to a deliveryman in his thirties. Promised a handsome groom, Nujood was later to tell reporters the man was in fact "old and ugly."[21] Her father, utterly out of his depth in dealing with a family of this size, claimed he only had Nujood's best interest at heart. One of his other daughters had been kidnapped by a rival clan, he said, and at least the husband had promised to "raise" Nujood and not have sex with her until she was twenty years old.[22]

We do not know if the groom did actually make that promise not to have sex with the girl until she was twenty, but we do know that if he did, it was not kept. On their first night together he insisted on sharing a mattress with Nujood, and when she resisted he beat her into submission. This was to become a nightly pattern. The girl several times complained to her family, but they told her they could do nothing, since she now "belonged" to her husband. Her mother was later to claim her heart "burned" and the father came to describe the husband as "a criminal, a criminal"—but that was only when Nujood had long since decided to take matters into her own hands.[23]

Astonishingly, after months of beatings and rape, the little girl, having asked the advice of an aunt, got into a taxi by herself (the first time in her life she had done so) and went to court to demand a divorce. At the courthouse, baffled officials at first had no idea what to do with her; then a female human rights lawyer, Shada Nasser, agreed to take on her case. It was Nasser, too, who alerted her contacts at the *Yemen Times*, and from there her story spread quickly around the world. The global publicity machine ground into gear: All the major U.S. newspapers got on the case, as did CNN. Finally, *Glamour* magazine flew the eleven-year-old Nujood to New York for a tacky award ceremony, where she was feted by such tireless fighters for the individual's right to wall-to-wall tabloid coverage as Hillary Clinton and Nicole Kidman. A tell-all book was commissioned, to be published in twenty-odd languages, whose authors promised a sizable proportion of the royalties would go to Nujood. Some kind, ordinary people in the United States donated money for the girl to attend a private school. By then she had been granted a divorce, and was back with her family.

But all, we subsequently learned, was far from well.

More than a year later Nujood was still angry, and, according to reports, not regularly attending the private school. Nasser said she pleaded with the family to make sure that she went, but the father told her there was no money for transport or food. The lawyer, however, believed that the family had been hoping for their share of what they thought must be a sizable cake, and were punishing Nujood when none of the money the global publicity had generated for the media industry devolved on them. The compensation for the husband had cost $250 after the court finally granted the child a divorce, which had been donated by a Yemeni lawyer, and the infamous book had not yet come out.

As usual, it was little Nujood who summed up her own situation most eloquently: "There is no change at all since going on television. I hoped there was someone to help us, but we didn't find anyone to help us. It hasn't changed a thing. They said they were going to help me and no one has helped me. I wish I had never spoken to the media."[24]

She added that, among her own family and friends, she now felt "like an outcast." However, according to a report in the *New York Times*, attitudes changed after the book was published and the royalties made Nujood the family's main breadwinner.[25] Nujood now apparently attends private school full time.[26]

In the Yemeni parliament there were attempts in the light of this case to pass a law that set the age of marriage at seventeen; and a number of other child brides came forward in the wake of Nujood's global fame.[27] The international media were not, though, interested in this fresh gaggle of child brides, since their story brought no "new" angle; and the proposed law was under threat from hard-line Islamist members of parliament who insisted that there is no fixed age of marriage in Islam. Nor is it clear how much weight such legislation would carry. Yemenis follow established customs more closely than the law, said Ahmed Al-Gorashi, chairman of the Yemeni child-protection charity Seyaj.

"Tribal leaders and imams have more influence than the state," he explained. "But it's important to amend our marriage laws to create a benchmark. We need a new place to start from."[28]

Among Islamic scholars and thinkers whose job it is to sort out this mess, the lines today are sharply drawn between what one might, with some reluctance, call the followers of liberal Islam and the supporters of Wahhabi extremism.

In this titanic contest, camel-toothed and milky of eye, stands that ineffable creep, the Saudi grand mufti Sheikh Abdul Aziz Al-Asheikh, willing poster boy for everything that is wrong with literalistic Islam. In what was to prove one of his more imaginative approaches to the question, this tireless scourge of the female driver (he is a vocal opponent of those who campaign for Saudi women to be allowed to drive) proposed in May 2009 to consider child marriage as a feminist issue. "We hear a lot about the marriage of underage girls in the media, and we should know that Islamic law has not brought injustice to women. It is wrong to say it's not permitted to marry off girls who are fifteen and younger. A female who is ten or twelve is marriageable, and those who think she's too young are wrong and are being unfair to her."[29]

He then rather knocked himself out by adding: "Our mothers, and before them our grandmothers, married when they were barely twelve." From a religious point of view that is irrelevant, but the mufti also represents the ideological arm of an authoritarian regime, sitting at the head of the Wahhabi Party Central Committee. And it is in this department that tribal tradition has assumed monumental proportions as a conversation stopper, hopelessly entwined as it has become with the struggle of the Wahhabi cleric's ancestor, Mohammed ibn Abdul Wahhab, against "innovation" in the eighteenth century—which is to say divergence from scripture and, especially, from the way Islam was practiced, or is thought by some to have once been practiced, in the very earliest years after the religion was founded.

Opposing the likes of the grand mufti, the lively Indian contrarian and journalist A. Faizur Rahman can stand for many with the following brisk summary of the main issues:

> A perusal of the Qur'an will reveal that marriage in Islam is a civil contract—meesaaq (4:21)—and as such it can be finalized only between persons who are intellectually and physically mature enough to understand and fulfill the responsibilities of such a contract. This can be further understood from the verse, "And test the orphans until they reach the age of nikah (marriage), and if you find in them rushdh (maturity of intellect) release their property to them." (4:6). It may be noted here that the Qur'an makes intellectual maturity (which always falls beyond the age of puberty) the basis to arrive at the age of marriage.[30]

Here a polemical element also lurks in the deft parenthesis claiming that intellectual maturity "always falls beyond the age of puberty." Well, that was the point the grand mufti was making, although the unkind might venture that by the mufti's own lights the age of intellectual maturity is either about eleven or never.

This, in any case, is broadly the state of the present debate, and according to many observing from the sidelines it represents in a nutshell the whole struggle for the very soul of Islam. But irrespective of these widely divergent present-day scholarly opinions, in her fine thesis Ali had earlier reminded us that the majority of Muslims in the developing world, especially among the lower uneducated classes, are still easily swayed by those who, for them, stand as local religious figures of authority. Unfortunately, the latter are rarely even qualified to be called teachers of any kind, let alone scholars. The Islam propagated at these levels is purely based on cultural norms and social and economic expedients.[31]

Little wonder that some of the juicier headlines about child marriage involve Saudi nationals, or come to us from Saudi Arabia itself.

In the Wahhabi kingdom many people take what we might call a pragmatic view of their religion, because it has morphed into the political ideology of their repressive state. While they may or may not see its core truth as absolute and nonnegotiable, many will, for peace of mind and a break from the constant sermonizing, do whatever the religious leaders tell them is permissible, without troubling themselves with yet more ethical questions on top of all the other things that are already supposed to be *haram* (from music to Valentine's Day cards). This is partly a side effect of Wahhabism, which effectively wrests the all-important element of discretion or interpretation *(ijtihad)* out of the hands of individual believers and renders it up to the jabbering old fools like Al-Asheikh who constitute the religious establishment. It takes little stretching of one's sympathies to see how a Saudi might well insist on one of the bare few rights the faith still seems to leave him: choosing his bride.

In 2009 an eight-year-old Saudi girl in Qaseem—in the deepest, darkest tribal heartland of the kingdom—was refused a divorce by her sixty-year-old husband, a decision a local court upheld.[32] Bear in mind that the girl, unlike Nujood in Yemen, still lived with her parents, and there was no suggestion that she would "enter her husband's house" until she was much older. Indeed, the court's apparently heartless decision was to prove purely a technical question of sharia law. The judge even tried to persuade the husband to divorce the girl, but the husband refused, apparently because he had paid good money as a dowry. The case was brought by the girl's mother. The judge, consistent with the medieval decisions quoted above, ruled that the girl could herself ask for a divorce once she reached puberty, but not until then. There was, to repeat, no question of compelling the girl to have sex with the man. It was simply that the man felt he had rights in a financial transaction, a kind of investment in his old age, which he had undertaken in good faith—to help out a friend, moreover, since the father apparently had debts—and he had put his trust in the legal standards that he believed to apply in a country that pretends to be governed solely by the strictest interpretation of sharia law. The case, then, far from demonstrating (as much of the Western coverage implied) an inveterate tendency to pedophilia among Arabs, let alone institutional support for it, instead represented an example of the tribal custom of selling off daughters upheld by medieval legal precedent in the present day.

Nevertheless, in the same year Saudi justice minister Mohammed Issa was claiming his ministry wanted to put an end to the "arbitrary"

way in which parents and guardians can marry off underage girls—
though he did not say he would ban the practice, for which he would
have some trouble finding an acceptable basis in Wahhabi Islam.[33] It
was apparently this remark, combined with the worldwide outcry about
the subject more generally, that prompted the grand mufti to utter the
nonsense, quoted above, about how Child Marriage is a Feminist Issue.
But only a year earlier the mufti himself had spoken out against marriages in which the age difference is more than fifty years. "Islam stipulates that both parties agree to the marriage contract. The woman
must express real consent to the suitor, and a guardian must not impose
his choice of husband on her . . . or force his son to marry someone he
doesn't want."[34]

In other words, though he occupies the reactionary side of the
debate by choice and inclination, and though his insistence that a
fifty-year age gap is a suitable cut-off point will provoke gasps of as-
tonishment by all but his most uncritical followers, Al-Asheikh was
evidently driven deeper into his reactionary corner the more the issue
became politicized. And there is no reason to doubt that he was defending what he genuinely thought was a set of values everywhere
under siege by the forces of Western-inspired corruption.

Consider, too, that the only reason the international media heard
about these cases is that they were first reported in the Saudi newspapers, which take as much delight in splashing examples of backward
tribal practices across their pages, holding them up for condemnation
and amusement, as the U.S. press does when weighing in on cultist
Christians and their habit of marrying, somewhere in the depths of the
Bible Belt, underage girls. Indeed, Al-Asheikh's own fatwa on child
brides and the fifty-year age gap was preceded by a chorus of argument
against the practice from less eminently placed but more rational Saudi

scholars. The previous year, the country's Shoura Council, an un-elected body that advises the king, had passed a resolution calling for a blanket marriage age of eighteen.[35]

What can be firmly laid at the doorstep of Islam, as it has over the centuries combined with local traditions, is the shape the sex tourism of some Gulf Arabs takes, where their behavior abroad mimics what is permissible at home. In the various short-term marriages of Shia and Sunni Islam, and in the uncertainties surrounding the age when girls can be married, Islam offers the more shameless opportunist a kind of gray area where he may see nothing wrong in becoming a fly-by-night husband to an underage girl in Indonesia, India, or Egypt.

Still, is the phenomenon of child brides really that common?

The answer largely depends on what one means by "child," and that definition certainly changes according to time and place. In the mid-nineteenth century Dickens liked to place his female heroines on the cusp of womanhood, which in the case of Little Nell was "not quite fourteen"; and Dickens himself was for much of his life obsessed with the memory of his sister-in-law, who died at the age of seventeen. Our present-day Western ideas of what a child is were largely shaped in the nineteenth century, and had a great deal to do with the circumstances in which the middle class of industrial countries was then able to live. The development of the education system has continued to push the age of maturity upward, to the point where there is now no very good reason why childhood should ever end for the sons and daughters of the well-to-do.

That is all for the good, I suppose. But it still seems, at best, odd to describe a girl of fourteen or fifteen as a child, in the same way we would a seven- or eight-year-old, especially if she lives in a country that does not enjoy twelve years of free compulsory education, that routinely sends children off to work, and that sets the age of consent for sex at fourteen or fifteen.

After summarizing the hysteria surrounding child prostitution in his book *Global Sex* (2001), and especially how the debate blurs "vital distinctions that exist between six- and fifteen-year-olds," the political scientist Dennis Altman sensibly states that "no-one would dispute that someone of eight is a child," but then provocatively asks: "what of a girl or boy of fourteen?"[36]

The age of consent in fact remains fourteen in much of Eastern Europe and Latin America, and it is fourteen even in authoritarian China, home to one fifth of the world's population. It is fourteen in Italy and Portugal, thirteen in Spain, and twelve in Malta. It would be incorrect to suggest that the moral panic about adolescent sexuality is confined to the English-speaking world (if only). But while Canada in 2008 raised the age of consent from fourteen to sixteen, and thus officially condemned Canadian teenagers to two more years of forlorn masturbation, Peru in 2007 lowered its age of consent from seventeen to fourteen (despite a campaign by "activists") and did so with public support and on the grounds that prosecuting people for having consensual sex over that age was a waste of everyone's time and resources.[37] However, the age for marrying is usually higher than the age of consent in all of these countries, often considerably so, and with very good reasons: Young people may be capable of deciding who they want to have sex with, but a decision about who they want to spend the rest of their lives with is a much weightier concern. More important, marriage by necessity involves consummation, but sex outside of marriage does not. That is why the convergence of prostitution and marriage of the temporary kind is particularly reprehensible even when it involves older adolescents.

More generally, the prostitution of adolescent girls is common in some, or perhaps most, parts of the world, because there is a market for them, and there always will be, though that is no excuse for not trying to reduce the number. Some of their customers are Arabs, but many more are not. The arrangements differ, too. Some girls are sold into bondage, held in brothels, chained to their beds, and forced to serve several customers a day (usually Confucians, Buddhists, and Hindus); some are willing freelancers looking for fun, money, and a break from the monotony of village life; some are naïve, or being lied to. There is a documented link to poverty and lack of education, but the existence of underage Danish hookers shows that, even in the best of all possible worlds, some girls will fall through the net.

Thankfully, press reports about Arabs in foreign lands abroad rarely seem to record any cases where the girl is prepubescent, but rather speak to a preference for what should be called "nubile girls"— nothing, if we are honest, out of the ordinary in any culture, and certainly not indicative, however frowned upon these days in the English-speaking world, of a tendency specific to Muslims.

In any case, and as we will see in the rest of this book, the overwhelming majority of Gulf Arab sex tourists are in search of neither children nor adolescents, but adult women.

CHAPTER *five*

PLEASURE ISLAND

The taxi driver first in line outside the arrivals terminal—middle-aged, bearded, slightly overweight—seemed friendly enough, and needed only the gentlest of reminders to switch on the meter. We set off for downtown Manama, capital of the tiny Persian Gulf island of Bahrain, and I told him the name of the budget hotel where I planned to stay. Here, as elsewhere, taxi drivers are the first point of call for travelers in search of forbidden local attractions, and to see if this one would take the bait I launched into an anecdote. After booking in at the same hotel about six years earlier, I recalled, I had not even had time to kick off my shoes before two Russian women came banging at the door offering their services. At the time, I was based in Saudi Arabia. The last thing I could have risked was getting caught up, however remote the possibility, in a vice sting, so I had nervously turned them away more quickly than I would normally have. I was making this latest visit, though, as a free agent, and specifically to research the island's notorious sex industry. That hotel, with its prostitutes roaming the corridors when not dancing in the bar with intoxicated Gulf Arabs, would be as good a place as any to begin the investigation.

The driver had been listening impassively, but suddenly stopped me in my tracks with a tut. Catching my eye in the rear-view mirror, he said that the hotel I mentioned was a two-star establishment, and all one- and two-star hotels had recently been banned by the government from serving alcohol, in a drive to curb prostitution. I had read about the ban, but dismissed it as gesture politics: aimed at generating nothing so much as a flurry of dramatic headlines to pacify domestic Islamist opposition groups and international NGOs, while bringing about no significant change at ground zero. Slightly disoriented by the driver's Gulf Arabic dialect, not that easy for me to comprehend because I speak Egyptian, I asked myself whether he was painting such a negative picture because he had taken offense that I had raised the subject or was trying to get me to go to another hotel so he could pocket a commission.

"No bar, no girls," he said.

So what, I asked, did he suggest I do?

"Stay," he said as if talking to an imbecile, "at a three-star hotel."

He knew one just a few blocks further down the main drag from my original choice. The room was ninety dollars a night, double what I intended to pay. But the hotel was crammed, he assured me, with women from all four corners of the globe. According to him, they included some of those who were previously based at the now dry budget hotels, who had scurried off to the more upmarket bars, discos, and dance halls after the alcohol ban came into effect. As we pulled into the courtyard, he reminded me that normally he did not use the taximeter: a not-so-subtle hint that his advice, offered—it turned out—without any moral misgivings, warranted additional compensation. The thunderous music coming from the hotel reassured me that he had not been bluffing about its desirability, so I was happy to oblige. Although it was four o'clock in the morning, there were still parties in full swing.

While the receptionist completed the formalities, I found myself staring at a solitary young Saudi man wearing a long, white thobe, who was singing an Arabic pop song and walking around himself in a tight circle like a dog chasing its tail. An Indian bellboy finally appeared and pushed him rudely in the direction of the coffee shop.

"No, no," the Saudi said in English, straightening himself. "Beer. Bar. Beer. I want beer," he said with deliberate emphasis, but also the desperation of someone lost in the desert who would breathe his last if not given water.

"I already told you three times the bar is closing," the bellboy barked back, handling him more forcefully. "Go to the coffee shop! You can get another beer there!"

Watching the mostly Indian staff so fearlessly push around and scream orders at the more unruly of their Saudi guests, and observing their glances of barely concealed contempt when leaving the better-behaved ones to their own devices, is my most cherished memory of the hotel. It was such a dramatic reversal of the situation I had grown accustomed to in neighboring Saudi Arabia, where the browbeaten Indian expatriates had little choice but to put up with the appalling treatment routinely meted out by their Saudi masters. Here, though, fear of bringing attention to their antics, forbidden back in the Wahhabi kingdom itself, helped to temper the Saudis' worst characteristics when dealing with their presumed third-world inferiors who dominate the service industry.

It was a deferential Egyptian, originally from Alexandria, who showed me to my room. It was not difficult for me to imagine how working in such a hotel, despite the relatively good salary (compared to Egypt at least), would sour anyone's appreciation of life, but particularly for this gentle man far from home, and on whose forehead was proudly displayed a *zabiba*, the prayer scar of the Muslim faithful.

However, I was in need of information.

To my surprise, he answered without hesitation a shameless question about how much the women cost ($60). And he listed, quite of his own accord, the house rules about picking them up and taking them back to the room. Perhaps doing so was part of his job description. Anyway, only one of the rules was so important that I am still able to recall it: staying away from the first floor, strictly reserved for Gulf families wanting to be shielded from the general mayhem.

There must be very few, if any, decent hotels in Manama free of such sinful delights, I suggested, if even the more pious families had no choice but to settle for this compromise. He said that was a pretty fair assessment of the situation, but was eager to point out that it was not unknown for married Saudi guests—who, he reminded me, may or may not be pious—secretly to rent an additional single room on another floor where they could take one of the hotel's resident hookers when the wife and kids were asleep in the dead of night.

My floor proved a hotbed of illicit activity, even—especially?—at that ungodly hour. Six diminutive Asian women immediately came running in our direction as we stepped out of the elevator. They uttered the tired mantras—You like friend? You like massage? I give you good time?—long established as the lingua franca of the global sex trade. One tried to grab my bags, seeking as much information from the Egyptian as her broken Arabic, and his air of indifference, permitted. Where was I from? How many nights would I be staying? What was my room number? Had I arrived alone?

"These girls are a big problem," the Egyptian warned me. As though to prove his point, he was forced to drag one, who had sneaked inside the room, back out with him into the corridor.

When I arrived in Bahrain in 2009, prostitution had already been the island's leading political controversy for months. I soon discovered that the debate was being kept alive by a local media that is relatively free to discuss sensitive social issues (as long as direct attacks on the royal family are avoided) and, when it comes to this issue, is predictably obsessive and sensational. It even appeared to have eclipsed the eternal feud between the majority Shia, who make up about two-thirds of the indigenous population, and the minority Sunnis, who rule over and oppress them.

Sunni fundamentalist politicians, who were behind the ban on alcohol, intended for it to mark only a first victory in their vociferous campaign to shut down the prostitution industry and eradicate all its related offshoots. "I'm sorry to say, but Bahrain has become the brothel of the [Persian] Gulf, and our people are very upset about it," an Islamist member of parliament told the *Wall Street Journal*. "It's not only the drinking that we oppose, but also what it drags with it: prostitution, corruption, drugs, and people trafficking."[1] The Islamists do have their supporters in Bahrain. Periodic riots break out, with a focus on trashing restaurants selling alcohol and any Saudi-registered vehicles that happen to be parked in the vicinity, although these riots are sometimes motivated by anti-Israel and anti-U.S. sentiment when Saudi vehicles are not trashed, and (to complicate matters further) can be the result of the interminable Shia-Sunni tensions or soccer matches between Saudi Arabia and Bahrain—or even, on occasion, a combination of all the above.[2]

The limited alcohol ban, as my taxi driver had indicated, was anything but a whitewash. Later I read estimates that it impacted a quarter of Bahrain's roughly one hundred and sixty hotels.[3] That is in contrast to the trend in Qatar and Abu Dhabi, which is toward greater liberalization. And in Cairo in 2009, when a Saudi prince tried to ban alcohol in the bar of a five-star hotel he owns, he was forced to back down because of negative publicity. However, the wonder really is that it took so long for the Sunni extremists in Bahrain to grind into action. Even among Arabs who live in countries where prostitution and alcohol are legal or tolerated, Manama is notorious, and its nightlife was already the stuff of legend by the 1940s when it was first referred to as Paradise Island.

After waking up late on my first day, I strolled through downtown Manama. It resembles nothing so much as a nondescript New Delhi suburb, the only Bahrainis around being surly drivers sipping tea at taxi stands. I checked out the hotel I had stayed at during my previous visit to see if the ban really had been enforced (it was shuttered), grabbed a coffee, and checked my email at an Internet café full of Indian boys watching porn and fiddling with their erections. My intention that evening was only a little more sophisticated: to sample my hotel's numerous entertainment venues.

To judge by the prominence given to a huge poster in the foyer I saw when I got back, the first point of call was a no-brainer. The poster featured four bleached-blonde female singers in their late twenties or early thirties, each trying a little more desperately than the next to look professionally glamorous. Towering over them was a man of about the same age billed as their manager and DJ, a balding man who had greased his thinning hair fetchingly over his forehead. His sleazy smile seemed aimed only at confirming the general impression the poster gave: that singing was the least important of the tasks his band had been brought to the island to perform. Any lingering doubts on that score dissipated as I entered the club. The women were on stage, half-heartedly miming the latest hit song from Egypt as they more carefully eyed the few dozen mostly Saudi customers. That they knew some of the lyrics was an indication that they were not newcomers to the region, but in and of itself no great accomplishment. The chorus goes: wa wa waaaaa, wa wa waaaaa, wa wa waaaaa.

The balding DJ stood behind a huge keyboard, although his sole task appeared to be pressing the play button on the music system. Indeed, as the next song started, he left the stage and made his way to each table, a routine the Gulfies seemed terribly uncomfortable with. When the man reached my table, it became obvious why: After introducing himself, he asked where I was from and what my name was. The very last thing anyone in such a club anywhere in the world wants anyone else to know, as he should be the first person to understand, is their identity, especially perhaps those who have nipped over from Saudi Arabia to get a drink and "change their oil" (as Arabic euphemistically has it). I gave him a false name and fictional home country, as I suspect did many of the others. During the rest of our two-minute exchange, he went fishing for compliments by apologizing for speaking "such awful English." Back on stage, he grabbed the microphone and announced that the next song was dedicated to "Ahmed from Riyadh" as he gave a cheery thumbs-up, causing the young man he had singled out almost to crawl under his table.

The waitresses were Indian, extraordinary beauties in their late teens or early twenties but not, it turned out, prostitutes. Their job, in addition to taking orders, was to walk around with huge leis of the kind

Elvis Presley had placed over his head by local girls to welcome him as he stepped off the airplane in Hawaii. Would I, a waitress presently asked me, care to buy a garland for any of the women on stage? Told they cost forty dollars, I firmly declined. But a few minutes later she was back, handing me a generic note from one of the singers, who waved as the waitress pointed her out. "Hi handsome," it read. "I'm ————. Would you like me to have a drink with you?" I declined that offer, too. Undeterred, the waitress returned one final time, bearing yet another note. It had a mobile phone number scribbled on it and the information that, should I change my mind about the drink, I could call her anytime.

As I left the club a little later, I could not help but notice, farther down the corridor, a large number of Indian men gathered around a door. The Indian music blaring from inside the place they were trying to get into was almost loud enough to drown out the Egyptian music in the club from which I had just stepped. That piqued my interest. To their bemusement, I pushed my way through toward the entrance. Inside, hundreds of Indian men, packed in like sardines, were watching a parade of Indian women dressed in multicolored saris, performing what looked like an amateur fashion show. The hostile glances from some in the all-male crowd made it clear that I was not welcome. White people can generally get away with doing anything in the Persian Gulf, especially if they are in the midst of a group of Indians. They have, as it were, the status of untouchables. Nevertheless, I took the hint that this was intended to be an exclusively Indian affair.

I was pleased to find a smattering of friendly Saudis in the bar, from teenagers in Western clothes to old men in Arab dress. The one thing they had in common, apart from their nationality, was an evident determination to drink as much as possible. There was only one woman. She arrived just as I did, and was completely covered. As far as one could tell she was middle-aged and (more obviously) obese. I could not take my eyes off her, try as I might, as she ordered a whiskey and sat alone to stare at a small stage, empty but for a solitary keyboard and amplifier.

I perched on a stool at the bar, and asked a man sitting next to me whether the woman was a prostitute.

"No!" he replied, almost choking on his drink. "She's from Saudi Arabia, but I think she lives in Bahrain. She comes here to listen to the music."

My neighbor, it turned out, was also from Saudi Arabia, more specifically its oil-rich Eastern Province that, like Bahrain, has a majority Shia population ruled by a repressive Sunni regime. The Eastern Province is also the Saudi region nearest Bahrain, where a bridge links the two countries. He said he drove over to Manama for a few drinks most nights after work, a journey that took him less than an hour even when he observed the speed limit. (Saudis famously drive like maniacs, and some of the others there that evening, especially the younger guys, improbably claimed that they could complete the journey on a weekday in about half that time.) He glanced down at a table of his fellow compatriots, three rowdy men in their fifties engaged in a drunken argument that had briefly threatened to turn into a brawl, and said that they made him ashamed of his country.

Saudis do not have a monopoly on behaving like clowns when they are drunk, I reassured him. He would be exposed to the same kind of mayhem in many British or American bars, I said. At least there was no fear that they were going to smash a bottle over his head. He was the last person, I subsequently realized, who needed that information, when he told me he had been educated at an American university and still spent much of the year in that country.

"Americans are nice," he later said, apropos of nothing. "They're not hateful, just ignorant. And you can't blame people for their ignorance."

And soon after offering that broad summation of the American mind-set, he announced that he was leaving. He paid for my drink, too, and gave me his almost full packet of cigarettes. I refused the latter, thinking his offer a gesture of kindness not supposed to be taken literally (something common in the Arab world). But he pushed the packet back toward me, and explained with a self-effacing smile that his wife, three years into their marriage, still had no idea he smoked. If she were to discover this packet, the consequences, he added melodramatically, would not bear thinking about.

What on earth would she do, I thought, as I watched him saunter away, if she discovered that he spent most of his evenings knocking down beer after beer in one of Manama's sleaziest hotels?

In considering the double life led by this Saudi man, and so many others like him, we should turn our attention to the Wahhabi kingdom itself. As good a starting point as any is the uproar, contrived or otherwise, caused by a new nonimmigrant visa application form issued in 2003 by the U.S. Embassy in Riyadh that, according to a Saudi newspaper report, was "met with dismay" throughout the kingdom.[4] Section 38 of the application, a new addition, was said to ask whether the applicant has been involved in past criminal activities, and "in particular prostitution."

A Saudi woman, Nahid Omari, who it seems almost suffered a hernia on being told the news, declared after finally regaining her composure: "What a weird and awful question. Imagine a husband filling out the application for his wife. The application is basically asking if his wife is or was a prostitute! What would he feel? This kind of question is totally unacceptable in our society. It is a possibility that they are doing all this to deter people from traveling to America."[5]

A married Saudi man, who for some reason asked not to be named, added: "Have they no respect? How dare they ask me if my wife or even I have ever been involved in prostitution?"

That "my wife or even I" is a curious turn of phrase, suggesting as it does that asking him is even more outrageous than asking his wife. Regardless, Americans should realize, he said, that "our society and our women are different from the women they have in America. What's next, are they going to start questioning whether our children are really our own?"[6] One can sympathize with the negative reaction. There is something distasteful, to say the least, in the American government thinking it has the right to invade the private lives of foreigners who have yet to set foot on its puritan soil. Nevertheless, the Saudi reaction was shrill. It is a country, after all, where the religious police have the power to demand of any man and woman found together in public documentary evidence that they are married or related and, if they are discovered not to be, tend to conclude on the spot that the woman is most likely a whore.

That contradiction tells us something important about the way the subject is dealt with, or more accurately not dealt with, inside the kingdom, where it is widely known that sex for money is as frequent an occurrence as it is elsewhere: from princes hanging out in Beirut's casinos to randy schoolboys paying the Filipina maid for a quickie before bedtime to the kind of men I was surrounded by that evening at the Manama hotel. Given that there are regular raids of brothels smack-dab in the heart of Mecca, Islam's holiest city, prostitutes are likely to be found everywhere, something that endless newspaper reports like-wise confirm.[7]

Equally well known, however, is that the subject of extramarital (or premarital) sex and prostitution is not considered suitable for frank public discussion. That is, unless it is presented, as in the reports on Mecca's brothels, as a heavily punished transgression (thousands of lashes seems to be par for the course), and preferably then picked up by the legions of Saudi op-ed writers—who specialize in producing di-atribe after diatribe against the evil, corrupting ways of dirty third-world immigrants and yet rarely vent their spleen about how Saudis are chiefly responsible, and on a far grander scale, for having created brothel cultures in Manama, Dubai, Beirut, Cairo, Damascus, Mar-rakesh, and wherever else they decide to spend the summer.

No carefully researched, objective assessment of the extent of do-mestic prostitution has yet been published by the Saudi media, which is otherwise free to cover social problems, and the reason is obvious. Digging deeper into this particular subject would risk cracking the façade of sexual puritanism fanatically defended by the religious po-lice, to the extent it might even suggest that Saudi women should not unquestioningly be considered different from "the women they have in America"—however unfortunate that choice of phrase may be.

Then again, considering the journalistic standards Saudis adhere to when they do discuss the subject, outright censorship for the time being seems the best option. For instance, Saudi-based e-newspaper *Kul Al-Watan* (All of the Homeland) was threatened with a defamation lawsuit in May 2009 when thirteen Saudi women journalists took issue with a report headlined "Saudi Women in Red Nights" about how prostitution, alcohol, and drugs had become prevalent in Saudi society. One of its many crude observations was that "women journalists rely on illicit relationships with newspaper bosses to get support and fame."[8]

From 1861 until independence in 1971, Bahrain was virtually a British protectorate. The terms under which the Bahraini ruling family and the British co-ruled were similar to those the British forged with other Persian Gulf states: The ruling family governed the territory, but could not establish any relationship with other governments without first obtaining British consent. In return, the British promised to protect the island militarily from any external aggression.

Data from the British Agency Annual Reports shows that prostitution flourished throughout the period, with a marked increase between 1926 and 1937.[9] The reasons given are vague, but what strikes me about those dates is that they correspond to the period when much of the Arabian Peninsula was conquered by the Al-Saud royal family and their Wahhabi foot soldiers. This was the third time the Saudis had tried to conquer vast parts of the Arabian Peninsula from their base in Al-Najd in the center, believing a vast empire their rightful destiny. Hundreds of thousands of Muslims were massacred because they did not subscribe to the Wahhabi version of Islam, an ultraorthodox ideology that essentially forbids everything but the Five Pillars of Islam. The Saudi state was officially founded in 1932, and its new God Squad was unleashed to hunt down and severely punish any stubborn manifestations of liberal Islam, which could involve anything from praying at saints' shrines to talking to a woman who was not a direct relative.[10] Bahrain found itself next to a giant neighbor bereft of any kind of entertainment outlets, a soon-to-be obscenely wealthy country, but one where even smoking and music and dancing were now outlawed. This likely caused an influx into Bahrain of Saudis, many seeking respite from their new Wahhabi tormentors in the arms of a prostitute—a trend that, as we have seen, grew rapidly during the following decades.

Whatever the reason for the initial increase in prostitution in Manama, the result was that two official brothel areas were established in what had already formed the de facto red-light districts; and in 1937 a court decree "ordered that prostitutes should live and work only in these two designated places," with those found living or working elsewhere to be deported.[11] The prostitutes themselves "were predominantly from Persia, Iraq, and Oman, with Persians commanding the highest prices, then Iraqis and Omanis, respectively. The prostitutes were known as Daughters of the Wind."[12] These designated districts remained the center of the Bahraini sex industry until the early 1970s, when it moved into the newly built hotels, nightclubs, and apartment buildings. During that decade, the oil boom created a new class of rich and superrich throughout the Persian Gulf, who flocked to Manama in ever greater numbers.

Although Bahrain had been the first country in the region to discover oil, its hydrocarbon reserves are small compared to those of Saudi Arabia, Kuwait, and Qatar, and after independence the island's rulers understood the need to diversify the economy (something they have achieved with admirable success). One sector with obvious potential was the entertainment and service industry, and it was given a boost by regional geopolitical events. In 1979 the Iranian revolution, an attack on the U.S. Embassy in Pakistan by an Islamist terror group, and a siege of Mecca by jihadis opposed to the Al-Saud's tentative moves toward liberalization all took place. A new wave of Islamic extremism swept the region. That made Bahrain's easygoing ways yet more of an anomaly, and so even more attractive.

In 1986, the bridge known as the Causeway opened, directly linking Saudi Arabia and Bahrain. Soon there was bumper-to-bumper traffic as hundreds of thousands of Saudis escaped the Wahhabi kingdom, and to a lesser extent Kuwait, for weekend breaks. (Unsurprisingly, there was no gridlock in the other direction on Thursday evenings, which marks the beginning of the Muslim weekend of Friday and Saturday.) One of the more predictable consequences of the bridge was yet another dramatic increase in the number of foreign prostitutes working Manama's ever-growing number of bars, discos, and hotels, who poured in with tens of thousands of other immigrant workers.

While soliciting is illegal in Bahrain, technically prostitution is not, although it is not legal, either. Almost all cases are officially filed under charges of adultery. Whatever resentment religious types may have had in the 1970s and 1980s regarding the direction in which their country was heading in the postdependence era was kept firmly in check by the ruling family by tried and tested means: severely restricting political participation and curtailing freedom of expression. The economy meanwhile continued to grow at an impressive rate.

The situation changed dramatically when limited political reforms were implemented in 2002. Elections, and a newly emerging freer media suddenly gave a national platform to the extremist Sunnis who were voted into office. In 1999, when Bahrain's longtime ruler died, his son and successor, Sheikh Hamad bin Isa Al-Khalifa, gambled that greater freedom would be more effective than outright repression in pacifying increasing demands by opposition groups for greater political participation. He "freed political detainees, fired a Briton who directed internal security and called on critics to join in drafting a program to change the political system."[13] He also changed his title from emir to king "and pronounced Bahrain a constitutional monarchy, suggesting that royal power would be constrained."[14] However, when it became clear that the key ministries and an upper house of parliament would be royal appointees with veto power over everything the elected lower chamber did, liberals boycotted the poll. The Islamists as a result were elected unopposed. Crucially, as parliamentarians, they were granted immunity from prosecution, meaning they could express opinions on previously taboo subjects, which they believed should be brought into the open. In turn, the media was given the green light from the ruling family to report what was debated in parliament, since not doing so would have rendered the whole democracy push pointless.

The Council of Deputies, as the elected chamber of forty members of parliament is called, is little more than a talking shop, the real power still resting with the royal family and unelected ministries. A soap box, though, is what extremist Sunnis crave more than anything else. Their goal is to create a climate of moral panic and fear to radicalize society from below and increase pressure on whoever rules to introduce sharia law. They deal best, that is to say, in slogans and insults while in the limited parliament, free of genuine responsibility and the need to make difficult and complicated choices, something that still rested with the royal family.

There could not have been a more obvious target for them than the foreign hookers right in front of everybody's eyes from Burma, China, the Philippines, India, Russia, Turkey, Egypt, Morocco, and Ethiopia.[15] Singling them out as representing a social menace was a sure way for the Islamists, who quickly formed a well-disciplined bloc in the elected chamber, to galvanize their core Sunni base and easily silence critics who risked being labeled anti-Islam if they dared to raise objections. By 2003, this was a risk fewer were prepared to make in the wake of the anti-Western backlash created by the U.S.-led invasion of Iraq. The campaign was also a way of introducing their strict Sunni agenda via the back door, the only way of doing so in majority-Shia Bahrain.

The Islamists' antiprostitution campaign, fought under the green banner of combating corruption within government and throughout society, soon gained the support of (or managed to silence) all the usual suspects: the mass media, which saw it as a circulation booster; Shia MPs, who usually cannot even bear to talk to their Sunni oppressors but who refused to offer any hint of criticism for fear of appearing soft on vice; human rights activists only too happy to highlight, even if they had an ostensibly liberal agenda, the country's moral decline, if doing so embarrassed the repressive ruling elite; the salvationists, posing as feminists; and those who make up the international anti-sex-trafficking industry. A few weeks before I hit town in 2009, their campaign, which we will turn to shortly, was given an unexpected shot in the arm: Manama made it onto a list of the world's top ten "sin cities" published by a popular U.S.-based men's webzine. The only Arab city included, and right up there with Pattaya in Thailand and Tijuana in Mexico, it was described as "the party oasis of the Middle East."[16]

That the Islamists are, so to speak, given to firing indiscriminately in all directions makes them especially dangerous in terms of political discourse, but it also means that they are the only ones likely to hit any of the right targets. No one could reject outright the argument that prostitution in Manama has long been out of control, is inextricably linked to local corruption, and involves some elements of exploitation of the women who work as prostitutes. A cleanup probably was long overdue. The problem with the issue being hijacked by Islamist rabble-rousers—quite aside from the most obvious one: that they do not allow for rational debate—is that they seek to shift the consensus from one of extreme tolerance to one in favor of total prohibition. But radically shifting the social center of gravity in this way brings a new set of problems, because scandal politics rarely goes to the root of the real issues. And the mess the Islamists are trying to clean up with such a hard-line Sunni policy in Bahrain is, all concerned would do well to remember, the result of the same permanent cleanup in Saudi Arabia. The mass exodus of Saudis to Bahrain over the Causeway every weekend makes one wonder where Bahrainis will escape to, if bans on everything considered haram are introduced in their own country, too.

Nevertheless, by rushing in where others fear to tread, the Islamists do make for great copy. Take, for instance, their merciless lampooning of Bahrain's cops and Ministry of Interior officials. In a February 2009 session of parliament, they claimed law enforcers deliberately left the "prostitution mafia" beyond the reach of the law because they themselves were busy accepting "free sex and other bribes."[17] They then accused the Ministry of Interior of deliberately turning a blind eye to the corruption and threatened to "demonstrate outside every hotel and apartment building to scare off prostitutes, if the government doesn't take action."[18] That threat was probably intended to put the fear of God into the rank and file of the Criminal Investigation Directorate, the agency responsible for clamping down on prostitution, more than the prostitutes themselves, because the former were alleged by the Islamists to be enjoying free dinners and prostitutes in the hotels in return for their continued silence.[19] Whatever the truth of these allegations, and they were never proven, the Islamists' narrative did sound more in tune with conceivable reality than anything the Ministry of Interior has ever said. The opening sentence of a February 2009 article in *Gulf News* is representative of the kind of coverage the latter prefers: "A Ministry of Interior officer denied there was a market for prostitution in Bahrain."[20]

It became clearer that the Islamists, rather than unelected government ministries who proffer blanket denials, are calling the shots in the wake of the infamous 2009 top ten article. It provoked such widespread coverage, much of it outright mockery, that an immediate crackdown was launched. Three hundred prostitutes and their pimps were rounded up, no doubt the most vulnerable, those who did not have connections to corrupt officials, as Bahraini religious leaders added their voices to the now nearly deafening din of outrage and condemnation.[21] All this at least had the positive result of highlighting—in addition to the Islamists' spunk, which no one can deny—the Bahraini regime's untenable position. It was cracking down, to the accompaniment of a flurry of official press releases, on a thriving prostitution industry that, according to another flurry of official press releases, did not exist.

Another evening in Bahrain, another bar, another smattering of Saudis. My companions were two nineteen-year-old Saudis, dressed in Western clothes, and arrestingly handsome: swept-back black hair, faultless olive complexions, shiny white teeth. They so resembled one another that I guessed they must be related, probably cousins. They were studying for their diplomas back in the Red Sea port city of Jeddah, they said, but since there was a school vacation they had driven over to the Eastern Province (it took a whole day), spent the night there, then crossed the Causeway. They were the kind of young Saudis—gentle, affable, generous—I had grown so fond of during my time in Jeddah, where in the mornings (in addition to working as an editor in the evenings) I had taught English to teenagers transitioning between school and university. And again, like those other Saudis, these teens were able, quite effortlessly, to switch to Egyptian from their own Arabic dialect. One reason is that young Saudis spend so much time in Egypt, another that so many Egyptians live and work in Saudi Arabia. But Arabs everywhere, even if they have never left their village, are able to understand the Egyptian dialect, and with a bit of effort to speak it, too, because Egypt for decades has produced the bulk of the region's movies, soap operas, and music. A Moroccan or Iraqi or Yemeni grows up with constant exposure to the idiosyncratic Cairo dialect.

Soon these two Saudi guys were regaling me with anecdotes about various discos and belly-dancing clubs they had visited in Cairo and the Egyptian tourist resort of Sharm El-Sheikh, but then lamenting that Egyptians are not only impoverished but, in their experience, inveterate tricksters, who had the impression all Saudis were brainless millionaires and therefore easy prey. That resulted in nightmarish trips, notwithstanding the occasional euphoric interlude, because the moment they were discovered to be from Saudi Arabia the Egyptians would charge them at least five times the local prices. Even inside the clubs, they recalled, everyone knew that there were two separate price lists: one for Egyptians and another for Westerners and Gulf Arabs. So, although in theory Bahrain was much more expensive than dirt-cheap Egypt, for them in practice the reverse was true.

"How much," one of them soon asked me, "do Egyptians pay to sleep with a prostitute?"

About twenty dollars, I said, unless she was a high-class hooker, in which case the sky is probably the limit.

"God damn them," he said, admitting that they had each been charged $150. "Even the whores here are half price," he reflected.

They patted each other on the back and ordered another round of drinks in celebration of this accidental confirmation that they had made the right decision to travel only to Manama in the future. I did not have the heart to remind them that, if the Islamists have anything to do with it, this bar would not be open for much longer. I also wanted to know why they felt the need to travel so far in search of fun. Jeddah is a relatively laid-back Saudi city where, for wealthy young men especially, more or less everything that is officially forbidden can be found with only a little effort: beer, rent boys, drugs, female prostitutes, and even Saudi girlfriends. They readily acknowledged the seedy side, but turned their noses up at the idea of indulging in sin back in Saudi Arabia.

"We have a lot of big problems, but we brush them under the carpet," one of them vaguely conceded, as though to change the subject.

"But it's better that way," his friend interjected. "I don't want to see Saudi Arabia turn into Bahrain. It's the home of Islam. It's different."

"Some would call that hypocrisy," I suggested.

"The truth is that he can't do anything in Jeddah even if he wanted to," the first lad said of his sermonizing friend, "because his father is a big shot. If he got caught . . ." He grabbed him and pretended to slit his throat.

Banter aside, the punishment for soliciting or consorting with prostitutes in Saudi Arabia is not death. However, it is considered a crime. Such charges can and frequently do result in lashings and jail time for both the client and the woman—more, much more, for the latter—or, in the absence of a formal, written penal code, whatever arbitrary sentence the Wahhabi judge feels like passing down that particular day after thumbing through the pages of the Qur'an.

Still, it struck me that a fear of dishonoring his family, rather than of any punishment he might face, probably determined the more conservative young man's attitude. That would be especially true if his father truly was a big shot and therefore could, however messy and undignified the process, get the incident brushed under one of those expensive silk Saudi rugs. His comment about Saudi Arabia being the home of Islam was claptrap; the country was a 1930s British geopolitical construct named after a corrupt royal family with borders demarcated by the heathen British, who brought the royal family to power with financial and military support. His brief defense of Islam was, if anything, even less credible, given that he made it while drinking alcohol in a hotel full of prostitutes. And there was something more than a little offensive in his implication that the Muslims of Bahrain were somehow inferior, and certainly beneath him, so unworthy were they, in his telling, of the same respect he would demand of them in his country.

I suppose he was trying to say, the only way he knew how, that he did abroad what, for personal and cultural reasons, he would not do at home, and that he would prefer, moreover, that others not do it at home, either. If so, he was no different than an American in a bar in a Mexican border town, say, or a British man living it up in Amsterdam's red-light district: indulging in behavior that is frowned on at home and so better acted out far from family and friends, and preferably in places where there is less chance of falling afoul of the law. In neither Britain nor the United States, notwithstanding the dramatically different legal consequences, is being caught with a hooker, after all, any more a badge of honor for a normal person than it is in Saudi Arabia. Moreover, such Britons and Americans who visit prostitutes in neighboring countries, I would argue, are just the type of people who (like these Saudis) would be among the first to object if a brothel opened near their homes back in Manchester, England, or Austin, Texas. They know better than anyone the virtue of taking dirty weekends abroad.

I did not express any of these opinions that evening, since I only formed them later on, and even if I had wanted to hold forth along those lines it would surely have been a colossal conversation stopper. In any case, our chat was interrupted by the arrival of a Saudi singer. Dressed in a thobe, microphone in one hand and beer in the other, he acknowledged the applause and settled down behind the keyboard. The bar had filled up in anticipation of his performance. The singer was soon performing songs from southern Arabia, but with a modern synthesizer backup. But it was when he pulled out a lute that its traditional twang worked the crowd on the small dance floor into a frenzy. This was an all-male affair. The men on the dance floor gradually paired up as the rhythms grew faster, swinging their hips, delicately twirling their hands, and casting deep glances into each others' eyes, as happy in their own bodies, it appeared, as they were in one anothers' close company.

This is the kind of scene that is most likely to provoke all sorts of nasty asides about Saudi hypocrisy, how they behave in one way at home and another abroad. To be sure, back in Saudi Arabia these men would be arrested, possibly even flogged and imprisoned, for transgressing so from the Wahhabi norm. But that tells us more about the ridiculous tenets of Wahhabi Islam than it does about their morality.

Anyway, who was I to judge them? Drunk myself, I offered little resistance when one of the two Saudi guys at the bar took my hand and led me to the dance floor.

※※

It was only a matter of time before the rhetoric of the Islamists in Bahrain became indistinguishable from that of conservative antiprostitution campaigners in the West. And sure enough, right on cue, in 2009 they dragged the twin scourges of sex trafficking and child prostitution into the Bahraini debate, as Western NGOs continued to make ever deeper inroads into this formerly mostly ignored playground. No one did so on the basis of any evidence, but that did not matter to either, because their goal was not to help prostitutes take control of their destiny but to save them from it. The end, therefore, always justified the means.

Enter yet another Islamist MP, who claimed—solely on the basis of hearsay—that he knew of Bahraini "schoolgirls" who were prostituting themselves in the local hotels.[22] But in another report I saw, they were described as university students, so in my view it may just have been a mistranslation that had the intention of titillating readers. Still, the MP himself insisted that, whichever educational institution they were supposedly studying at, they were minors. And having thus slyly associated child prostitution, for whose existence he provided no proof whatsoever, with consenting adult prostitution, he went on (and in the very same sentence) to link prostitution in drinking dens to the imminent collapse of society. "Besides associating minors in prostitution, I want with the help of other lawmakers to eliminate problems caused by furnished apartments that are promoting vice activities," he said. "I have been receiving calls from citizens complaining of disturbances they are facing because of vice operations taking place in their neighborhoods."[23] He had learned every last trick in the Western anti-sex-trafficking campaigners' book, concluding with the tired cliché that prostitution is "an industry and it promotes crimes and human trafficking."[24]

The antitraffickers themselves eventually got the attention of the Bahraini government, to the extent that "trafficking in people" was said in a newspaper report to be "under intense scrutiny from the Bahraini authorities following local and international calls that more efforts are needed to tackle the issue."[25] In March 2009, the island even hosted an international conference "dedicated to the discussion of national strategies to combat human trafficking and ways to enhance coordination with the private sector."[26] This three-day event was held under the patronage of none other than Shaikha Sabeeka Bint Ebrahim Al-Khalifa, the king's wife, in the presence of "government officials from the [Persian] Gulf."[27] A Bahraini rights activist, Faisal Fuladh, was telling anyone who would listen that "the failure of some government parties, the private sector and NGOs to act decisively on the issue meant that little progress has been achieved in stopping the exploitation of women." And then, buried right at the end of the article in which Fuladh was quoted, came the all-important caveat that nobody thought important enough to discuss: "The true scope of human trafficking is not known."[28]

Do the women who work as prostitutes in the city's entertainment venues end up there because they were trafficked from distant lands against their will? No one has provided any reliable statistics on the issue. The reason why those who are working there by choice are doing so is obvious enough: They are earning at least ten times, and sometimes much more, than they ever could in their own countries working in a dead-end job (if they can find one). Some no doubt have personal problems, perhaps even what everyone in the world but me likes to call "psychological issues," and we can safely assume—judging by the pimp in my hotel—that pretty much all of them have an awful boss. But then so do many other people working in many different fields.

There were no signs in the bars and clubs I visited of the school-girl hookers the Islamist MP claimed had become a fixture. A Chinese woman I spent a few hours chatting with was typical of what was actually on offer. She was twenty-six years old and had originally come, she said, from a small city in China, where she had been working in a garment factory since she left school. After spending a few years in Shanghai as a prostitute, she had arrived in Bahrain a few months earlier to meet up with a group of long-established Chinese working women. She paid half the normal price for a room in the hotel, she told me, and since she shared it with two of the other Chinese women, that meant it was basically free. She ate for free, too, at the hotel's restaurant, as long as she restricted herself to the (extensive) buffet. And she made, she said, about four thousand dollars in a good month. She planned to stay for about a year, when she would have saved enough to return to China and open a small business.

Of course, we cannot generalize about all prostitutes on the basis of her experience, but neither should we discount it, and I highlight it here because it is the sort of narrative that so often gets lost in the more sensational coverage of the issue in Bahrain and elsewhere. Her situation is also typical of the half dozen or so other working women I talked to at length while in Bahrain.

⁂

In 2005 Mohammed Al-Maskati had founded the secular Bahrain Youth Society for Human Rights, when he was just eighteen years old.

The organization flourished, not least because it had an excellent website and has established links with the major Western human rights organizations.[29] However, he has been given the constant runaround by the government, who initially refused to acknowledge his application for the group to be registered and then cynically took him to court for running an NGO without an official license. The society is run by volunteers, he told me in the course of our morning together, but he makes some money working as a trainer with international human rights organizations. All that sounds admirable, and it is, but I still had my doubts about his motives and intentions. This was because no one, apart from the Islamists, had done more to publicize the prostitution issue in Bahrain. His popular website was littered with stories about sex trafficking and exploitation based on what I subsequently made clear to him I believed to be the worst kind of generalizations, and yet it was quoted widely in the local English-language media.[30] Still, I told myself that I should listen to what he had to say, since if anyone could provide concrete evidence about sex trafficking it would be him. It was a testament to his sincerity, and his winning personality, that even though we disagreed on almost everything, when I left him I liked him so much that I feel terrible writing even a single negative word about what he does.

We met in one of Manama's horrible malls early one morning when it was nearly deserted. He was wearing Western clothes and had thick black hair and a charming, welcoming smile. The first thing I wanted to know, as we settled down with our coffees, was whether he would get into trouble with the powers that be for talking to me, but he assured me that he was free to say and do whatever he wanted, although he was sure, too, he was being watched even at that very moment. We played spot-the-secret-policeman for a while (not that difficult in a deserted mall), and then, to get things going, I asked him how the women who worked as prostitutes got into Bahrain in the first place, given its strict visa policy. Obviously, there were those brought in on valid work visas for other jobs, who then ended up working as prostitutes on the quiet. But that could not account for all of them. The other main way, he said, was the use (or as he put it "abuse") of the local family law.

"If I'm a Bahraini, I can marry four women," he explained. "So anyone who wants to have a group of women travels to countries like Morocco, Tunisia, Egypt, or Thailand. When the new wives come back with him, the government can't do anything, because it's his right to marry four times."

Many of these marriages, he claimed, were in reality crude business arrangements.

This person has married these women only so they can work in local hotels, and every month he takes 20 percent of whatever she earns. The government has no idea who is married legitimately and who is using the marriage as a front. And it helps if this sponsor—and I call them sponsors, not husbands, because that's what they are—has good relations with someone in the royal family. Then they have protection. Also, the hotels where the women work have the same kind of protection. At the same time, the women have their passports confiscated, so they are the only ones who have no protection. Many can't even speak Arabic, which is the only language spoken in the police stations. So if they are exploited by their sponsor and go to the police station, the cop says okay we'll take care of you, give you a ticket, and fly you home. But the one who created the problem has impunity, because of his royal patronage.

That made some sense, but it still left many other situations unaccounted for. What about women who came on their own? What happened at the airport? "You must have a sponsor. You can't get a tourist visa," he insisted. I told him about the Chinese woman I had met, who told me she came in as a tourist and ate and stayed at the hotel for free. Was she lying? Visitors from China, Thailand, and Russia, I reminded him, were granted two-week visit visas on arrival at the airport in Manama. "The other way is the Formula One race every year," he said, not really addressing my point, "and when it takes place, the government gives everyone a three-day visa on arrival at the airport. Then they stay on illegally." But most had probably been staying at the one- and two-star hotels, which had now been banned from selling alcohol, and surely that meant that the government was responding to the pressure to take action.

Not according to Mohammed.

We not only have stars given to the hotels officially, but unofficially the owners are rated the same way. You can have a five-star hotel, but you may not be a five-star owner. Now, what do I mean by this? For example, if you don't have a close relationship with the police in your area, if you don't have connections with the royal family, if you don't have connections even to someone who is himself close to the royal family, or the Ministry of Interior . . . well, you own a five-star hotel, but you're not a five-star owner. On the other hand, one of the hotels here in Manama is officially a one-star hotel, but the owner is five-star, so he can still do whatever he likes.

What was in it for the protectors? Obviously, they took a cut from the profits, he said, and they "get to use the facilities when members of other royal families in the Gulf visit Bahrain, when they insist for example that the hotel owners provide them with girls for free."

"Is that on the record?" I asked.

"Everything I say is on the record, and I have a lot worse than that if you'd like to hear it," he declared.[31]

If true, that raised the issue of parliament, I suggested, and how powerful it really was.

"The government has two parts," he continued. "One is the Shoura, which is appointed by the king, and has a veto on everything the elected parliament does." But the Shoura, he said, was "full of businessmen." And in Bahrain, if you were a businessman and "you don't have connections with the royal family," you would fail.

> It's guaranteed. Let me give you an example I personally know about. There was recently a businessman who wanted to build a huge shopping center, but it was rejected by one influential individual who demanded to be a partner. The individual said he would not take on any risk or put in any investment, but would take a percentage of the profits. When the businessman rejected this, the individual told him: Fine, let's see how you get on without water, without electricity, without anything. So he couldn't do anything, because these people are also the ones who have the influence.

That, then, left only the Sunni MPs. Did he, as a liberal Shia, support them? And did he in turn get their support? No, he did not get any support from them, he said, because "most of the MPs, and especially the Sunni Islamists, are pro regime"—because, I assumed he was saying, their loyalty to one another as members of the elite Sunni Muslim minority overrode any political differences they had about the pace of reform. They might want to stop prostitution, he added, but in reality they were part of the problem rather than the solution.

> For example, when they give the Ministry of Interior permission to close hotels engaged in the prostitution business, the ministry knows which hotels have links with the royal family and which don't. So they just close three or four hotels. It's propaganda, and gets them publicity, but it changes nothing. The Islamist MPs are playing this game, they are part of the problem. It means the Islamists can get credit for cleaning everything up, the regime can get credit for cleaning everything up, but in reality nothing has been cleaned up. It's only superficial. The [Islamists] know that not everyone is equal. There are red lines. You say they are banning alcohol in one- and two-star hotels, but they know this will never happen for high-class hotels. It just cannot. Everyone knows that not only the Bahraini royal family, but the Saudi one as well, have a lot of money invested in the hotels.

So it all boiled down, as I had guessed, to the economy.

The Shoura would not move against the bigger establishments because the economic fallout would be too punishing not only for their masters but also for ordinary people. So how could Mohammed expect to get the support of the people, if he was supporting a ban on prostitution across the board? He was effectively telling ordinary people they were going to have to lose their jobs so that he could assuage his conscience. But he had been waiting for that question, and deftly drew a distinction between the "Bahraini economy" and the "royal family" economy.

The royal family has its own economy. It's more powerful than the real economy. The parliament here has authority over the budget in Bahrain, but they never ask about the king and royal family's finances. Never. In Manama you see hotels, malls. But go inside the real Bahrain. There the people are extremely poor. They don't have a single dinar. They go for days without eating. The government says if there are visitors to Formula One it will benefit the economy, but where is the money? We sell oil. But where is the profit? It's the royal economy that takes most of it, not the real economy. If you stop prostitution in Bahrain, it will not ruin the economy. We have thirty-seven islands here in Bahrain, but we cannot go to any but four of them. The royals own the rest. They are huge and beautiful. This is a parallel economy. The royal family think they own the country.

His analysis was spot on. But that still meant that unless a complete ban on prostitution was enforced at the same time as a popular revolution that sent the royals packing—which was highly unlikely—it would mean the royals would continue to maintain their privileged position but just with a little less money in the bank, while the workers (and prostitutes) would still lose their jobs.

However, instead of pressing him on that point, I challenged him more generally. Isn't prostitution necessary? Lots of people argue, for instance, that with so many immigrant workers, many of them single, it provides an outlet, which if they did not have it might result in more sex crimes against women. Or did he have some kind of moral or religious objections?

"Okay, if you want to have freedom of choice, that is your right," he said. But he then pointedly stated that I should not misquote him as suggesting that he was in favor of prostitution, which he once again pointed out he was not. "We can't tell everybody: do this and don't do that," he nevertheless resumed. "But the main issue is . . . I mean, if you have a girlfriend, okay have sex. But our issue is trafficking in persons. How are these girls used, or told, to have sex?"

I knew it would come up sooner or later.

"But I can't find any evidence that they are trafficked." I said. "The ones I spoke to came here of their own accord."

"Let's take Morocco as an example," he said calmly. "The women there are earning maybe a hundred dollars a month. But when they come here, they can earn more than three thousand. So I exploit these girls if I have sex with them, because they are very poor and vulnerable."

"Yes, but we're talking about two different issues," I countered. "One is exploitation, if you want to call it that, of those who come here willingly, with all of the facts, the other is forced trafficking. If you don't like your office hours, you form a union, you don't abolish office work altogether just because someone might not get a fair deal. Anyway, what about their freedom of choice? I'm sure forced trafficking of women exists, but aren't such women a tiny minority? Do you have any figures for me? I can't find reliable figures about this anywhere in the Middle East."

Yes, he did. Or then again, he did not:

"I can't tell you how many. Maybe 40 or 45 percent. It's not that they have a gun put to their head. They just maybe find that they can't earn enough working as a secretary to save any money, because the rent is so high here for apartments, so it's the impossible situation that forces women into prostitution. But when they return home, they have jewelry, lots of money. She says she's worked in hotels in Manama, and then all her friends want to come as well."

"So what?" I asked. "Would it be better if they stayed in their dead-end jobs back in Morocco?"

"The problem is the money and the laws," he said, surprised that I was getting so worked up. "We have export countries and import countries. We want to have new laws, for example, that will ban single women in Morocco under the age of twenty-five from coming to Bahrain."

"But why would you want to do that?" I asked, now incredulous. "If she is twenty-three and wants to come, what has it got to do with anyone else? What would you say to her if she told you to get out of her life?"

"Okay, let's argue that these women want to come here to make money," he said. "Why? Because they don't have any. Maybe they support their families. The father died, maybe there are a dozen children in the family. So the problem is poverty. If we resolve the poverty, they will not need to come here."

"Well, that's the theory, the ideal," I said. "And good luck to you in trying to solve world hunger. But the reality is that there is poverty, nobody is going to get rid of it anytime soon, so we have to deal with that reality. What if a woman was here now, she was twenty-three years old, and she said to you: 'Leave me alone, I want to work like this. Go and save someone else.' What would you tell her? Is it a moral question for you? Just that prostitution is wrong? Is it a question of them corrupting Bahrain?"

"No, no," he said firmly, before elaborating.

"The problem is not only with these girls, it's the reputation of the Moroccans that is being tarnished. All the women get a reputation for being prostitutes. I would tell this girl I'm not so much protecting her as her reputation, and the reputation of her family, and other Moroccan women, and the reputation of Morocco itself. We cannot say they can stop this, but we can try to have more development and education in Morocco. If you solve these two problems—poverty and lack of education—then you solve the problem of prostitution."

So prostitution, after all, was first and foremost a "problem."

The reputation of Moroccan women in the Middle East has indeed hit rock bottom, as he explained, and as we will see later in this book. But I was more at a loss than ever as I left Mohammed to understand what that had to do with the forced trafficking of women for sex, for which he had provided no evidence at all. I could, though, easily picture the cartoon image that had formed in my mind of the human rights campaigner in full flight, trying to dodge a hail of stiletto heels aimed squarely at his cerebellum.

That was unfair to Mohammed. He did have a grievance against the political and economic organization of his country that struck me as fully legitimate. By human rights, though, I think he actually meant civil rights, or it would have been better if he had. On his grievance with the royal family, his analysis was penetrating and eloquent, and I am grateful to him as well for elucidating some of the intricate mechanics whereby the Bahraini sex industry continues to flourish and the hypocrisy of all involved in saying they want to impose the bans. Equally understandable is that, in his courageous struggle for a hearing in adverse circumstances, he was just using all the ammunition he could get his hands on.

At the same time, let us not pretend that his primary concern is the real feelings or circumstances of the prostitutes for whose welfare he affected to be concerned. And why, thinking about it, should it be? Having chosen his sizable cause, it was only natural that all others should fade into lesser significance.

For him, as with the Islamists, the end justifies the means.

Caught up in all this chaos are the owners of the hotels and entertainment venues, many of them staring at the prospect of losing their considerable investments. They have made timid calls to be left alone, so the service and entertainment sectors could continue to help the economy grow. But the Islamists remain as keen as ever to enforce a wholesale ban on the sale of alcohol. The Council of Deputies passed a law in 2009, shortly after the one- and two-star hotel ban was enacted, which calls for just such an outright ban, but as of this writing it is still awaiting approval from an unelected cabinet that has the power to veto it.

And that, oddly, is what it may well decide to do.

The ministers, after all, do not have to pander to the masses to seek reelection, and as royal appointees they also clearly serve the interests of an elite that has itself invested heavily in the local entertainment, service, and retail sectors, as Mohammed had pointed out. Nor is there any evidence that the Islamists, although they are adept at making the most noise and providing the best media sound bites, have anything approaching majority support among ordinary Bahrainis for their Wahhabi manifesto. That is something highly unlikely because they represent the Sunni minority, and as we have seen they came to power because liberals boycotted the elections. All of this gives the cabinet the space to take a more pragmatic, long-term view. And they actually have at their disposal a perfectly sensible counterargument.

A study in June 2009 revealed that the tourism sector alone was set to contribute around $1.7 billion to tiny Bahrain's economy that year, representing 12.1 percent of GDP, a figure projected to rise to $4.9 billion (or 14.5 percent) by 2019. If realized, that latter figure would in-

crease the number of people employed in the industry to 78,000 people (some 17.5 percent of the workforce), compared to the present 13.7
percent.[32] Given such high stakes, and the global economic downturn,
the cabinet would be rash, to put it mildly, to endorse an immediate
blanket ban on alcohol. At the back of their mind must be the impact,
too, on the potential boost to the tourism sector by a new Causeway
connecting Bahrain with wealthy Qatar, scheduled to open in 2013
with a rail link alongside the highway, that will cut traveling time from
the countries to less than a half hour.

The Islamists claim that they would make the tourism industry
more family centered, and one is reminded of Las Vegas, which, having tried to rebrand itself as family oriented, had then gone to the sales
pitch "What happens in Vegas stays in Vegas." It is true that not all
Saudis who head to the island do so with the sole intention of getting
drunk and screwing a prostitute. There are also cinemas and discothe-
ques, like everything else banned in Saudi Arabia. But Bahrain, remarkably for a country so long known as Paradise Island, does not even
have a decent beach; and the one thing the four million Saudis who
visit annually have more than enough of at home is shopping malls,
ranting clerics, and sharia law.

Even the most idealistic Islamists must realize how Herculean will
be the task of luring them to Manama if its hotels are dry.

CHAPTER *six*

MORAL PANIC

Yemen, the most impoverished country in the Middle East, is also among the poorest on the globe. North of Sanaa, the capital, right up to the smuggling haven of the Yemeni-Saudi border, it has always been essentially lawless: a traditional, tribal heartland as near as exists to the way the Arabian Peninsula was at the time of the birth of Islam. Yemen's unique architectural inheritance includes Shibam, the first-ever skyscraper city built (eight stories high) in the sixteenth century; and it is also home, as clichéd as it sounds, to perhaps the most hospitable people on earth. However, it is a terrible country in which to live if, like me, you would like to spend a string of afternoons idly watching the world go by while puffing through a packet of cigarettes, sipping a succession of strong coffees, and chatting with the locals.

When I arrived in Sanaa in 2004 for a four-month stay to brush up my Arabic, what most struck me on my first walk around the city—more than the eerie lack of other tourists (scared away by periodic kidnappings), the wonderfully conserved old city (a UNESCO World Heritage site since 1988), and the proud custom of men and boys displaying huge daggers, called *jambayas*, in their belts—was the dearth of coffee shops. That would be remarkable anywhere. But it is especially so in the Middle East, where cafés remain important social and intellectual gathering places and, in the major cities, are as numerous as they were in eighteenth-century London or early-twentieth-century Paris.

It did not take me long to discover that in Yemen *qat*, or *khat*, was the reason for the absence of coffee shops. It is a flowering plant whose leaves are chewed for hours so they eventually mush into a great ball gathered against the inside of the cheek, and its red juice is said to make the chewer slightly high.

It only made me feel nauseous, though, the one time I tried it. Another reason to avoid it is that these days it is cultivated with the use of harmful chemicals and pesticides (at least with cigarettes you know what you are inhaling). However, Yemenis continue to spend huge sums on the plant, and the doorman at my apartment building told me that he and his friends set aside about half of their monthly salaries to buy it fresh each morning from the local qat market. By midafternoon the streets are deserted, as almost everyone retires to designated qat-chewing rooms in the home.

Because this beloved activity is such a private affair, and an excuse for catching up with friends and family, the inhabitants of the Yemeni capital have little passion for café culture. Early evening and the masses reemerge, cheeks painfully stretched as though someone had forced a tennis ball into the side of their mouths, their eyes glazed over. No one is in any apparent way happier or friendlier for the indulgent interlude. Indeed, quite the reverse—if my experience is anything to go by.

I headed south from the capital for a long weekend in Aden at the first opportunity. Although that city was also conservative and almost as qat-obsessed as Sanaa, I had hopes that it would be more modern and cosmopolitan. Its people's mind-set, I reasoned, would be shaped not only by the customs of a tribal inheritance but also decades of Communist rule before north Yemen and south Yemen were unified as a single country in 1990. In contrast to the rest of the Arabian Peninsula, "the former socialist south Yemen enforced many reforms for women. Girls went to mixed schools with boys, women were encouraged to work and leave the headscarf at home, while polygamy was banned."[1] It had a centuries-long tradition of welcoming foreign guests, in addition to importing unwilling ones as slaves. Aden's integration into the global community was accelerated by the city's status as a Free Trade Zone from the late 1960s, with the end of British rule, until 1990, when South Yemen and North Yemen were unified as a single country. I was relieved to discover that there were a few coffee shops dotted along the main drag, even if they were just rickety tables and chairs strewn haphazardly on the street. One of the men I talked to on my first afternoon there held out the promise that, down by the port, there were a number of establishments that sold alcohol and afforded wonderful views of the docking ships. He lowered his voice as he added that they were also known as good places "to make new friends."

In the blazing heat of an intensely humid afternoon, after spending half an hour following the map this man had scribbled for me (which made the district seem much nearer than it was), I located one of the bars. A large, ramshackle shed with windows blacked out by grimy curtains, it did not look like much. But since I had come all that way and now was desperate for a drink, I went inside and stepped into a strange encounter.

The bar was sparsely furnished but bright and airy, the huge windows on the far side, away from the road, wide open and offering, as promised, a spectacular view of the port. There were about a dozen locals inside who, at first glance, struck me as sailor types. Mostly they were sitting alone and staring at empty beer bottles neatly lined up on the table in front of them. It was as though the bottles were a manifestation of their honor or manhood, or a way of marking out the slow progress of a lazy afternoon. It was still only about four o'clock, but most of the men were already too drunk to take much interest in the solitary Westerner who had wandered into their midst.

I found a table, ordered a beer from the uncommunicative bartender, and requested a menu, then decided to freshen up in the washroom. When I emerged, my beer and the menu were being placed on my table, not by the barman but by a woman dressed in a black *abeyya* and *niqab*, the face-covering veil; even her hands were covered by tight-fitting black gloves. I had arrived in Yemen after spending two-and-a-half years in Saudi Arabia, so was used to being surrounded by similarly attired women. In fact, I had routinely interviewed such women for jobs at the newspaper. But those meetings, of course, were never set even remotely in a place that looked like this seedy sailors' bar. Unsure whether to thank, or even acknowledge, this covered waitress, since in Saudi Arabia even the briefest exchange would be taboo, I eventually said that I would order something from the menu a little later.

"Oh, you speak Arabic," she exclaimed in English, her heavily made-up eyes darting this way and that. "Where are you from?"

Before I could answer, she had pulled up a chair, and was presently sitting beside me. The other patrons, roused from their drunken slumber, started to take an interest. We had become the center of attention, unsurprisingly so, given that I was the only European guy there and she the solitary woman. Nervously, I fumbled with my packet of cigarettes, pinched my shirt between finger and thumb to let the cooler sea breeze

from the open windows tickle my torso. I was about to offer her a cigarette, then thought better of it. It would be best not to encourage her,
and the prospect of witnessing her smoke underneath a full-face veil
was just too absurd.

She, however, displayed no such inhibitions. Taking the lighter
from my hand, she offered me one from my own packet. She lit it for
me, and allowed her fingers to caress mine as we shielded the flicker-
ing flame from the persistent breeze.

"I'm from England," I said. "And you?"

"Somalia," she replied, volunteering the additional information
that she spoke fluently not only her own native Somali language but
also English and French, and Arabic, too.

Her English was impressive. I found it impossible to picture this
woman in terms of the news reports I had seen about Somalis
crammed on a small boat with hundreds of other refugees at the mercy
of gun-wielding pirates known to throw crying babies overboard and
risking their lives on the crossing from the war-torn Horn of Africa.
Was she the exception to my stereotype, or was my inability to picture
her just a symptom of the outsider's failure to appreciate who such
people are beyond a teeming mass of unfortunates? Her covered face
made her story all the more intriguing, but by now the other customers were as transfixed by our exchange as they would be during
the soap opera later that evening, so my sense of discomfort out-
weighed my fascination.

I ordered a sandwich and another beer, hoping that, by having to
deal with the order, she would leave me to my own devices. Instead, she
turned and repeated it in Arabic to the barman, who disappeared into
the kitchen. Again I had her full attention, and I told myself she would
probably be sitting next to me right to the very end of my visit.

"So where are you staying?" she asked solicitously, pressing her knee against mine under the table. Her eyes narrowed when I told her the truth: a budget hotel in the center of town.

"Why aren't you staying at the five-star hotel?" she wanted to know, the definite article appropriate, there being just the one in Aden.

"Because I don't have that kind of money," I told her.

That was a lie. It was the hotel's reputation as a hangout for wealthy Gulf Arabs looking for prostitutes that kept me away from it. Anyway, what was it to this woman? She hung out at the five-star hotel bar during the evenings, she explained, and if I were staying there she could easily make her way to my room. But it was impossible to pull that off in the budget hotel. So this, I was left in no doubt, is what the young man at the coffee shop had meant when hinting that I could "make new friends" here.

I think she mistook my lack of immediate response to her proposition for brooding contemplation, or perhaps shyness. A moment later, she declared with conclusive bravado that the only option was for us to go to a furnished apartment rented by the hour.

"What if someone saw us walking down the street together?" I asked.

"I'll go first, and wait for you in the room," she reassured me, with the confidence of someone who had performed the ritual countless times. "The owner will wait for you outside."

I told her I would just have another beer and something to eat, thanks all the same, and she rested her chin on her hands with a sigh.

I still had no idea whether the message had got through, still less what her reaction to the subtle rebuff was. Then she asked me in a gentler voice, as the barman leaned between us to put the sandwich and beer on the table, whether I would like to see her face. I have an inveterate, quintessentially English aversion to causing a scene in public, or being rude to someone's face (even if, as on this occasion, I had yet to see it), so I gave her my assent while scolding myself for not telling her, once and for all, to leave me alone. There was at least still the possibility that she might be possessed of an extraordinary beauty, the kind that can transform a lonely man's peripatetic life with a flutter of her eyelashes.

She glanced around the bar, turned to me, and lifted her niqab. Revealed was the pudgy, surprisingly nervous visage of a woman in her midtwenties, her cheeks so pockmarked that even crude layers of makeup could not conceal the skin complaint.

In a flash, she was covered again.

I wolfed down my sandwich, drank the beer in two swigs, and called for the check. She followed me right to the exit, tugged on my arm, demanded a more generous tip and a promise to return the next day. I was able to escape only when three more covered women arrived, to whom she turned her attention. They were Somalis, too, it appeared, since they spoke to each other in a common, but to me entirely unfamiliar, language.

That veiled seductress was, I think, one of the roughly thirty thousand Somalis and Ethiopians who, according to the United Nations, make the hazardous sea journey to Yemen annually, numbers that have steadily been increasingly since the Somali capital Mogadishu descended into civil war in the 1990s. Somalia continues to slide ever deeper into intercommunal bloodshed as the U.S.-backed Ethiopian and Somali regimes battle an Islamist insurgency linked by the Western media to what they call Al-Qaeda.

In any case, Somalis are immediately granted refugee status in Yemen, a credit to the basic decency of a nation that can barely feed its own people, and there are refugee camps run by international aid organizations with assistance from the central government. About ten thousand Somalis who have made it to Yemen's shores currently survive from day to day there, but most new arrivals head instead for a slum district of Aden called Basateen. It is often described as Mogadishu without the warlords, and has been home to both Somali immigrants and Yemenis with historic trading and family ties to Somalia for more than a century.

That historic trade between East Africa and Yemen is intimately entwined with the history of prostitution in Aden. It started with the slave trade, of which Aden was an important center by the time of the Prophet. After the British occupied the port in 1839 to stop pirate attacks against British shipping, they set about regulating the already flourishing prostitution industry. In 1867 the Bombay Act III mandated that prostitution be regulated and prostitutes should live in areas set aside for them. But by 1877 there were still just nineteen registered prostitutes, meaning many more remained unregistered. The occurrence of sexually transmitted diseases, though, was relatively small. Most of the prostitutes were Somalis. These working women were required to pay a daily sum for the hire of a house, furniture, clothes, and ornaments, and were known to be alcoholics.[2] In 1907, the British rulers' main complaint remained that most prostitutes remained unregistered, and a notorious red-light district in Aden, called Sheikh Othman, was eventually placed out of bounds to all British troops because of health concerns.[3] Still, in the 1950s "open prostitution . . . in the port towns of South Yemen attests to the absence of strong legal or social disincentives against it,"[4] and Western expatriates recalled Aden as a seedy, decadent port city as late as the 1960s, when an especially notable character by the name of Maalla Mary, either of Somali or Indian origin, would wander the streets at night intoxicated, trying to pick up clients.[5] After South Yemen gained independence from Britain in 1967, the new Communist government closed the red light districts and employed public prostitutes in factory work. It was then that prostitution began to center "in restaurants and nightclubs and developed also in the form of direct contacts between customers and sex providers."[6]

However, the Yemeni constitution adopted in 1990, upon unification of the north and south, was based on sharia law, and prostitution was officially outlawed throughout the country. With such dire prospects for earning a decent (or any) living in this dirt-poor country, the Somali-dominated districts of Aden nevertheless remained a major source for Aden's prostitutes. The going rate for a brief tryst, I was later told, was about $30 for a Yemeni client, $100 for a visiting Gulf Arab or Westerner, and double for the whole night. The latter sum is not inconsequential anywhere, but a jackpot in a country where half the population survives on less than $3 a day. Hence the magnetic attraction of a roaming prostitute to any white man. A Gulf Arab, though, is a much bigger catch, especially a client from Saudi Arabia, because, in the event that the sexual liaison becomes a more permanent relationship, she will find getting a visa to that country, although not an easy process, is definitely easier than getting one to Europe.

Oil-rich Saudi Arabia is the ultimate destination for most Somalis who arrive in Yemen. For about fifty dollars, they can be smuggled over the border and into a kingdom already legally home to fifty thousand of their compatriots, and many more without residency permits. I became acquainted with some of those Somali exiles when I lived in the old district of Jeddah, which is where many of them live. They were a clique of intellectuals who read a column I wrote for the English-language daily *Arab News*, where for my sins I was working as managing editor. At our occasional buffet lunches in a local hotel, these gregarious Somalis would sometimes introduce me to a male newcomer who, having arrived from Yemen, was being welcomed into their circle.

Back in Sanaa I resigned myself, in the absence of coffee shops, to hanging out at a smattering of bars and nightclubs similar to the one I had stumbled on in Aden. They were hidden in alleyways and advertised by word of mouth—two Yemeni boys studying English at my language school initially pointing me in the right direction. The nightclubs had security personnel at the door and charged extortionate entrance fees, a sizable percentage of which, we can take for granted, went to buying the silence of corrupt officials. A number of local budget hotels were infamous for offering rooms by the hour, and some of them had the bonus of free access to pornographic satellite channels. One assumes the sex channels were available to spice up the sex, rather than as a draw in themselves, because anyone with a satellite dish in the Middle East can watch them at home.

The prostitutes I encountered when I went to such clubs were mainly Yemenis, although there were immigrants as well. They were friendly, but not pushy, and seemed to enjoy what they were doing, which mostly involved flirting with visitors while being bought drinks and wrangling a tip as the customer left alone. I was told they took a small percentage of the final bar tab from the owner, but kept all the tips for themselves. They were selling friendship and company more than sex, although it was obvious from my conversations with them that most were prepared to have sex as well for money.

The clientele were locals and visiting Gulf Arabs, and I never saw another Westerner. By observing the unspoken rules (discretion and prudence), which trumped the officially illegal status of prostitution in Yemen, the industry was able to prosper, and so provide a source of income for poor Yemeni and immigrant women in the safety of clubs closely monitored by their slightly paranoid owners. Their fear of scandal and exposure encouraged them, I think, to step in swiftly on any demonstrative behavior, which they did. The clients were anyway kept in check not by what the law said—who cared?—but by the need to safeguard their reputations, as well as that of family and tribe, notwithstanding the antics of the occasional drunken Saudi. An awareness of such relative acceptance of the phenomenon is what led to the prostitutes in the sailors' bar in Aden donning the niqab, but in Sanaa they shed the abeyyas and niqabs on entering the nightclubs, because they were located so far from the collective public gaze.

I do not recall seeing any articles, either in the English- or Arabic-language newspapers, dealing with this clandestine nightlife, nothing anyway sensational or prominently displayed. Most locals seemed content to ignore it, too, as long as the veneer of Islamic social normality was maintained outside the secluded spots where the clubs were located. My private Arabic teacher at the language school was a normally veiled Yemeni woman in her early twenties, full of verve and wit, and always eager to hear about my latest escapades so long as no information too crude was conveyed. I remember her telling me during one lesson, when I admitted to having got drunk in one of the clubs the previous evening (I was explaining, like a naughty schoolboy, why I had not done my homework), that she was fully aware of their existence, as was everyone she knew. But she added it was not the sort of thing discussed in polite company. I pressed her for an opinion, despite the hint she had given, and she told me she considered such behavior haram, or religiously forbidden, but it was up to God to deal with such transgressions.

The tribal Islamic garb was worn by the prostitutes, that is to say, in almost mock deference to the superficially conservative social norm. In this way an essentially liberal Islamic game played out, between an ever-present demand for public order on the one hand and, on the other, a general reluctance, common to tribal societies, to encroach on the private lives of individuals. Not that the results were always as one might have expected. Yemen, as elsewhere in the Middle East, gets more socially conservative by the year, but back in 2004 being covered from head to toe in black was still not a popular fashion statement among the younger women of Yemen's major cities, least of all those who lived in the wealthier quarters of Sanaa where the clubs were. Most women preferred simple, and sometimes colored or patterned, veils that, like that of my teacher, covered the hair but not the face. One consequence of the fact that it was prostitutes who were always conservatively dressed was that any completely covered young woman going about her business in districts where the nightclubs were located was thought, and probably correctly, most likely to be a hooker.

These days, even the residents of Mogadishu must be asking themselves whether traveling to Yemen is worth the risk to life and limb.

The issue now is not so much what might happen during the terrifying sea voyage: that is a long-established fear, if exacerbated in recent years by the emergence of more brutal gangs of pirates in the local shark-infested waters. Rather, it is what they will encounter if they do finally reach land. No group will be debating that question with greater urgency than the Somali women who, in the past, considered Yemen at least stable enough to allow them quietly to work as prostitutes, while saving enough money for the next leg of their journey to Saudi Arabia. A witch-hunt against prostitutes has spread like wildfire throughout Yemen, led by peaceful Islamists of the kind who, as by this stage in our journey we need little reminding, always crawl out of the woodwork in the Middle East during social crises. Their goal in Yemen, as elsewhere, is to exploit collective uncertainties and anxieties to impose on the majority their own strict morality.

Before we look at the witch-hunt, a little background. After I left Yemen in 2004, the social and political situation rapidly began to deteriorate, and the country has since descended into near anarchy. As of this writing, it is the nearest the Arab world has to a failed state. One little-noticed consequence is that the issue of prostitution, and other forms of vice, have been dragged out of obscurity, to take center stage in a new discourse about the country's identity. That the witch-hunt against prostitutes in Yemen started at the moment the country began to fall apart is not mere chance. The warning signs of imminent collapse were there before I left, and I tried to convey them in a number of dispatches at the time.[7]

As the only Western journalist recently to have reported freely from Saada, the northernmost city in Yemen near the Saudi border (now strictly off limits to foreign correspondents by government decree), I was told in 2004 by members of the Shia minority, who have

long complained of discrimination, about their anger at the arrest of a
Shia cleric on trumped-up charges of sorcery. A few miles outside
Saada, I spent the afternoon at what is the largest open-air arms bazaar
in the world. Machine guns, grenades, ammunition, and even rocket
launchers were displayed as though fruit and vegetables.[8] During the
more than two hundred kilometer road trip back down to Sanaa, the
soldiers accompanying me (for my safety) were repeatedly stopped by
makeshift roadblocks set up by local tribes. The officer in charge would
have to negotiate our pass with bribes or, if that did not work, rely on
the assistance of one of his soldiers who was from that particular tribe
or another on friendly terms with it. If the palpable tension in this region boils over, I remember thinking at the time, no antigovernment
militia in the world could more easily arm itself to the teeth than any
that might spring up here.

The followers of another Saada-based Shia cleric later in 2004 declared open war on the Yemeni government, and it proved no idle
threat. More than four thousand rebels and soldiers have thus far been
killed in the ensuing conflict, which has also displaced hundreds of
thousands and drawn in the Royal Saudi Air Force on bombing mis-
sions in support of the Yemeni army. No Western troops are officially
involved in the war, which has now drawn in so many domestic enemies
of the central Yemeni government that even longtime Yemen observers
do not have a clue as to what is actually going on anymore.

The same is true about coverage of militant groups that have kept
up their decade-long nationwide campaign of terror by targeting both
government forces and symbols of the West. Predictably, the U.S. Embassy is a favorite among the latter, coming under repeated attack from
terror cells armed with an endless supply of missiles. In addition, a
separate revolt has broken out in southern Yemen.

Deep resentment was felt by the majority of southerners at unification in 1990 because of the government's funneling of the nation's resources to northern tribes close to the president's own. Scores have
been killed and injured in unprecedented street protests, awakening a
long-dormant succession movement calling for the reestablishment of
an independent South Yemen. Mass strikes and riots by workers and
students are now frequent across the south, and in at least a half dozen
other Yemeni provinces whose aggrieved populations also sense the
time is right to push for autonomy. The Yemeni president, in power for
the predictable three decades, has managed only to unite all these dis-
parate factions in opposition to his own rule, in no small part because
of his support for the U.S.-led "war on terror." That has included invit-
ing American Special Forces to train a new Yemeni antiterror squad
and, more controversially, granting the United States permission to
assassinate the country's alleged Al-Qaeda leader.[9]

How is this social and political disintegration linked to rising concerns about prostitution?

Like any other, the sex trade is fundamentally governed by the laws
of simple economics, with the crucial difference that the prostitute is
not selling goods but her own body. Still, it ultimately amounts to the
exchange of cash between those who need a service and those who are
willing and able to provide it. Its regulation, however, is a much more
complex process, and in the modern age crackdowns are often orchestrated during periods of radical upheaval, and the issue resonates like
no other precisely because the service involves the selling of a body.
As one human rights group, writing about the targeting of young male

prostitutes in Iraq during the fallout from the Anglo-American invasion, put it:

> When deep uncertainties about rapid change gather to a head, peo-
> ple look for scapegoats: not just to explain, but to incarnate the un-
> settling transmutations around them, shifts that they cannot fully
> articulate but are determined to stop. [These] are battles to define
> who belongs in a community and who does not.[10]

In quasi-democratic countries like Yemen, which has an elected
parliament and one of the freest media in the Arab world, such moral
panics are especially dangerous. The governments are elected not by
overwhelming majorities of the entire voting-age population, but by a
highly motivated core minority of the population whose leaders are
savvy at manipulating the process. As in Western-style democracies,
conservative groups flex their muscle to galvanize public opinion into
electing amenable politicians, and the media is apt to whip up the panic
with sensational reporting.

In January 2004, as the various wars between the Yemeni government and its ever-multiplying enemies broke out on all fronts, the first
shots were also fired by the Islamists in Yemen's parallel culture war, the
outcome of which will likewise determine who does and does not belong to the community of whatever country emerges from the chaos.
In Aden, a budget hotel was raided following a tip that it was fronting
as a brothel. Fourteen Saudi nationals and thirteen Yemeni women received six-month suspended sentences, the three Yemeni hotel owners
got a year behind bars, and their hotel was closed for the same period.[11]
The defendants' lawyers unsuccessfully tried to get the official charge
of "adultery" dropped, because the prosecution could not provide four

witnesses to each alleged act of sexual intercourse as required by sharia law to prove guilt.[12] But what is more interesting is that this raid appears to have been the first carried out by police in Yemen solely on the basis of complaints by "concerned citizens."

Soon, scattered reports of similar incidents were coming in from all over the country: stick-wielding vigilantes attacking not only suspected brothels but unrelated male and female teenagers who happened to be walking together in public. In the Red Sea port city of Hodeidah, a lovely holiday destination similar in its more laid-back social climate to Jeddah in Saudi Arabia, vigilantes teamed up with local police to storm, out of the blue, three homes suspected of being used as brothels. One homeowner died during resulting clashes with police, and several of the women living in the raided homes were subsequently put on trial.[13]

In a column published in the *Yemen Times* in August 2005—headlined, somewhat rhetorically, "Gulf Tourists: Are they People of Lust and Corruption?"—journalist Hakim Almasmari had addressed this apparent sudden and dramatic spread of vice.[14] Unfortunately, I was left with the impression that it addressed none of the relevant facts and provided no social or historic context, restricting itself instead to discourse of the kind that will be familiar to any people in the English-speaking world still in the habit of buying a newspaper. The article placed all the blame for the apparent wave of depravity on sex-obsessed, diseased foreigners, specifically wealthier Gulf Arabs (a possible pandering to popular prejudice because Yemenis, generally speaking, cannot stand especially their Saudi neighbors). It suggested that AIDS cases in Yemen were the exclusive result of said foreigners "importing" it. It casually linked such foreign men who pay to marry very young local girls with those who pay for sex with consenting adult prostitutes. It categorized grown women who choose to work as prostitutes as passive victims who, along with children, must be rescued. It made a desperate plea for greater research on the phenomenon by global and domestic nongovernmental organizations. And it implied that prostitution had only recently become widespread in the country, and as such threatened the wholesome fabric of traditional Yemeni society (whatever that is). Reading it, one is reminded of the quote from the human rights organization above about how, in the midst of dramatic upheaval, societies look for scapegoats to explain disorder "they cannot fully articulate but are determined to stop."

A certain Colonel Hussein Yahia Hussein, spokesperson for Aden's security office, was quoted in 2005 as saying that police were now "regularly" raiding "brothels" in the city and arresting "gangs" running sex-trade rackets. "It's organized prostitution," he said solemnly. "It's growing very fast, and needs to be addressed."[15] By 2009 the pro-government *October 14th* newspaper, based in Aden, wrote that vigilantes were now so established in the city that they were setting up sting operations, which amount to entrapment (a copycat tactic used by vice squads in the West). The group "telephoned some young women, claiming that they want to have a forbidden relationship with them and then making an appointment to meet them," and the women were then handed over to the police. The vigilantes testified against them in court.[16]

Almasmari's call on NGOs to take a greater interest in the subject did not fall on deaf ears, and two months after his 2005 column appeared the Yemeni-based human rights group the Women's Forum for Research and Training issued the first ever report on prostitution. After interviewing seventeen female sex workers in two of the country's southern governorates, the authors reportedly came to the conclusion that such women "are often forced into the profession out of dire economic circumstances." Most of the sex workers interviewed "are without jobs," the study further noted, before adding that this is "why they sell sex as a source of income to support themselves and, in some cases, their families."[17] None of that tells us anything we did not know, but what was surprising is that the study raised no discernible objection to the fact that a large percentage of the women they interviewed were in prison.

Ever more spectacular raids on suspected brothels were carried out across Yemen during 2009. One of the biggest, in Sanaa, targeted massage parlors and restaurants run by Chinese immigrants and located in one of the wealthier districts of the city. Police, accompanied by a now formidable and well-disciplined God Squad and gangs of photo-snapping journalists, dragged Chinese women into the streets and posted signs on the façades of the business premises that read CLOSED BY THE AUTHORITIES. The way such establishments were increasing in number "was very suspicious," the Saudi-funded Al-Arabiya news station quoted an anonymous Yemeni official who supervised the clamp-down as saying, although he could offer no further justification for the raid.[18] Buying into the now dominant narrative of blaming foreigners for the spread of vice and corruption, the official added that all the establishments raided were "run by foreign women," and, for good measure, he pointed out they were all illegal immigrants.[19] If that was the case, their status as employees, and the ability of their bosses to set up multiple businesses in a central part of town without official hindrance, pointed to a much bigger story about local corruption that neither the official nor Al-Arabiya thought it significant to highlight (leaving aside the question of how the women got into the country in the first place).

The religious vigilantes in Yemen had meanwhile come out of the closet, publicly forming a committee in 2008 to alert police, they said, about violations of sharia law (as interpreted by them) and help locate places and hunt down people who spread vice. This new group called itself the Committee for the Promotion of Virtue and Prevention of Vice, the exact same name of the official Saudi goons who for the past six decades have beaten Saudi citizens into observing prayer times and avoiding the female gaze. The self-appointed head in Yemen is Sheikh Abdul-Majeed Al-Zindani. A Wahhabi cleric, he is head of Imam University in Sanaa, an infamous breeding ground for extremist students who have included the "American Taliban" John Walker Lindh.[20] He is also the sometime spokesman for the Yemeni branch of the Muslim Brotherhood, and a vocal supporter of Yemen's main Islamist political party, Islah (the Arabic word for Reform), which is a powerful bloc in the national parliament.

A busy man, back in 1984 orange-bearded Al-Zindani founded (and continues to run) something called the Commission on Scientific Signs in the Qur'an and Sunnah. Based in Saudi Arabia, it is funded by the Wahhabi kingdom's religious establishment (via the Saudi-funded World Muslim League), and has predictably been mired in controversy from day one.[21] Any organization funded by the Wahhabis is almost certain to be cuckoo, either obsessed with the tedious minutiae of literalistic Islamic dogma or just propagating deep-seated bigotry against Jews, Christians, and Shia, and this outfit is no exception. Its goal is to sideline rational, scientific discourse, in favor of praising Allah for miraculously having revealed in the Qur'an all scientific discoveries we foolishly think have only recently been unearthed. This is possible if you imaginatively read between the lines of the Islamic holy book. For the unquestioningly devout—and there is, we should remember, an equivalent trend among anti-Darwinian, right-wing Christians in the United States that resulted in the acclaimed movie *Creation* (2009) failing to find a distributor in that country[22]—this approach explains everything that might once have been thought worthy of doubt and therefore serious scientific investigation. It renders redundant, too, any independent thought, dissenting viewpoints, or objective analysis. In this context, of substituting fact for fiction and faith for reason, we should briefly mention Al-Zindani's claim—taken, it seems, quite seriously by his followers, if by nobody else—to have found a cure for AIDS.[23]

Al-Zindani is on America's Most Wanted list of suspected terrorists, accused of once having been a pal of Osama bin Laden, which comes as no surprise, either.[24] But since just about everyone Washington does not like in the Middle East ends up on one terror list or another, we can probably give him the benefit of the doubt when it comes to this accusation. Even the usually compliant Yemeni government has refused to hand him over. For balance, we should also give Al-Zindani credit where it is clearly due. He has encouraged at least one healthy new pastime among bored Yemeni zealots, namely, the chasing down of foreign Christian missionaries. For years these individuals have been preying on the poor and ignorant in the remoter regions. Now, after Al-Zindani's followers have handed them over to the authorities, they are deported.

But let us return to the grimmer reality.

Al-Zindani is the proud issuer of a fatwa, or religious edict, that sanctioned the demolition, carried out by his committee's rank and file and some members of the public, of a house in a Sanaa suburb, the owner of which had been accused—again, merely accused, not found guilty—of running a prostitution network.[25] However, prostitution is just one of many vices Al-Zindani and his like-minded "scholars" have demanded the government take action against, under the rubric of fighting what they call "moral corruption." Others include mixed dancing, the consumption or sale of alcohol, racy television soap operas, fashion shows, coeducation, pop concerts, women politicians, mannequins displayed in shop windows, and nightclubs of any and all description. Rahma Hugaira, chair of Yemen's Media Women's Forum, summarized the threat the Islamists' agenda poses:

> This new vice and virtue movement has the potential to undermine the government. Civil society groups are working hard to modernize society, to establish a social contract grounded in our constitution and reflected in our laws. A group using religion as a weapon threatens all the progress we have achieved."[26]

In other words, it threatens to turn Yemen into Saudi Arabia. That this new, apparently spontaneous movement against "moral corruption" is named in homage to the Saudi religious police, and is headed by a cleric with close religious and financial ties to the Saudi regime, is the heart of the matter. The history of Yemeni-Saudi relations is too long and complex to delve into here. But one pertinent fact that is important to highlight is that Saudi Arabia has done its best to undermine the central Yemeni government since unification in 1990. They have done so largely because they fear the consequences of a democratic country on their doorstep, and the precedent such popular participation in the democratic process may set for the Persian Gulf.

Rather than being a genuine grassroots movement, tapping into the concerns of the majority of Yemeni citizens, the Committee for the Promotion of Virtue and Prevention and Vice is more of a Trojan horse. As such, it is arguably the real source of corruption in Yemeni politics today—its followers as reprehensible, in many respects, as the foreign Christian missionaries they round up.

The meeting in 2007 called to found the Committee for the Promotion of Virtue and Prevention of Vice in Yemen drew around six thousand attendees, mainly tribal and religious leaders but also elected members of parliament. The latter consisted of about sixty Islamists from the Al-Zindani-backed Islamist parliamentary group Islah, which simultaneously launched an attack on the "spreading moral corruption" in Yemen. As in Bahrain, they hit some of the right targets, if for all the wrong reasons. Officials, they said, run "shady businesses," while police turn a blind eye to citizen's complaints about how alcohol, drugs, prostitution, and bars were "increasingly common" in the major cities. "This laxity is what caused these places to spread and prosper," as one Islamist put it.[27] That it was a group of Saudi sex tourists who first fell victim to the raids back in Aden in 2004, Saudis who like millions of others had tried briefly to escape their repressive and hypocritical society patrolled by the same religious police, was an irony as usual lost on everyone. As was the fact that Saudi Arabia, the most undemocratic country in the Arab world, is deftly exploiting the relatively vibrant Yemeni political process to further its own backward theocratic agenda.

A barely functioning Yemeni state is the Saudi royal family's preference. However, a failed state would be a nightmare, this because militant Yemenis have a role in training and then smuggling Islamist militants across the northern border to carry out terror attacks in Saudi Arabia. Nothing if not politically astute, the Saudis appear (and this is just my reading of the situation) to have made a move on the vice front in the hope that a friendly, reactionary Islamist regime might seize power and thus redefine mainstream Yemeni political discourse through the unifying (and for the Saudis unthreatening) call of a return to fundamentalist Islam.

An exhausted, corrupt, deeply unpopular government; a widespread perceived increase in lawlessness that essentially amounts to a break-down of the fragile social contract; official collusion in the lies of the "war on terror"; surrender of tentative social advances; and increas-ingly high-pitched political rhetoric, calling for ever more draconian measures against scapegoat causes, especially immigrants and "vice"— these but for the peculiarities of dress and climate could be an account of Broken Britain under Tony Blair or Bush-era America. In Yemen, a sham ideological debate—Islam and virtue on one side, freedom and vice on the other—is being used to bully, harass, and intimidate soci-ety's most vulnerable and erode established liberties, while providing a cover for quite different and largely unseen interests (the Al-Saud, re-ligious extremists) to assert greater control. The difference is that in Yemen, government control has broken down to such an extent that even the undermining of individual freedoms and the assault on weaker members of society—the last stronghold of the state in the West—has been, as it were, outsourced.

But the founders' meeting in Yemen did not involve any academ-ics or prominent intellectuals—crucial groups Saudi Arabia has been more successfully able to co-opt—despite invitations being sent to more than a hundred of them. And female journalists were also turned away from the meeting. Khaled Ayesh, director of the Yemeni National Human Rights Forum, openly called such morality guards a joke. "What gives these people the right to interfere with others' freedoms and personal lives?" he asked. The majority of Hodeidah residents were angry, he further noted, but also conceded that "a few people in Hodeidah are happy about some of what this group is doing."[28]

Apparently not enough of them to sway officialdom.

In mid-2009 Hodeidah governorate's new security director, Abdulwahab Al-Rathi, publicly denounced the morality goon squads as "a group of vagrants on the streets." Their activities had now been stopped, he claimed, and their leaders arrested and referred to prosecution, as Yemeni law quite properly allows no one except police to conduct such activities. He wanted to put an end to the harassment once and for all, he concluded, to "get citizens back to walking around freely without fear."[29] Since Al-Rathi seems to be such a nice man, we will refrain from sarcastic remarks about the other fears in chaotic Yemen that have in fact left people with little freedom of movement, goon squad or no goon squad.

In the press, meanwhile, the reaction against the committee was so strong—not in favor of prostitution, to be sure, but against the general trend of vigilantes taking the law into their own hands and the erosion of hard-won civil liberties—that Al-Zindani was reduced to accusing the media at every opportunity of having launched a smear campaign against him: a sure sign, coming from determined manipulators of public sentiment, that their end is nigh. Ali Saif Hassan, director of the Political Development Forum, also felt that Al-Zindani had overplayed his hand, arguing: "The media's response was so strong the fundamentalists have lost their case. They're in a weaker position."[30]

In fact, a more likely cause for a lack of recent coverage of vice-related issues in Yemen is that the wars and secessionist revolts have left no room for articles in the newspapers on anything else. Still, even if the interregnum appears to be running out of steam, so must be the women who work in the sex industry. Now more vulnerable to attack and degradation than ever, they can find no lobby or journalist to support them as equal members of society—whichever way the political wind blows.

CHAPTER *seven*

VEILS AND VICES

Agadir, the principal tourist resort in Morocco, is all flash tourist hotels near the public beach, amid their own infrastructure of pricey bars, restaurants, and clubs where leafy avenues meander through an Identi-Kit resort landscape of bougainvillea and pebbled embankments. The other part of the city is a dreary Arab urban sprawl, at whose center budget hotels catering to backpackers and Gulf Arab visitors double as brothels, and where streetwalkers are as common as the tumbleweed blown down the dusty main streets. Unemployment and poverty in the city, as ubiquitous as elsewhere in Morocco, mean that along the alleyways the "psst, psst, my friend" tendency of drug pushers and rent boys in the region are a permanent nuisance to anyone not looking for those particular indulgences, directed as they are at any foreign male who happens to be walking by.

In April 2005 a Moroccan was browsing through a bundle of pornographic DVDs for sale in his local Agadir souk. The cover of one of the DVDs made him perform a double take: Could that really be his fiancée on the cover, a leash tied round her neck as a Western man sodomized her from behind? In a rage, he made his way home to confront the woman, a forty-two-year-old teacher called Samira.[1] She could not deny that it was her in the picture, and he beat her up and threw her out onto the street, unable to countenance listening to any explanation she might have.[2] Samira decided to go to the police station to file a complaint against the Westerner, an illogical move on her part that remains today as confusing to all observers as it was at the time. It was an even graver mistake than posing for the photographs in the first place, because she inadvertently set in motion a train of events that would culminate in Morocco's biggest-ever sex scandal.

Initially, she claimed the Westerner had taken and distributed the photographs without her consent, but what the cops saw on the DVD did not persuade them that the coercion story could be true. The production and dissemination of pornography being illegal in Morocco, she was arrested. Eventually, Samira was sentenced to a hefty fine and a year in prison. She was also disowned by her family and friends and fired by her school.[3]

Any chance of ever leading a normal life had disappeared the second she stepped inside the police station, as did that of countless other women featured on the DVD who became involved with the scandal, because on the basis of the evidence she provided the local vice squad launched a dragnet for the other eighty or so women featured on the DVD. All but one had also engaged in sadomasochistic sex with the same Westerner, sometimes being sodomized while bound and gagged, and invariably photographed in the most degrading sexual positions. Many were smiling, but some were grimacing, and one was clearly in distress. The emphasis on sodomy might at first glance appear a fetish of the aggressive pornographer, related to his evident need to dominate and humiliate; but it probably had as least as much to do with the reality of prostitution in Morocco, where women are expected to be virgins when they get married. A recent study of five hundred professional prostitutes in the country found that 13 percent of them were still virgins, their hymens intact.[4]

The Westerner had of course blacked out his own face, but he made no attempt to hide the women's identities. Within days, more than a dozen other women he had photographed had been arrested. Most hailed from three of the city's poorest districts. Like Samira, thirteen of them were given fines and sentenced to prison at hard labor for between six months and one year.[5] However, the ramifications for those who were close to the women, and the women themselves, went far beyond the courthouse and the indignity of the stinking, rat-infested prison cells. The husband of one woman reportedly went insane, two of the women sent to prison apparently tried to commit suicide, and a number of others the cops could not locate had fled the city or were believed to have either killed themselves or been murdered by their disgraced families.[6] Even the one woman featured in the pictures who was fully dressed, and whose inclusion on the DVD was thought to have been some kind of sick joke at her expense, became a social outcast, after her neighbors were said to have labeled her a prostitute and the local shops refused to let her in.[7] The parents of some of the women fell ill, relatives were unable to go to work for fear of being ridiculed, children from the families became the butt of constant mockery on the school playground, and the brother of one of the jailed women openly vowed to murder her the minute she was set free.[8]

The city's inhabitants, one Moroccan columnist reported, "talked of nothing else."[9]

The scandal went national, because as long as they stay away from direct criticism of the royal family journalists in Morocco are free to publish what they like. All the country's newspapers reported every twist and turn of the vice squad's investigation on the front pages, and no detail was spared. Many even reproduced the photographs, along with warnings that the content was not suitable for children. It was the kind of trial that comes to define an era by focusing a society's sexual preoccupations and anxieties, much as the Michael Jackson trial did, for instance, at the height of the pedo panic in the United States during the 2000s.

Soon the Moroccan press launched an investigation of their own, with the aim to out the Westerner. It did not take them long to expose him: Philippe Servaty, it turned out, was a forty-two-year-old economics correspondent for Belgium's leading French-language newspaper, *Le Soir*. When he posted the photographs on a porn website he may have concealed his identity. Sad nonentity that he was, he had however told all the women he picked up in Agadir his real name and nationality, while boasting about his job with *Le Soir*. A self-proclaimed "serial fucker,"[10] he seems to have been the kind of conflicted deviant about whom forensic psychologists like to say: "He always wanted to be caught."

However, Servaty was not responsible for producing the DVD or sanctioning its distribution in Agadir. It was a local who downloaded the pictures from the website, compiled them into an attractive package, and sold them in the souk for two dollars—the first of many hypocrisies that surround this scandal. Evidently, it was okay to sell the DVDs, and no one ever complained that Samira's husband-to-be had been shopping for one that day. As long as the women were somebody else's wife, somebody else's daughter, somebody else's sister, the men were happy to amuse themselves at their degradation.

Still, Servaty must have been aware, not least because of his extensive journalism experience, that the Moroccan vice squad, like that in other Arab countries, does monitor the more popular sex tourism websites for evidence of local debauchery. Such photographs, which are posted on websites geared toward other sex tourists who compete with each other to provide the most graphic images and commentary, literally threaten to tarnish the country's image abroad. The consequences of their distribution are not as easy to turn a blind eye to as a prostitute sneaking into an apartment. And here we are introduced to the other main hypocrisy in the Arab world's sex industry: if there is one rule for men and another for women, there are often none at all for Westerners. The Belgian had been briefly detained in 2004, a year before the scandal broke, when word reached the cops that he was one of the more prolific and violent of the Western pornographers who creep about—"creep" being the operative word—the Arab side of town. "The police kept me for eighteen hours, but they released me because Morocco has good relations with Belgium where I am a well-known person," he is said to have crowed on the web.[11] In a later television interview, he confirmed that he had been questioned, and following a search of his laptop had been told to leave the country and never return.[12]

Fortunately for him, and undoubtedly to the secret relief of the Moroccan authorities, when the story broke Servaty was in Belgium. Nevertheless, in the wake of the newspaper reports, a flurry of activity among senior Belgian and Moroccan diplomats raised the prospect of Servaty being charged with some kind of crime, if not in Morocco then in Belgium, where a then decade-old law allows for citizens who commit crimes abroad to be tried at home. However, pornography is not a crime in Belgium, and neither is prostitution. The law was introduced to combat child-sex tourism, meaning Belgians having sex abroad (consensual or otherwise) with under-eighteens. The Moroccan press did its best to try and find a child-sex angle—you cannot have enough of a good thing where circulation is concerned—but all they could come up with was a seventeen-year-old. Technically, that made her a minor, as one Moroccan author eagerly wrote, bringing into play a potential pedophile angle.[13] Servaty would later claim that the constant false accusations that he had had sex with minors was for him the most "catastrophic" part of the scandal.[14]

When this seventeen-year-old "child" revealed in court that she had been married to a Moroccan since she was fourteen, all the efforts at finding a vulnerable youngster went up in smoke. Indeed, according to Moroccan newspaper accounts of the trial, she was just launching divorce proceedings when she met Servaty, who if anything bizarrely came across in her retelling of the tale as something of a godsend in the hour of need. "I had marital problems, my husband's family kicked me out of the house, and my husband was in and out of the mental hospital," she reportedly told the judge. "I needed money to survive, and [Servaty] gave it to me."[15] Not much potential there then for a pedo headline, and the absence of the vital ingredients of kiddie porn and child prostitutes is perhaps why no major English-language newspaper covered the scandal. Then again, it may just be that no English-language newspapers have permanent correspondents in Morocco, do not generally monitor the French-language media, and take little interest in developments in the country unless a bomb goes off and it can be linked to Al-Qaeda.

Servaty was never charged with a crime, although criminal investigations continued in Belgium until 2007.[16] His fellow Belgian jour nalists labeled him the new Tintin, putting a sarcastic spin on the idea of the intrepid reporter, but it fell to a liberal, French-language Moroccan magazine, *TelQuel*, to first offer its readers a psychological portrait of the man. He was indeed one of the most respected journalists in Belgium, the magazine said, a pillar of the establishment, who mingled with the rich and powerful. But it added that he had also written extensively and sympathetically about third-world issues such as external debt and the 2004 tsunami. Acquaintances quoted by the magazine described him as "quiet and polite," which is what is usually said in retrospect about college gunmen after they have been on their rampage. Under the peaceful veneer, the article added, he was "a cold-blooded monster."[17]

If Servaty had not been identified as holding such a prominent position in Belgian society, the story might not have taken off in the way it did even in the French-language media. Perhaps what really made it the Moroccan sex scandal of the decade was that he had posted extensive commentary online along with the porn that was so cruel, exploitative, and Islamaphobic that many deemed it more offensive even than the photographs. Both the commentary and the photographs have since been removed from the original website, but before their deletion countless media outlets (including all of the Moroccan media) had reprinted the comments verbatim. He had a preference, he wrote, for "mom-and-pop" girls: ordinary women rather than professional prostitutes, and of no particular type—women going about their daily business who could, within minutes, be charmed into accompanying him back to his apartment. Detailed graphic descriptions were given of the activities that ensued, full of bluster and demeaning allusions to these women's faith.

The media presented him as a fully rounded monster. His behavior, and continued freedom, was in the liberal Moroccan press contrasted with the women's vulnerability, whom he had promised to marry, then betrayed, and who now were rotting in Morocco's notoriously decrepit prisons.

Servaty had been visiting Agadir for years. He said in his commentaries that he had had sex with an average of three or four women a day during his trips. Perhaps most shocking of all for Moroccans, he also claimed that he had only had to pay one of them for sex, and won the rest over by declaring his love and holding out the hope of a visa to Belgium. Some of the women's testimonies at the trial, as reported by the local media, corroborated his version of events. Samira, for example, had been in a relationship with Servaty for two years, was convinced that he loved her, and had confided in him "all her secrets." She agreed (she finally admitted) to be photographed because he claimed the pictures were mementos for his exclusive use, to remember her by when he was in Belgium, from where he kept up a regular email correspondence with her.[18] Manal, a twenty-four-year-old who worked in a fish-processing factory, insisted that her relationship with Servaty had "never been about money." She offered him, she said, her body, and "performed all his wishes." She agreed to let him take photographs because he "quickly convinced me that he loved me and intended to marry me and take me one of these days to Belgium."[19]

These particular stories read like they are authentic. We should remember, though, that Servaty claimed to have had his way with hundreds of Moroccan women. He may have been boasting about the numbers, but that there were at least eighty of them is evident from the photographs the cops found on the DVD. Many of them went with him to his apartment within minutes of meeting him, according to his commentaries, and in some of the photographs there are two naked women together. It is unlikely that both these women believed he was going to marry them, still less that he was in love with either of them. Nor is it easy to accept that Servaty, a nondescript little man, was always getting freebies. These women would have had every social and personal incentive to claim they were not prostitutes. That way, they at least stood an outside chance of being viewed by the judge and their loved ones in a more sympathetic light, subject to a moral lapse rather than engaging in an immoral trade.

Servaty was at least eventually made to resign from *Le Soir*—which covered the scandal and its aftermath extensively and published petitions calling for a royal pardon in Morocco for the women—but the reason was not his treatment of the women. He had made anti-Islamic remarks, and his chief fantasy seems to have been performing and recording these lewd acts while they were naked but for the veil.[20] Predictably, it was this angle the Moroccan media obsessed on, along with the fact that Servaty is Jewish. That allowed them to trot out popular conspiracy theories, and he was even described by at least one newspaper, as though it seemed to explain everything, as being pro-Israeli.[21] Many of the women were reportedly pictured in positions that made it look as though they were praying, but given that they were submitting to sodomy that was possibly a coincidence. In any event, Moroccan Islamist groups put a bounty on Servaty's head, and he went into hiding.[22]

It is true that Servaty obsessively returned in his miserable commentaries on the photographs to the triumph of having sex with veiled women. One of Servaty's followers on the porn site, a sane voice among those who otherwise constantly egged him on by requesting more photographs of veiled women, anticipated the looming catastrophe. "These girls are Muslims," he reportedly wrote in a comment. "They live in a Muslim country. You are exposing them to a grave danger by exposing them in such a way."[23] The website's U.S.-based moderator suggested Servaty might perhaps cover the eyes of the Muslim women to make identification more difficult, but they never were concealed.[24]

One can understand the tendency, given all this, to view Servaty's antics in light of the clash of civilizations, but on sober reflection that will not wash. For a start, he had also visited, and with the same intentions, Cameroon, Ghana, and the Dominican Republic,[25] none of which are Muslim-majority countries. His fixation on the veil in Morocco had more to do, it seems to me, with sexual barriers and fetishizing taboos, rather than Islam. There is in any case something silly in suggesting that one man's actions can define the attitudes of an entire people or culture.

Instead, Servaty should have been seen as an individual acting out his personal obsessions, rooted in a culturally nonspecific hatred of women born of a culturally nonspecific sense of inadequacy. After all, Muslims in turn often rightly point out that suicide bombers who happen to be Muslim should not be seen as representative of Islam, or of contemporary Muslim cultures and beliefs. The fact that he was instead taken as a symbol in Morocco of something much more profound tells us a great deal about how the scandal fed into the country's domestic politics, and in particular men's unease at the improving status of its women, and the Islamists' eternal preoccupation with women's sexuality and independence.

When we look at the cause of the sudden proliferation of blatant female prostitution in Agadir, and Morocco generally, over the past decade, the pointlessness of seeing Servaty as symbolic of the West's decadent encroachment on sacred Islamic land becomes clearer, as by extension does the reaction of the Islamists. In the late 1990s numerous senior members of the Saudi royal family built palaces in the city and started to spend their summers there. The notoriously corrupt defense minister, Prince Sultan bin Abdul Aziz (nicknamed by critics of the Saudi royal family the "Sultan of Thieves"[26]) convalesced in his Agadir palace in the 2000s after surgery, and he was visited on numerous occasions by the entire Saudi royal family and its entourage.[27] The city therefore become well known to Gulf Arab sex tourists, and wherever there is a sudden mass influx of them, female prostitutes, as we have seen, inevitably multiply. After the Servaty scandal, mass raids were carried out on the city's hotels. It should have come as no surprise to anyone that it was mainly Saudis and Kuwaitis, not Westerners, who were found to be the prostitutes' clients. In one of the biggest raids, in August 2005, which resulted in sixty more Moroccan prostitutes being summarily tried and sent to prison for up to four months, twenty-eight Saudis and nine Kuwaitis were also apprehended. However, these foreigners, like Servaty, were not charged with any crime, and instead were deported.[28] The Islamists loudly cheered these prostitutes' arrest, and the clampdown on Western-style debauchery, as ever oblivious to the reality that most of the men involved had flown in straight from the Land of the Two Holy Mosques.

What the Servaty case, and the scandal of Abu Ghraib that it in so many ways echoes, does underline is the folly I drew attention to in the introduction to this book, namely, the labeling of Arab men as somehow uniquely repressed and sexually conflicted; and by extension the hubris of suggesting they have anything to learn from the West when it comes to the complex question of human sexuality. Perhaps no one summed that up better than the man himself. In an interview on Belgian television in July 2005, in which he appeared with his face blurred, Servaty claimed to receive "death threats on a daily basis," admitted that he was "a pervert, a sicko," and explained that he was "undergoing medical treatment." He further stated that he had "nothing against Islam" and "it was just lust that led me to veiled women."[29] His therapist presumably got him thinking hard about whether "just lust" was the most unsparing way to describe what drove him. Otherwise Servaty put it in a nutshell—which, as vessels for the man's psyche go, seems about the right size.

❈

A primary purpose of the veil is to create mystery, which is why it attracted Servaty. However, it also has a political purpose. For the Islamists, what the veil hides is valuable, sacred even, not to be exposed to the eyes of lustful and sinful men. Veiling is meant to separate the sacred from the profane, the private from the public. That is part of its allure, and that is why its central role in the porn scandal so outraged ordinary Moroccans, especially the Islamists.

Veiling women performs a central social function in a society like Morocco's, which is dominated by males, where women still play a circumscribed role. In short, the veil is a form of control, both of men and women. It inherently postulates that women are weaker, need to be protected, cannot be trusted, are subject to the whim of men, and indeed are their possessions. Traditionally, the veil in Islamic countries has played an important role in keeping social order. It sanctified privacy, separated the private from the public. Everyone knew the rules of the game—in public women were off limits, and public violations of the rules brought punishment from the offended parties, families whose honor was breached. This, too, was, and is, a male thing, and it was generally a private undertaking of righting a public slight. True, there was always the possibility of the restoration of honor getting out of hand, threatening the public order, and this is when the state stepped in. For there are few things more disturbing to regimes, not only in the Middle East, as disorder.

Yet, at the same time, the veil is the subject of curiosity, the mystery behind it tempting and alluring precisely because it is hidden. Were it not valuable, if it were not forbidden, it would not be hidden. In the Moroccan porn scandal, the veil, as Servaty's chief fetish, subversively revealed as much as it hid when the photographs of the women naked but for the veil became publicly available. Perhaps, given this context, what was most absorbing of all about the scandal to those who would subjugate women is that the veil came to symbolize, if accidentally, their women's drive for independence, leading ultimately— the women clearly hoped—to a new life in a non-Muslim land, far away from the controlling menfolk of their families.

As the personal becomes politicized, so, too, does politics become increasingly personalized. There is, as I have made clear, much to be said for the separation of the public and private. When the state becomes responsible for upholding social order or rectitude, its failures to do so become an indictment of the rulers on a personal level, especially in the eyes of those who present themselves as the alternative to the existing state. This is different from an Eliot Spitzer getting caught with his pants down in New York, and exposed for personal hypocrisy. Rather, it goes much deeper when the regime does not provide the goods of social and economic development, and when the state at the same time squashes debate. The opposition readily turns to a subject that is close to everyone's heart, not least because we are all involved with the sex issue. Ironically, its resonance is perhaps something the Islamists understand, and exploit, better than anyone.

The Servaty scandal could not have come at a worse time for Morocco's embattled liberals and secularists, or a more opportune moment for the country's ascendant Islamists. The radicalism that plagues Morocco is a product, many argue, of the royal palace itself. According to one observer of the Middle East, in the 1980s and 1990s the present king's father, Hassan II, embarked on an initiative to Islamize Morocco:

> Seeking both to solidify his image as Commander of the Faithful and to weaken the secular left-leaning opposition forces that had gained support in the 60s and 70s, Hassan led a relentless effort to remake education and popular culture, infusing school curriculums with radical Salafi [extremist Sunni Muslim] teachings. The monarchy sought to divert attention from the sad reality of daily life by associating all secular thinking with colonialism and western domination—a powerful charge for a country that lived under French rule for nearly five decades—engaging the population in a search for lost identity. More imagined than real, the new identity focused on the religious character of the state: a Sunni, Salafi Morocco.[30]

Morocco's present ruler, King Mohammed VI, further cultivated so-called moderate Islamists as a bulwark against terror outfits. Moderate Islamists may condemn the violence of the Al-Qaeda franchise, but their cultural extremism is far more threatening to the long-term stability, and certainly social progress, of any country that wants to be part of the modern world, and nowhere is that truer than where women are concerned. The Al-Qaeda terrorists have little active support among ordinary people in any Arab country;[31] but even when their bombs do go off, the damage is at least contained to the site of the blast.

The cultural terrorism of the so-called moderate Islamists, on the other hand, knows no limits, and—despite the fact that they, too, have only minority support—it is relentless. As we have seen from the suicides of the women arrested in Agadir, and the threat to murder another, the moral climate they cultivate can also be deadly. Nor does the political Islamists' usurping of the mainstream, we should remember, stop the bombers from detonating their explosives, as was seen when multiple suicide attacks were carried out in Casablanca in 2004, and as is evidenced by the endless arrests, both within the country and in Europe, of Moroccan terrorists before and since those blasts took place.

The Justice and Development Party, known by its French acronym PJD, is presently the second largest parliamentary opposition group in Morocco, after the even more conservative (but pro-monarchy) Istiqbal Party. It seems only a matter of time before the PJD forms a majority, because only about 40 percent of Moroccans vote in parliamentary elections. That means the PJD does not have to win the support of the majority, but only of the majority of the most politically committed minority. And there are few more committed minority voting blocs anywhere in the world than those that support religious parties. Part of the PJD's recent agenda has been "to impose Islamic morality on all manifestations of Western behavior," and it argues "passionately in favor of the veil and holds up the traditional Islamic family unit as an ideal of private behavior."[32] More generally, the PJD promotes itself as a strict enforcer of moral standards, as defined by a strict interpretation of sharia law; and many liberals fear, and with not a little justification, that it wants to turn Morocco into a purist Islamist state. Its current leader, Abdelilah Benkiran, is so extreme that when he was once interrupted during a parliamentary speech by a woman wearing jeans and a T-shirt, he refused to continue talking until she had left the chamber.[33]

The PJD is also famous for its sheer pettiness: a Miss Morocco contest had to be held in secret because the party deemed it "un-Islamic," and its members instigated the prosecution of fourteen heavy-metal fans ultimately imprisoned on charges of "Satanism" and "corruption of public morals" merely for listening to such Western music.[34] The party is partly made up, I would argue, of the border-line insane: Its mouthpiece published an article in the wake of the 2004 Indonesian tsunami stating that it was God's punishment "for sex tourism, homosexuality, and child trafficking in South East Asia."[35] One singer with a local rock band summed up the liberals' contempt for the PJD's agenda: "When someone holds a concert, these populists always trot out their favorite themes: Zionists, Satanists, drugs, homosexuality."[36]

The king's precarious position, and the way he has boxed himself into a corner, is best exemplified in the contradictory reactions to his signature family law called the *mudawana*. Introduced in 2004, it was supposed to give women equal rights within the family. It did so by changing the rules of polygamy, so a man could not have more than one wife unless he could prove (according to Islamic tradition) that it was necessary for procreation or he could guarantee the same quality of life to them. It raised the legal age of marriage for girls from fifteen to eighteen, allowed a woman to ask for divorce without her husband's approval, and made it illegal for men to repudiate their wife arbitrarily by making divorce conditional on a court decision.[37]

The introduction of this law had followed a pro-women's march in 2000, when more than a million people took to the streets in support of a reformed mudawana. It was countered by an even larger protest against the law organized by the Islamists. It was in that year that anonymous Islamists threatened to assassinate Aicha Ech-Channa, who for two decades has worked to help give shelter to unmarried mothers, on the grounds that she was "an infidel" who encouraged "sinful behavior."[38] The same year, however, the king gave Ech-Channa a medal and financial support, and by 2009 her work resulted in her becoming the first Arab Muslim woman to win the $1 million U.S. Opus Prize, awarded to individuals for outstanding achievements in resolving serious social problems. She dedicated it to King Mohammed and the Moroccan people.[39]

This mutual back-slapping might suggest some kind of victory for the liberal trend. But when we look at how compromised Ech-Channa's position is, it is obvious that it is the Islamists who, despite the legislation, have won in the social arena. For a start, her organization—called Women's Solidarity and offering thousands of unwed women a stable future so they do not have to abandon their offspring—categorically refuses to have anything to do with prostitutes, and it has what can only be described as a Victorian attitude to the women it saves: teaching them "skills that can bring them an income such as cooking, baking, sewing, make-up, and hairdressing."[40] Morocco has women in most professions, including the police and several cabinet ministers, and a minimum of 10 percent of female legislators are elected under a quota. But instead of preparing these women for the real, modern world, there is nothing in the lifestyle of cooking and knitting they are being groomed for by Women's Solidarity that could upset the Islamists, even if the focus of those training courses is more a reflection of Ech-Channa's difficult circumstances than her beliefs.

If the king has created a monster in the form of the Islamist opposition he may not for much longer be able to control, the liberal Moroccan media is culpable, too, in promoting an Islamist agenda essentially at odds with its own. By obsessively reporting the Servaty case, and so many others before and since, even if at times to highlight the plight of the women, it has contributed to the moral panic the Islamists are exploiting. The only ethical response to the Agadir scandal from a journalistic perspective, it seems to me, would have been not to report it at all, or at least only briefly. The main reason the media did promote it so relentlessly and graphically was, of course, to boost circulation. There is nothing particularly Moroccan about that kind of yellow journalism, but in an Islamic country, one might argue that these secular but not atheist publications transgressed even the most liberal interpretation of sharia law.

"In the broadest view, Islamic legal practice strives to permit behaviors that people are inclined to do anyway, provided that the behaviors or their modes of practice are not harmful to the institutions of family and community," write Walter G. Andrews and Mehmet Kalpakh in their book *The Age of Beloveds* (2005), which examines portrayals of sexuality during the height of the Ottoman Empire. "Sex and sexuality," they add, "are seen as natural, God-given drives of the body, whose repression can result in (socially) dangerous actions." But there is an important balancing act between the need to punish transgressions and protect social harmony, in other words a clear distinction between the public and the private. They write:

> The principle of concealment requires that the public punishment
> of private behavior . . . must always be weighed carefully and avoided
> when making the offenses public would itself be "pornographic" and

subvert the moral character of the community or result in a punishment that the community would find unacceptably harsh.[41]

It would take a very coldhearted individual not to conclude that
the "pornographic" coverage of the women's behavior in Agadir by the
Moroccan mass media led to consequences that for everyone involved,
excluding Servaty, were "unacceptably harsh."

Agadir was devastated by an earthquake in 1960, just as Tangier, the
world's most notorious playground for Western expatriate pederasts
during the first half of the twentieth century, was being cleaned up after
it lost its status as an international zone and joined Morocco upon the
country's independence in 1956. The government rebuilt Agadir as a
tourist resort, the Western pederasts headed south, and the local boys
followed. That was how it was when I visited in the late 1990s. The epi-
center of the boy sex trade was a square of budget hotels and surrounding streets, where elderly Western gentlemen of a vaguely
colonial description would holler *rendez-vous* at the top of their voices
at any boy who took their fancy, who would invariably then enter into
negotiations. In addition to the crackdown on female prostitution in
the wake of the Servaty scandal, the Moroccan authorities also arrested
a number of these Westerners who had sex with male youngsters, who
in the intervening years had become the very definition of sitting
ducks. Perhaps the more astute among them had read the writing on
the wall and decamped before the raids and show trials got underway.
What is clear is that those who stayed had done little to hide what they
were up to, nor had there been much reason to do so, accepted as they

had been until then by most of the locals as the latest generation in a century-long file of European gay men relocating to a North Africa teeming with boys who were eager to become their new friends.

Indeed, when I was in Agadir I was told that many were living with the families of their kept boys, or had them shacked up in their own apartments; and they could be seen hanging out together in restaurants and coffee shops (not at all an uncommon sight elsewhere in the region). Most of the youths were in their late teens, some were adolescents, and others were in their twenties. Regardless, because most had hit puberty, still considered for boys throughout the Middle East (apart from among the Westernized elites) to mark sexual maturity, no one as far as I could tell batted an eye. If the boys did not want to be with the Westerners, the logic seemed to be, they would not go to their apartments, even if ultimately the only reason most of them did so was for the cash. This may be difficult for Westerners to comprehend, but people in impoverished communities in the third world do not have the same inclination of taking a moral stand by denying those given a chance to escape the poverty trap. Abdellah Taia's autobiographical coming-of-age novel *Salvation Army* (2009) gives an insider's glimpse of this reality. It recreates his adolescence in the late 1980s in the Moroccan town of Salé, where in addition to having sex with other Moroccan boys he hooks up with foreign sex tourists, finally making it to Switzerland after being sponsored by an older Swiss man he met.

There are, then, obvious material benefits such relationships with foreigners can bring: food, clothes, school fees, electronic gadgets, a safe place to sleep for the homeless, and even the possibility of the longed-for European visa. That is one reason they are accepted throughout the Arab world. Another is the widespread assumption that the Westerners are the passive partners: An Arab taking on the active role in sex with a man is considered no different from one performing the same role with a woman, so it involves no loss of masculinity or status. Of course, who does what to whom behind closed doors is anyone's guess; and when it comes to sex among Arab boys, there has to be a bottom to every top, so at least half of them are lying. The necessary duplicity this setup involves is one of Taia's main themes in *Salvation Army.*

However, if everyone is willing to play the game according to the rules (discretion, no gay-identity politics, no discussion of the specifics in public), sex among and with boys is tolerated. Dealt with in this discreet way, it has the societal benefit of providing a sexual outlet that, on the one hand, does not involve girls losing their all-important virginity and honor and, on the other, does not cause social rupture. That boys go with boys is an inevitable consequence of keeping girls pure until they are married, and that men continue to have an inclination to boys, regardless of whether they get married, is also accepted as inevitable (it would be odd for a man's tastes and habits suddenly to disappear after the wedding night).

As institutionalized female prostitution became part of Arab societies within a few centuries of the Prophet's death in the seventh century, so did pederasty.

"Such illicit sexual practices were known and tolerated from the earliest days in Islam," writes Dror Ze'evi in *Producing Desire: Changing Sexual Discourse in the Ottoman Middle East, 1500–1900* (2006). "They were denounced in Islamic moral and legal literature in the strictest terms, but in practice very little was done to curb or inhibit them, provided they were done away from the public eye."[42] In the Qur'an, homosexuality is not condemned because it is not conceptualized as a state of being or a separate identity. Instead, it is the sexual act of anal penetration between two males, called *liwat*, that is proscribed, although uniquely in the Islamic holy book there is no specific punishment given for this particular sexual transgression, and the community is advised to rehabilitate those who have been punished so long as they repent and promise to change their ways.[43]

So while it would clearly be better not to indulge at all (as is made explicit a number of times in the holy book), what males do in the privacy of their own homes should in the final analysis be nobody else's business; but at the same time the individuals concerned should not cause a social disturbance by bringing public attention to it. Because it is the sexual act, rather than falling in love with boys or admiring boys, that is forbidden, a great deal of freedom for openly indulging in the latter is given. In the Qur'an itself, one of the rewards offered to believers in heaven is to be served by beautiful adolescent boys, described as "eternal" in the sense that they will never mature into adult men, and thus become unlovely to look at.[44] Poets would later assimilate these boys of paradise into their work, sometimes directly comparing the real beloved boys addressed in their poems to them.[45] "Falling in love with a teenage youth and expressing this love in verse were not punishable offenses," one historian writes, "and a significant number of Islamic scholars, though not all, asserted that such behavior was not objectionable."[46] In contrast to European history, there is not a single recorded case of any man being executed for homosexuality in the Arab world since the birth of Islam, nor are there any instances of mass persecution or crackdowns.

The first great modern Arab poet (and many argue the greatest Arab poet ever), Abu Nuwas, wrote in the eighth century at the height of the Abbasid era, and was a notorious lover of boys (as was his patron the Caliph Al-Amin). He was the first to throw all caution to the wind. Many of his poems are about him seducing gorgeous "beardless youths." Abu Nuwas set a precedent that would be emulated with countless variations (from the symbolic and religious to the apologetic and profane) until the turn of the twentieth century, with the second golden age of Arabic boy-love poetry after the Abbasid era occurring between 1500 and 1800.

In *Producing Desire*, Ze'evi points out that during this later period sex between adult men "is seldom discussed, and when it is, there are insinuations that this is a 'sickness' of some sort."[47] He adds that male sexuality was still widely assumed to manifest two distinct phases. In the first, until the end of puberty, "the boy's sexuality could best be described as untamed, drawn to older men as well as to boys or women." In the second phase, once they have fully matured, "men's sexual behavior changes. From that time on they are expected to be attracted to women or to younger males, but not to men in their own age category. Those who do not complete the transition are somehow flawed."[48] In *Before Homosexuality in the Arab-Islamic World, 1500–1800* (2005), Khaled El-Rouhayeb concurs that there is good reason to resist "the temptation to bring the modern concept of homosexuality to bear on the positions expressed in belletristic comparisons of the charm of women and boys." The participants in the disputations were, he explains, "adult men who expressed their preferences for either women or *boys*. None of the positions involved adult men being attracted to adult men with masculine features."[49]

This is, as I have written in my previous two books on the Middle East, pretty much how things continue to play out in the region.[50] While in the West the dominant social stratification is now based on age (why is that strange man hanging out with those adolescent boys?), in the Middle East it is on sex segregation (what is that strange woman doing in this coffee shop, and is she related to one of those men she is with?). The current hysteria about pederasty in the West has found little traction in the contemporary Middle East apart from in Morocco (as we will see below). Perhaps the most useful parallel for the treatment of the phenomenon is nineteenth-century London, prior to the trial of Oscar Wilde in 1895. There, too, a large number of men, many of them married, habitually engaged in sex with boys, and male brothels packed with adolescents were widespread. More importantly, there existed, nurtured by the all-male boarding schools and universities, a pervasively homoerotic climate.

Since Saudi Arabia is the most sexually segregated Arab country, it is there that homosexuality is still most common, to the extent that it could fairly be described as universal, especially in the kingdom's schools and colleges. "A particularly beautiful boy always gets top marks in the exams because he's some teacher's favorite," an English teacher in a government high school told me when I was living there, as I reported in a dispatch for *The Independent*. "On the other hand, I know many older boys who deliberately flunked their final exams so they can stay with their younger sweethearts." Another Saudi friend, a student at a private college, said there had been no shame at all in having a boyfriend in his private high school. Although he firmly rejected the label "gay," he admitted that he then had a "special friend" in college, too. "It's those who don't have a boy who are ashamed to admit it. We introduce our boy to our friends as *al-walid hagi* [the boy who belongs to me]. At the beginning of term, we always check out the new boys to see which are the most *helu* [sweet] and think of ways to get to know them."[51]

Except in a small number of high-profile cases, invariably targeting those who are Westernized and have come out and so threaten the peaceful social harmony, the authorities turn a blind eye, as they did in Victorian England, and I suspect not least because many members of the establishment came of age in the same schools and colleges and have fond memories of their boyhood trysts and still have a keen eye for cute boys. In nineteenth-century England, again as in contemporary Saudi Arabia, great emphasis was also placed on the manliness of such pursuits. Taking their cue from the Greek obsession with athleticism, proponents of the cult of the beautiful boy would tend to argue that an all-male world if anything made more of a man out of the beloved than the promiscuous mingling with women, which many felt had a polluting, emasculating influence. It was a youth who spent too much time with women, rather than one who spent all his time around other boys or men, who was suspect.

Pederasty in the Arab world remains as ubiquitous as the call to prayer. So long as the sexual behavior is not spoken of publicly, it does not subvert existing homosocial norms, and it is not therefore perceived as a threat. The trick seems to be not to mention the subject in categorizable terms, not to acknowledge its existence if at all possible, and therefore not to have to deal with it as a distinct aspect of social reality. When it comes to the broader question of social and sexual independence, adolescent boys enjoy far more freedom in most Arab countries than adult women, and they are still as desired and fought over by adult men as they were during Abu Nuwas's time. The golden rule for all, tough, remains always to keep up manly appearances in public, and certainly to avoid behaving in such a blatantly queer fashion that it becomes impossible for the community to pretend there is nothing more to the relationships than friendship. Among ordinary men, the idea that sex "corrupts" the boys is also as alien today as it ever was. The pseudoscience we call psychiatry, and its various sex-obsessed offshoots, never took off in the Middle East, apart from among the superrich who have more money and time on their hands than they know what to do with, and Islam is entirely bereft of such beliefs. What matters is reputation, and the boy should guard against everyone finding out if he enjoys the passive role, although he is forgiven his youthful transgressions as long as he adopts the active role with younger boys when he gets older. What Arabs cannot stand, throughout history and up to the present, is adult men who make a song and dance about how they prefer to take the passive role in sex with other adult men, although if such individuals keep quiet about their preference they are, with a few inevitable exceptions, left alone. When told by snickering Arab friends in numerous Middle Eastern countries during the past decade about individuals in their communities who "take it in the ass," as the matter is usually indelicately put, I have always made a point of asking whether they suffer violence or discrimination as a result of having such a reputation. Their response is always the same: a look of total bafflement. The idea simply does not enter their heads.

Still, this way of dealing with the subject only works if the country concerned is not in the midst of a full-fledged moral panic. The Oscar Wilde trials, which, we should remember as we return to Morocco, Wilde brought on himself by insisting on going to trial, changed everything in England by bringing the subject out into the open and allowing society to categorize and stigmatize homosexuals as a distinct and separate group, especially in the sense that they "corrupt" and "groom" boys. These days, Morocco appears to be going through what may turn out to be an equally defining moment.

Unlike the foreigners arrested for engaging in female prostitution during the 2000s in Agadir, the gay Europeans were not quietly deported but sentenced to a year or so in prison. The reason is that they were suddenly presented as predatory pedophiles by the Francophone media, well-versed in the negative rhetoric surrounding pederasty in the West, and newly established local NGOs also inspired by the global child abuse panic. We saw with the Servaty affair how desperate "journalists" can be to sniff out a pedo angle even where none exists, and in Morocco the media has adopted an even more ridiculous definition of pedophilia (properly speaking, the attraction of adults to prepubescents) than have the Western tabloids. No one in their right mind could object if there was a genuine effort to help children, or for that matter adults, who are being exploited, sexually or otherwise. But the impression one gets from the media coverage in Morocco, as in so much of the coverage in the West, is that this is not what has happened.

One local French daily, for instance, even described a Westerner as a "pedophile" because he had been caught in a sting having consensual sex with two Moroccan men aged seventeen and eighteen.[52] More generally, an indication of how thorough were the investigations into this new group of scapegoats in Agadir became apparent when an Irishman, a year after being sentenced in 2006 for having sex with two youths under sixteen, was acquitted on all charges after an appellate court judge declared there was no evidence against him.[53] More grounded in reality, though, was the 2006 sting on a studio specializing in gay pornography in Marrakesh. Dozens of Moroccan men aged between eighteen and twenty were arrested. Like Servaty, the French head of the movie studio that produced and distributed the videos was outside the country at the time,[54] but unlike Servaty he had paid the men and they knew what they were involved in. A court sentenced thirteen of the local gay porn stars to prison terms ranging from six months to six years,[55] and this scandal, too, came to dominate the local media for months.

All this boy-related commotion set the scene for Morocco's biggest gay scandal in 2007. It involved only Moroccans, but again was viewed as a symptom of encroaching foreign cultural decadence. When rumors of a "gay wedding" spread through the northern town of Ksar Al-Kebir, the only proof produced was a video on YouTube of what appeared to be a man dancing in women's clothes. Still, thousands took to the streets, chanting antihomosexual slogans at the local mosque before moving on to trash the house where the event had taken place. An MP for the Islamist PJD, who claimed the demonstration and riot were spontaneous and not organized by religious figures, chimed in nevertheless to denounce the alleged gay wedding as yet another sign that Muslim values and traditions were disintegrating, while demanding the government "combat those who want to turn Morocco to a brothel."[56] What a gay wedding, imaginary or otherwise, has to do with brothels remains as much a mystery today as the identity of the alleged groom at the event, who was never found and most likely never existed. The "bride" himself meanwhile was married and had two kids.

The current debate over gay weddings in the United States is reported frankly in Morocco, but usually in the manner of someone holding his nose because of the engulfing stench, and it is probably

this association in the popular consciousness that allowed the Moroccan "wedding" to be presented as a foreign import. That meant again
ignoring home-grown realities, in this instance a long tradition of gay
marriage in the Middle East, from North Africa to Sudan and the Persian Gulf, which involved men taking boys as their brides, a practice
only clamped down on in the early twentieth century.[57] In any event,
according to the guests, this particular Moroccan party had actually
been the culmination of a Sufi ritual. A black bull was paraded through
the streets and sacrificed to appease a feared demon under a local bath-
house, while local Gnawa musicians, known for their poverty and
pleasure-seeking lifestyle, provided entertainment.[58]

Most noteworthy, however, was the trial testimony of the alleged
"bride," a wine merchant and former circus artist named Fouad Frettet, who was eventually given a ten-month prison sentence. He reportedly told the judge that "he had been a homosexual in his youth but
pointed out that he was now married with children."[59] The original
transcripts of court proceedings are not made public in Morocco, but
that English-language summary of Frettet's statement strikes me as a
very loose translation of what he said, because Arabs do not use binary
terms like homosexual/heterosexual to define their sexuality. He more
likely said something like: "When I was young I had sex with boys, but
then I got married." Either way, his confession begs the question: Why
did he volunteer this information during a trial in which he was plead-
ing not guilty to gay-related criminal charges, and when the proceedings were being observed by his close family and friends and followed
by the whole country through the media? Though unremarked on at
the time, I think the confession represents the one moment of honesty
in this whole charade. Frettet had alluded to an unspeakable truth in
order to present himself, in his transition from a youth who had sex

with boys into a married adult, as a regular kind of Moroccan guy, and perfectly in step with the country's quietly tolerated tradition of homosexuality with and among the young.

⟡

By appearing to crack down on gay vice in all its manifest variety, the Moroccan regime was further able to demonstrate its Islamist credentials. At the same time, the gay scandals helped to reinforce the standard narrative that all vice is a Western import. But with pederasty, which is to say sex between men and adolescents, the idea that it is Westerners who created the phenomenon is especially absurd. As late as the 1920s, boys were still being sold off to locals in Morocco's public markets as sex slaves, and it was in fact French colonization that first stigmatized pederasty.[60] "Homosexuality between man and boy was never considered in any way abnormal or shameful in Morocco," one historian points out, "until the infiltration of European opinion with the French."[61] At the same time, the reason Westerners flocked to North Africa was precisely because pederasty was a part of the social fabric, and has been since time immemorial. Anyone knows that if they have read Flaubert's reminiscences about Cairo's nineteenth-century bathhouses, where he writes about how locals talk about "skewering" boys without shame, or Andre Gide's early-twentieth-century autobiographical novels set in Algeria and Tunisia where he learned to accept his own love of young boys in a welcoming climate that contrasted with his repressive native France, or Joe Orton's diaries detailing his endless exploits with adolescent boys during the 1960s in Tangier, which was likewise seen as remarkably libertine in this regard compared to Britain.

The new drive in Morocco to desexualize adolescent boys—and demonize those who are attracted to them—is the culmination of a century-long struggle in the Arab world to rid itself of the ancient boy-love tradition in the name of modernity and the adoptions of Western sexual norms by the Westernized elite. In his monumental study *Desiring Arabs* (2007), Joseph A. Massad draws on a vast array of Arabic sources from the nineteenth and early twentieth centuries to chart an increasingly shy and troubled discussion of Abu Nuwas's licentiousness during the period. This, he shows, was often in the context of the adoption by local writers of Western conceptions of "civilization" and "progress":

> In the course of writing classical and medieval Arab history these modern historians encountered an ancient Arab society with different sexual mores and practices that were difficult to assimilate into a modern Arab nationalist project informed by European notions of progress and modernization and a Victorian sexual ethic.[62]

Secular Arab nationalists were especially eager to purge their history of boy-love sentiment, which they came to see as an embarrassment, and imported Western concepts such as "decadence" and "degeneration" further helped them to bury it. By the early twentieth century, such poetry had been censored from Arabic-language schoolbooks, and mentioned only to condemn it. As one commentator put it, boy love was now to be considered a "disgrace" to Arab literature.[63]

"The advent of colonialism and Western capital to the Arab world has transformed most aspects of daily living," writes Massad in *Desiring Arabs*, adding that it has "failed to impose a European heterosexual regime on all Arab men, although its efforts were successful in the upper classes and the increasingly Westernized middle classes."[64] But now a new push by "progressive" outsiders threatens to eradicate the practice itself, in addition to its literary representation. A Spanish-based Moroccan gay rights organization, KifKif, was set up in 2005. It has a mere fifty members in a population of some thirty million, but the impact it has on the ground is revealed by a steady stream of local press coverage, and the fact that Islamists regularly hack its website. Massad points out that such Western-based gay rights organizations have no constituency to speak of in the Arab world, and by trying to impose on their home countries Western gay lifestyle choices, they have the effect of reducing the number of practicing homosexuals, because once homosexuality is defined and dragged out of the closet in such terms nobody wants to have anything to do with it.[65] These gay activists also give credence to the Islamists' argument that homosexuality is something foreign, because it is defined in Western gay terms; and it also gives Middle Eastern regimes an excuse to round up self-identified gay men who can be associated with that foreignness. The push for Western-style gay rights therefore creates more problems than it solves, if it solves any. According to Massad, on the back of all this the press and Islamists "soon begin to call for specific laws that criminalize same-sex practice."[66] Most cynically, the Western gay organizations can then point to the resulting roundups, calls for new legislation, and media hysteria in order to garner more publicity and funding.

Now living in France, Taia, the Moroccan author of *Salvation Army*, has also adopted a Western gay identity, turning his back on his home country and criticizing it for being mired in repressive social and religious mores that encourage males to define their masculinity in terms of the sexual role they perform. *TelQuel* put Taia on its cover in 2007 under the banner headline "Homosexual,"[67] and as a result he is now preposterously referred to as "Morocco's only gay man," a moniker he seems to wear with pride. But who were *TelQuel* and Taia trying to kid? Yes, Taia had come out, much to the jubilation of the Western gay community (the principal audience, we should remember, for this author's books: *Salvation Army* appeared in the United States with an introduction by Edmund White, that country's leading gay writer); but that is something few others in Morocco who have sex with boys would dream of doing. So why should their lives in Morocco be compared, one way or the other, to Taia's in Paris? By presenting him as a martyr rather than a shameless self-publicist, *TelQuel* was crucially able to avoid discussing the elephant in the room: that there are few Moroccan men who have not had sex with boys, and the chances of anything happening to them as a result are pretty slim so long as they do not run around the streets with a rainbow flag in one hand and a copy of *Gay Times* in the other. Instead, the article was carefully headlined, in reference to Taia, "Toward Homosexuality and Against Everyone." However, in a 2009 interview with an English-language website about his youth in Morocco, the worst thing even Taia could recall was how, when his friends found out he preferred the passive role, they let it be known that they would welcome him bending over when they got the urge.[68] Many a sex-starved, isolated gay boy in the West would surely feel a pang of jealousy on reading that. The truth ignored, then, in this farcical game of shadows is that while unmarried Moroccan men remain as boy crazy as ever, they for the most part do not see any benefit, either personally or politically, in reminding the world of the fact at every opportunity. For them, the personal is not political. The British sociologist Jeremy Seabrook has highlighted the hubris of those who nevertheless insist on imposing on others Western concepts like "gay" and "bisexual" that bear no historic relation to other cultures' sexual identities:

To impose such categories—except upon a small minority who have been much influenced by Western gay experience—is to bring alien concepts to the people involved; it is arrogant and disregarding of other cultures; and far from the respect for pluralism and diversity which the West now claims as one of its most characteristic attributes.[69]

A more basic question is whether the Western gay lifestyle is really something that anyone should take as a role model, but that is rarely asked because we casually adopt a supremacist, imperialist stance in discussing the issue. Why on earth would they not want to live like us, with our prejudices and hang-ups and strict definitions of what is and is not normal, acceptable, and desirable? Well, for me, there are in fact few if any more dispiriting sights in the big cities of the individualistic West than their gay ghettos: their armies of men in Identi-kit outfits, drinking gay coffee in gay cafés, sniffing gay poppers in gay discos, and looking forward, as a break from the norm, to their gay holidays in their gay hotels on one of the gay beaches on the Greek island of Mykonos. Admittedly, a higher common denominator is provided by a handful of vapid, superannuated pop stars and a taste for violently colored soft furnishings. But such people cannot conceivably share much else but what they like to do in the bedroom, any more than straight people can, so a whole evening's conversation must therefore be stitched together from what is in effect a collection of ready-made linguistic quirks—in countries where you do not speak the language, or places where the music is too loud, the same thing can be done by off-the-peg gestures with no perceptible loss of meaning.

Proponents argue that the ghetto offers protection, and it does, but the fact that such protection is needed further highlights the absurdity of promoting the Western gay model in the Middle East, where random social homophobia in the form of gay bashing, and the relentless, cruel bullying of boys who fancy boys, is so uncommon as to be statistically negligible. The most obvious reason is that, to one degree or other, everyone is implicated. Another is that the sex act does not magically transform itself into a defining personal trait. It is an act, and when completed it is sensibly forgotten. In contrast, and for all the official talk about equality, homophobia remains depressingly widespread in my home country of Britain (as it does in the United States), where boys in high school routinely get beaten to a pulp for any perceived expression of gayness, where the word "gay" (or "fag") is the most common playground insult, and where self-identified gay teens are far more likely to commit suicide than other teens. An extensive 2007 study concluded that two-thirds of the homosexual pupils in Britain's schools have suffered homophobic bullying. Almost all experienced verbal bullying, but 41 percent said they had been physically attacked, and 17 percent even claimed that they had received death threats.[70] So when it comes to the question of tolerance and a respect for others' privacy in relation to homosexuality, we in the West might have something to learn from the Arabs, and certainly very little to justify preaching to them.

However, the self-criticism should only begin there. As in every community based on a wholly spurious notion of common identity, in the gay one the walls are up and the thought police are stalking the perimeter, ever ready to make an example of subversives who threaten to undermine the unity of the collective as the unelected leaders of the gay-rights lobby ingratiate themselves into the mainstream. Thus a gay man in the acceptable Western sense is now an adult who, by some fluke of genetic wiring, is attracted exclusively to other adult gay men—though how he is usually said to have "known" he was gay, in the stock account, from an early age, thus suffering the frustrating, alienated adolescence from which the Coming Out moment was to liberate him, is not explained. In having put up these walls, and having attained positions of power and influence, the gay community's leaders these days enthusiastically pander to the worst instincts of the mainstream, especially when it comes to laying down the rules about what is permitted and what is not in their ranks, and out-Haroding even the hetero Harods as far as the pederasty issue is concerned.

A good example is the British journalist and self-appointed gay community spokesman Johann Hari. In 2009, he berated the popular British playwright Alan Bennett for daring to suggest that there may be worse things for a boy in mid to late teens than being propositioned by an older man. Bennett is something of a British institution, and most famously the author of the play *History Boys* (2004), on which the successful 2006 movie of the same name is based; but he also wrote the screenplay for the movie *Prick Up Your Ears* (1987) about Joe Orton that dealt frankly (and without any concessions to the moralizers) with Orton's sexual encounters with teenage Moroccan boys in the 1960s. Hari admitted that in his own case such propositions during his adolescence, which of course he made crystal clear he turned down, had no adverse effect, but he nonetheless concluded: "The taboos protecting young people from sexual abuse took a long time to build up. They have to be protected from erosion."[71] Hari is rightly troubled that almost all historical "gay icons" rarely conform to the new gay community standards, and would more accurately be described as pederasts. But instead of rationally discussing the implications of that pederastic inheritance, for example by exploring the difference between morality and convention (the dominant theme in much of Gide's writing) or even challenging those new "taboos" and the reactionary commentary they provoke on a daily basis among his fellow hacks, he asked: "Did the violent suppression of homosexuality perhaps have a deforming effect on their sexualities?"[72]

One can hear the waves of derisive laughter still sweeping from the Bosporus to the south of the Arabian Peninsula. The following comment by the far more erudite and sophisticated Camille Paglia was written before Hari polluted cyberspace with his, but it reads like a stinging rebuff. It should serve, too, as a warning to anyone in the Arab word who values his literary history and wants to preserve his distinct cultural identities about the dangers of embracing the vacuousness Hari and his ilk now so proudly stand for in the West. Paglia explained that she has long lamented how gay male culture in the wake of the 1969 Stonewall riots "suddenly went off track" toward politics and away from an aesthetic appreciation of the beautiful adolescent boy. The result, according to her, is a "trivialization of gay sensibility":

When I look around and I see the kind of act up style, with the short shorts and the combat boots and a kind of skinhead look, I think, first of all, how childish, and secondly, how desexualized, no matter what people say, how utterly neutered. That is the end result of [a] turn away from aesthetics in the gay male community . . . a loss of feeling for the beauty of this archetype of the boy, which was seen everywhere in late nineteenth century photography, in poetry, and going back all the way to these beautiful dreamy statues of the high classic Greek period. Contemporary gays who try to distance themselves from this issue of boy love are in effect committing cultural suicide. . . . These assertions of discontinuity may seem highly academic, but they are the breeding ground of opportunism and fraud.[73]

CONCLUSION

I have illustrated in this book how the events of 1979 in the Middle East, and in particular the Iranian revolution and the siege of Mecca, ushered in a wave of Islamic fundamentalism at a moment when the region was in tremendous flux. Rapid social and economic changes have since fed into and changed the region's political and religious discourse surrounding personal choices, including the most fundamental ones involving sex. But we should importantly remember, too, that in 1979 and 1980 elections also brought to power Ronald Reagan in the United States, with the support of the Christian evangelicals, and Margaret Thatcher in Britain, whose "family values" rhetoric was no less extreme for not being explicitly couched in religious rhetoric.

The late American evangelical preacher Jerry Falwell once let slip to an associate in an unguarded moment: "If homosexuals didn't exist, we'd have to invent them."[1] For once, he was making an interesting point, namely, about the way sex, religion, and politics have become inextricably entwined in his country, and how those on both sides in the resulting culture wars need and feed off each other to promote their opposing agendas. In their book *Perfect Enemies* (1996), in which the Falwell quote about homosexuals first appeared, American journalists Chris Bull and John Gallagher convincingly showed that the religious right and the gay movement in their country have more in common than either would like to admit. Both are considered fringe groups by the general population, but each, they argued, bring the other to national attention and galvanize their supporters.

Just as the religious right in the United States would have needed to invent what it describes as sexual deviance if it did not exist in order to prosper, so would the Islamists in the Middle East. As a result, we all find ourselves in the midst not of a clash of civilizations, as is popularly thought, but a convergence of religious fundamentalisms. No longer can the powers that be in the Middle East keep a careful but tolerant eye on the prostitution industry, indulge in the sins of the flesh themselves, and expect everyone to turn a blind eye to the hypocrisy of their claim that they are defending Islam, now perceived as the victim of a full-frontal assault by the West. It is equally unlikely, though, that an American politician would be elected to high office if he offered even a timid argument in favor of legalizing prostitution, or declared categorically that he did not believe in God. Remarkably, there are few, if any, senior American politicians who are self-declared atheists. With this intermixing of sex, politics, and religion, hypocrisy has inevitably grown in the West, too. Deviation is increasingly defined as disorderly, dirty, and sinful by puritans of various stripes, and this book has drawn attention to the central paradox that, as intolerance has increased, so has vice, because as the range of acceptable behavior decreases so the definition of vice broadens and more people therefore are by default engaging in unacceptable behavior.

Which brings us back to the question of hypocrisy. It certainly is everywhere in the Middle East regarding discussion about sexual behavior, but is just as widespread in the United States. Perhaps this was best encapsulated by Falwell's fellow antivice preacher, Ted Haggard, who fell from grace in 2006 after he was found to be using drugs and a male prostitute. His shenanigans were mirrored by that other evangelical antipederast crusader, Mark Foley, who resigned his seat in the U.S. Senate the same year, after he was discovered to have engaged in explicit sexual banter with teenage boys. There are countless other examples, and the Catholic Church of course comes immediately to mind, but the point is made that viewing sex as profane or sacred is ultimately dysfunctional for any society, and perhaps especially those who try to live up to impossible standards they set for everyone else. I have made clear my stand, as a secularist and libertarian, that it is better to view sex instead as a private transaction, completely separate from religion and politics, and that the media and self-serving lobby groups have played a disgraceful role in forcing onto our own societies such hysterical discourse on the issue.

The state's role, in the East and West, should be the exact opposite of the one it is playing now: to ensure that, in clearing a rightful space for itself, morality does not intrude too far into the space immorality has a legitimate claim to. Minority interests must be safeguarded—safeguarded, not elevated above those of other minorities, or the majority—and it is in that delicate task, rather than in bullying and posturing and the hounding of scapegoats, that a state can come into its own, divorced from any symbiotic relationship to sex and religion. That is why, in retrospect, there is much to admire in the example offered by Tunisia. However, the country is too politically and geographically marginalized to act as a trendsetter for the region, and is, if anything, itself up against it when it comes to keeping at bay the rising tide of fundamentalism encroaching from all sides. For one result of this radical social and political upheaval in the Middle East, as we have seen, is the bringing into the mainstream of the Islamist political parties and the concomitant marginalization and shunning of liberal, let alone secular, voices. Even for Arab regimes that are historically secular, as in Syria, or those that favored a permissive society, as in Bahrain, it has become impossible for ordinary folk even to hint at opposition to the Islamists' antisex agenda, for fear of being labeled stooges of the West, and therefore anti-Islam.

At the same time, one cannot help but be struck by the remarkable resilience of liberal cultural identities and attitudes toward sex in the countries we have visited, how a diverse and vibrant underground continues to flourish in private and sometimes even in the open in the local, strongly rooted communities, despite the strange, faceless, sexless rules the minority fundamentalists want to put all over public life. "In such matters the most draconian measures seldom last and their promulgators are driven to writing pamphlets or preaching sermons against prostitution, always to no avail," wrote Bouhdiba in *Sexuality in Islam*.[2] Four decades after his book appeared, the promulgators are preaching louder than ever, but equally to no avail, and one can confidently predict that, four decades hence, we will encounter the same scenario.

NOTES

INTRODUCTION

1. Seymour M. Hersh, "Annals of National Security: The Gray Zone," *New Yorker,* May 24, 2004, www.newyorker.com/fact/content/?040524fa_fact.
2. Ralph Patai, *The Arab Mind* (New York: Scribner's, 1973), p. 160.
3. Ibid.
4. Ibid., p. 162.
5. Ibid., p. 160.
6. Ibid., p. 356.
7. Lionel Tiger, "Obama Bin Laden's Man Trouble," Slate, September 28, 2001, http://www.slate.com/id/116236/.
8. Martin Amis, *The Second Plane: September 11: Terror and Boredom* (New York: Knopf, 2008), p. 87.
9. Ian Buruma, "Extremism: The Loser's Revenge," *The Guardian,* February 25, 2006, http://www.guardian.co.uk/world/2006/feb/25/terrorism.comment.
10. Ian Buruma, *Murder in Amsterdam: The Death of Theo Van Gogh and the Limits of Tolerance* (London: Penguin, 2006).
11. Patai was born in Palestine, so he presumably knew some Arabic, but he was from a Jewish family and spent his entire adult life in the United States, Europe, and Israel, and was a lifelong advocate of Zionism. He does not appear ever to have visited any of the Arab countries he writes about in *The Arab Mind.* See "The Zionist Diatribe Underpinning American Attitudes Towards Muslims and Arabs," *Muslim Media,* July 2004, http://www.muslimedia.com/ARCHIVES/special04/ziondiatribe.htm.
12. "The Suicide Bomber," PBS, November 14, 2005, http://www.pbs.org/news-hour/bb/terrorism/july-dec05/bombers_11-14.html.
13. George Orwell, *1984* (New York: New American Library, 1961), p. 133.
14. "Fourteen-Year-Old New Jersey Girl May Get Sex Offender Status for Posting Naked Pictures on MySpace," Associated Press, March 27, 2009. http://www.nydailynews.com/news/2009/03/26/2009-03-26_14yearold_new_jersey_girl_may_get_sex_of.html.
15. Abdelwahab Bouhdiba, *Sexuality in Islam* (London: Saqi, 2001), p. 189.
16. Vern Bullough and Bonnie Vern, *Women and Prostitution* (New York: Prometheus, 1987), p. 76.
17. Ibid.
18. Bouhdiba, *Sexuality in Islam,* p. 189.
19. Ibid., p. 190. See also Leila Ahmed, *Women and Gender in Islam* (New Haven, Conn.: Yale University Press, 1992), p. 264 n. 34.

20. Bahar Colak, "Portraits of Women in the Late Nineteenth Century Ottoman Empire From the Pen of Ahmed Midhat Effendi" (Master's Thesis, Bilkent University, Ankara, 2002), pp. 101–2, http://www.thesis.bilkent.edu.tr/0002043.pdf.
21. Ibid.
22. Ibid.
23. Bouhdiba, *Sexuality in Islam*, p. 192.
24. Bruce Lawrence, *Messages to the World: The Statements of Osama bin Laden* (London: Verso, 2005), p. 229.
25. A transcript and video of the show are available at http://www.aljazeera.net/NR/exeres/BA1EB338-F7A8–4401–928C-EEFD02B07291.htm.

1. DISSENT IN DAMASCUS

1. Sami Moubayed, "Sexual Repression in Syria," *PostGlobal*, January 27, 2007, http://newsweek.washingtonpost.com/postglobal/sami_moubayed/2007/01/sexual_repression_in_syria.html.
2. Ayman Nour, "Egypt: 29 Years Between a President and His Heir," Ayman Nour website, October 17, 2009, http://aymanoormasr.blogspot.com/2009/10/egypt–29-years-between-president-and.html.
3. Moubayed, "Sexual Repression in Syria."
4. Noy Thrupkaew, "The Crusade Against Sex Trafficking," *Nation*, October 5, 2009, www.thenation.com/doc/20091005/thrupkaew.
5. See, for example, Dorchen A. Leidholdt, "Demand and Debate," Coalition Against Trafficking in Women website, 2004, http://action.web.ca/home/catw/readingroom.shtml?x=53793&AA_EX_Session=944f35563eb48eaae22c40a95f509c5f.
6. As stated on their website here: http://www.catwinternational.org/campaigns.php#prostitution.
7. See http://action.web.ca/home/catw/readingroom.shtml?x=114598&AA_EX_Session=c3d4e7e54ca36cdee3fc35d40b6c4710.
8. Jerry Markon, "Human Traffic Evokes Outrage, Little Evidence," *Washington Post*, September 23, 2007, http://www.washingtonpost.com/wp-dyn/content/article/2007/09/22/AR2007092201401_pf.html; Nick Davies, "Inquiry Fails to Find a Single Trafficker Who Forced Anybody Into Prostitution," *Guardian*, October 20, 2009, http://www.guardian.co.uk/uk/2009/oct/20/government-trafficking-enquiry-fails.
9. Kamala Kempadoo, ed., *Trafficking and Prostitution Reconsidered* (Boulder, Colo.: Paradigm, 2005), p. xxi.
10. Ibid.
11. Laura María Agustín, *Sex at the Margins: Migration, Labour, Markets, and the Rescue Industry* (London: Zed Books, 2007), p. 38.
12. Joshua E. S. Phillips, "Unveiling Iraq's Teenage Prostitutes," Salon, June 24, 2005, http://dir.salon.com/story/news/feature/2005/06/24/prostitutes/print.html.
13. Charity Tooze, "Syria Attempts to Combat the Rise of Human Trafficking," CNN website, September 8, 2009, http://ac360.blogs.cnn.com/2009/09/08/syria-attempts-to-combat-the-rise-of-human-trafficking/.
14. Katherine Zeopf, "Iraqi Women Survive in Damascus by Prostituting Themselves," *New York Times*, May 28, 2007, http://www.nytimes.com/2007/05/28/world/africa/28iht-syria.4.5900916.html?pagewanted=1&_r=1.
15. Will Everett, "Sisters of the Good Shepherd," World Vision Report, May 16, 2009, http://www.worldvisionreport.org/Stories/Week-of-May–16–2009/Sisters-of-the-Good-Shepherd.

16. "Syria: New Law Targets Sex Traffickers," IRIN, March 17, 2008, http://www
    .irinnews.org/report.aspx?reportid=77311.
17. "First Shelter for Trafficked People Opens in Damascus," IRIN, February 2,
    2009, http://www.irinnews.org/Report.aspx?ReportId=82686.
18. "Syria: New Draft Law Targets Sex Traffickers," IRIN, March 17, 2008, http://
    www.irinnews.org/report.aspx?reportid=77311.
19. Kempadoo, *Trafficking and Prostitution Reconsidered*, p. xxii.
20. Allen J. Beck, Paul Guerino, and Paige M. Harrison, "Sexual Victimization in Ju-
    venile Facilities Reported by Youth, 2008–09," U.S. Bureau of Justice Statistics,
    January 7, 2010, http://bjs.ojp.usdoj.gov/index.cfm?ty=pbdetail&iid=2113.
21. "NSPCC Says Extent of Child Sex Offenses 'Shocking,'" Reuters, January 25,
    2005, http://uk.reuters.com/article/idUKTRE60O1WF20100125.
22. Nick Davies, "Prostitution and Trafficking: The Anatomy of a Moral Panic,"
    Guardian, October 20, 2009, http://www.guardian.co.uk/uk/2009/oct/20/traf-
    ficking-numbers-women-exaggerated.
23. The video can be watched here: http://radioviceonline.com/1996-secretary-of-
    state-500000-dead-iraqi-kids-worth-it/.

2. ISLAMIC FEMINISM

1. "Tunisia Tops Competitive Rank in Africa," Afrol News, June 17, 2009, http://
   www.afrol.com/articles/33565.
2. Abdelwahab Bouhdiba, *Sexuality in Islam* (London: Saqi, 2001), p.193.
3. Ibid.
4. Ibid., p. 192.
5. "Tunisia Ranks Top of Arab Countries in Life Quality," Global Arab Network,
   January 11, 2010, http://www.english.globalarabnetwork.com/201001114313/
   Travel/tunisia-ranks-top-of-arab-countries-in-life-quality.html.
6. "Committee Experts Commend Tunisia's 'Great Strides Forward' in Promoting Equality Between Women, Men," U.N. Committee on Elimination of Discrimination Against Women, press release, June 14, 2002, http://www.un.org/
   News/Press/docs/2002/wom1348.doc.htm.
7. Ahlem Belhadj and Hafidha Checkir, "A Situational Analysis of Commercial
   Sexual Exploitation of Children in Tunisia," ECPAT Report, March 2003, p. 6,
   http://www.childtrafficking.com/Docs/ecpat_2003_situational_analysis_studies
   _cse_children_tunisia_3.pdf.
8. Iason Athanasiadis, "Future Shock," *The National*, May 29, 2009, http://www
   .thenational.ae/article/20090529/REVIEW/705289979/1008.
9. Nick Pisa, "Gadaffi's Girls: When in Rome . . . ," *The Daily Mail*, November 17,
   2009, http://www.dailymail.co.uk/news/worldnews/article–1228196/Colonel-
   Gaddafi-demands–500-beautiful-Italian-girls-convert-Islam-Rome-summit
   .html.
10. Alfred E. Montesquiou, "Tunisia Economy Thrives Amid Restrictive Politics,"
    Associated Press, October 29, 2009, http://etaiwannews.com/etn/news_content
    .php?id=1094558&lang=eng_news&cate_img=35.jpg&cate_rss=news_Business.
11. The historical summary in the paragraph is drawn from the account given of
    Bourguiba's early years in power in Toine Van Teeffelen et al. (eds.): *Changing
    Stories: Postmodernism and the Arab-Islamic World* (Amsterdam: Rodopi Bv Edi-
    tions, 1995), pp. 58–61.
12. Quoted in Suha Sabbagh, *Arab Women: Between Defiance and Restraint* (New
    York: Olive Branch Press, 1998), p. 34. See also Richard H. Curtis, "Tunisia's
    Family Planning Success Underlies Its Economic Progress," Washington

Report on Middle East Affairs, December 1999, http://www.wrmea.com/back issues/1196/9611072.htm.

13. Sabbagh, *Arab Women*, p. 34.
14. Ibid.
15. Eric Pace, "Habib Bourguiba, Led Tunisia to Independence From France," *New York Times*, April 7, 2000, http://www.library.cornell.edu/colldev/mideast/bourgnyt.htm.
16. Ibid.
17. Gautam Naik, "Tunisia Wins Population Battle, and Others See a Policy Model," *Wall Street Journal*, August 8, 2003, http://online.wsj.com/article/0,SB106028926761045100-search,00.html?collection=wsjie%2F30day&vql_string=tunisia%3Cin%3E%28article%2Dbody%29.
18. Ibid.
19. Montesquiou, "Tunisia Economy Thrives Amid Restrictive Politics."
20. "Tunisia Ranks Top of Arab Countries in Life Quality."
21. Ibid.
22. "Tunisia: Country Observes World AIDS Day," All Africa News, December 1, 2009, http://allafrica.com/stories/200912020291.html.
23. "Creation of 11 Free AIDS Clinics in Tunisia," *TunisiaMag*, December 25, 2008, http://www.tunisiamag.com/20081225222/Society/Health/creation-of-11-free-aids-clinics-in-tunisia.html.
24. Trevor Mostyn, *Egypt's Belle Epoque: Cairo and the Age of the Hedonists* (London: I. B. Taurus, 2006), p. 145.
25. Margot Badran, *Feminists, Islam, and Nation: Gender and the Making of Modern Egypt* (Princeton, N.J.: Princeton University Press, 1996), p. 194.
26. Ibid.
27. Yunan Labib Rizk, "Al-Ahram: A Diwan of Contemporary Life (393)," *Al-Ahram Weekly*, June 7, 2001, http://weekly.ahram.org.eg/2001/537/chrncls.htm.
28. Ibid.
29. Ibid.
30. As quoted by Ibid.
31. Ibid.
32. Mostyn, *Egypt's Belle Epoque*, p. 198.
33. Jo Doezema, "Loose Women or Lost Women? The Re-Emergence of the Myth of 'White Slavery' in Contemporary Discourses of 'Trafficking in Women,'" *Gender Issues* 18, no. 1 (Winter 2000), http://www.walnet.org/csis/papers/doezema-loose.html.
34. Badran, *Feminists, Islam, and Nation*, p. 189.
35. Ibid., p. 198.
36. Gretel C. Kovach, "Why the Bellyaching About Belly Dancing?" *Newsweek*, October 21, 2002, http://www.newsweek.com/id/65979/page/7.
37. Magdi Abdelhadi, "Egypt's Sexual Harassment 'Cancer'," BBC News, July 18, 2008, http://news.bbc.co.uk/2/hi/7514567.stm.
38. See, for example, "Egypt Deports 'East European Prostitutes,'" BBC News, June 27, 2002, http://news.bbc.co.uk/2/hi/middle_east/2070639.stm.
39. Safaa Abdoun, "HIV Increases Six-Fold in Egypt, Says Government Study," *Daily News* (Egypt), January 12, 2010, http://www.thedailynewsegypt.com/article.aspx?ArticleID=27055.
40. Rizk, "Al-Ahram: A Diwan of Contemporary Life (393)."
41. Ahlem Belhadj and Hafidha Checkir, *A Situational Analysis of Commercial Sexual Exploitation of Children in Tunisia* (ECPAT, 2003), p. 4.

42. Ibid.
43. Ibid.
44. Ibid.
45. Ibid., p. 5.
46. Montesquiou, "Tunisia Economy Thrives Amid Restrictive Politics."
47. See Dennis Altman, *Global Sex* (Chicago: University of Chicago Press: 2001), pp. 145–48.
48. Tunisia, U.S. Bureau of Democracy, Human Rights, and Labor, U.S. State Department, 2005, http://www.state.gov/g/drl/rls/hrrpt/2005/61700.htm.
49. "A Situational Analysis of Commercial Sexual Exploitation of Children in Tunisia," p. 6.
50. U.N. Committee on Elimination of Discrimination Against Women, "Committee Experts Commend Tunisia's 'Great Strides Forward' in Promoting Equality Between Women, Men," press release WOM/1348, June 14, 2002, http://www.un.org/News/Press/docs/2002/wom1348.doc.htm.
51. "Tunisia Balancing Islam Against Islamists," Associated Press, October 23, 2009, http://sify.com/finance/tunisia-balancing-islam-against-islamists-news-business-jkxvpofeffd.html.

3. TEMPORARY MARRIAGES

1. John R. Bradley, "Iran's Ethnic Tinderbox," *Washington Quarterly*, Winter 2006–2007, www.twq.com/07winter/docs/07winter_bradley.pdf.
2. Juliet Lapidos, "How to Spot a Persian Prostitute," Slate, April 23, 2008, http://www.slate.com/id/2189816/.
3. Ibid.
4. Nazila Fathi, "To Regulate Prostitution, Iran Ponders Brothels," *New York Times*, August 28, 2002, http://www.nytimes.com/2002/08/28/world/to-regulate-prostitution-iran-ponders-brothels.html.
5. http://www.youtube.com/watch?v=J7ptTtRdXWo.
6. Spengler, "Jihadis and Whores," Asia Times Online, November 1, 2006, http://www.atimes.com/atimes/Middle_East/HK21Ak01.html.
7. Ibid.
8. "Iran Juggles With Taboos, Holds First Session of Prostitutes and Police," IRNA, December 7, 2002, http://www.netnative.com/news/02/dec/1032.html.
9. "A Police Chief Incarcerated: Prostitute Scandal Rattles Tehran Government," *Der Spiegel*, April 28, 2008, http://www.spiegel.de/international/world/0,1518,550156,00.html.
10. Ibid.
11. Monique Girgis, "Women in Pre-Revolutionary, Revolutionary and Post-Revolutionary Iran," *Iran Chamber Society*, 1996, http://www.iranian.com/main/news/2009/12/23/women-pre-revolutionary-revolutionary-and-post-revolutionary-iran.
12. Ibid.
13. Shahla Haeri, *Law of Desire: Temporary Marriage in Shi'i Islam* (Syracuse, N.Y.: Syracuse University Press, 1989), p. 110.
14. Ibid., p. 90.
15. Robert Tait, "Premarital Sex in Iran on Rise as Iranians Delay Marriage, Survey Finds," *The Guardian*, December 29, 2008, http://www.guardian.co.uk/world/2008/dec/29/iran-gender.

16. Ibid.
17. Ibid.
18. Elaine Sciolino, "Love Finds a Way in Iran: 'Temporary Marriage,'" *New York Times*, November 4, 2000, http://www.nytimes.com/2000/10/04/world/love-finds-a-way-in-iran-temporary-marriage.html.
19. Ibid.
20. Kikki R. Keddie, *Women in the Middle East: Past and Present* (Princeton, N.J.: Princeton University Press, 2007), p. 303.
21. Kimia Sanati, "Temporary Marriages Degrading for Women—Critics," Inter Press Service, June 26, 2007, http://ipsnews.net/news.asp?idnews=38316.
22. "Temporary Marriages Surge by 122 Percent in Six Months," Middle East Online, November 3, 2002, http://www.middle-east-online.com/english/?id=3088.
23. "Debate on the Legitimacy of Mutaa," IslamOnline, http://www.al-islam.org/encyclopedia/chapter6a/9.html.
24. Sciolino, "Love Finds a Way in Iran: 'Temporary Marriage.'"
25. Francis Harrison, "Iran Talks Up Temporary Marriages." BBC News, June 2, 2007, http://news.bbc.co.uk/2/hi/6714885.stm.
26. Sanati, "Temporary Marriages Degrading for Women—Critics."
27. Sciolino, "Love Finds a Way in Iran: 'Temporary Marriage.'"
28. "Temporary Marriages Surge by 122 Percent in Six Months."
29. "Significant Increase in 'Temporary Marriages' in Iran," Right Side News, December 19, 2009, http://www.rightsidenews.com/200912207862/global-terrorism/spotlight-on-iran-update-december–19–2009.html.
30. Sanati, "Temporary Marriages Degrading for Women—Critics."
31. See, for example, Lily Mazahery, "The Silent Screams of Women and Girls," *Jerusalem Post*, January 15, 2007, http://www.jpost.com/servlet/Satellite?cid=1167467739732&pagename=JPost%2FJPArticle%2FShowFull.
32. Girgis, "Women in Pre-Revolutionary, Revolutionary and Post-Revolutionary Iran."
33. Ibid.
34. Richard Greene, ed., *Graham Greene: A Life in Letters* (London: Little, Brown, 2007), p. 156.
35. Hassen Fakih, "Misyar Marriage Enrages Gulf Women," Middle East Online, April 25, 2006, http://www.middle-east-online.com/english/?id=16308=16308&format=0.
36. "Pleasure Marriages," Women24, http://www.women24.com/Content/HomeAndAway/Travel/2537/e5e2d32177bb4d439d6eadedea372a8b/05–04–2006–12–40/Pleasure_marriages.
37. Gihan Shahine, "Illegitimate, Illegal, or Just Ill-Advised?" *Al-Ahram Weekly*, February 18–24, 1999, http://weekly.ahram.org.eg/1999/417/li1.htm.
38. Riham Adel, "Married, or Maybe Not," *Al-Ahram Weekly*, December 10–16, 2009, http://weekly.ahram.org.eg/2009/976/feature.htm.
39. Shahine, "Illegitimate, Illegal, or Just Ill-Advised?" *Al-Ahram Weekly*.
40. Mariz Tadros, "Secretly Yours," *Al-Ahram Weekly*, June 2, 1999, http://weekly.ahram.org.eg/1999/417/li1.htm.
41. Fakih, "Misyar Marriage Enrages Gulf Women."
42. Adel, "Married, or Maybe Not," *Al-Ahram Weekly*, December 16, 2009, http://weekly.ahram.org.eg/2009/976/feature.htm.
43. Ibid.
44. Somayya Jabarti, "Misyar Marriage: a Marvel or Misery?" *Arab News*, June 5, 2005, http://www.arabnews.com/?page=9&section=0&article=64891.

45. Adel, "Married, or Maybe Not."
46. Ethar El-Katatney, "No-Strings Marriage," *Egypt Today*, June 2009, http://www
.egypttoday.com/article.aspx?ArticleID=8531.
47. Ibid.
48. "Pleasure Marriages," *Women24.*
49. Ibid.
50. Ibid.
51. Ibid.
52. "Man Dupes Naive Misyar Hopefuls," *Arab News*, December 6, 2007, http://
arabnews.com/?page=1&section=0&article=104371&d=6&m=12&y=2007.
53. Ibid.
54. Saud Al-Barakati, "Jail and Lashes for Misyar Woman," *Saudi Gazette*, August 17,
2009, http://www.saudigazette.com.sa/index.cfm?method=home.regcon&con-
tentID=2009081746995.
55. Ibid.
56. Fakih, "Misyar Marriage Enrages Gulf Women."
57. Adel, "Married or Maybe Not," *Al-Ahram Weekly.*
58. "Pleasure Marriages," *Women24.*
59. Shahine, "Illegitimate, Illegal or Just Ill-Advised?"
60. Thomas Mann, "Das Gesetz" [The tables of the law], in *Gesammelte Werke*
(Frankfurt/Main: Fischer, 1960), vol. viii, p. 756.
61. Amira K. Bennison, *The Great Caliphs: The Golden Age of the 'Abbasid Empire*
(New Haven, Conn.: Yale University Press, 2009), pp. 34–35.
62. Vern Bullough and Bonnie Vern, *Women and Prostitution* (New York:
Prometheus, 1987), pp. 75–76.

4. CHILD BRIDES

1. John R. Bradley, "Waking Up to the Bloody Threat in Southern Thailand," *The
Straits Times*, May 27, 2004, http://yaleglobal.yale.edu/content/waking-terror-
threat-southern-thailand.
2. "Indonesia V.P. Encourages Arabs to Pay for Temporary Marriages to Local
Women," Associated Press, June 28, 2006, http://www.foxnews.com/story/0,293
3,201533,00.html.
3. "Cleric Defiant Amid Controversy Over Marriage to 12-Year-Old Girl,"
Jakarta Post, October 25, 2008, http://www.thejakartapost.com/news/2008/
10/25/cleric-defiant-amid-controversy-overmarriage–12yearold-girl.html
?page=2.
4. P. K. Abdul Ghafour, "Temporary Marriages With Indonesian Women on Rise,"
Arab News, April 18, 2009, http://www.arabnews.com/?page=1&section=0
&article=121653&d=18&m=4&y=2009.
5. Ibid.
6. "Indonesia: Five Saudis Deported for Muslim 'Prostitution' Marriage," *Free Republic*, April 8, 2006, http://www.freerepublic.com/focus/f-news/1678183/posts.
7. Ghafour, "Temporary Marriages With Indonesian Women on Rise."
8. Mohammed Wajihuddin, "One Minor Girl, Many Arabs," *Times of India*, September 4, 2005, http://timesofindia.indiatimes.com/articleshow/1219601.cms?
headline=One~minor~girl,~many~Arabs~ .
9. Ibid.
10. "Egypt Battles 'Sex Tourism,' Bans 92-Year-Old From Marrying Teen," *Haaretz*,
June 14, 2008, http://www.haaretz.com/hasen/spages/992636.html.

11. Ibid.

12. Ibid.

13. "Child Marriage: What We Know," PBS, October 12, 2007, http://www.pbs.org/now/shows/341/facts.html.

14. The State of the World's Children 2009, UNICEF, 2009, http://www.unicef.org/sowc09/docs/SOWC09-ExecSummary-EN.pdf.

15. Anjum Ashraf Ali, "Child Marriage in Islamic Law" (Master's Thesis, McGill University, Canada, 2000), http://digitool.library.mcgill.ca/R/?func=dbin-jump-full&object_id=31082&local_base=GEN01-MCG02.

16. Ibid., pp. 18–19.

17. Ibid.

18. Ibid.

19. Ibid., p. 32.

20. Ibid., p. 40.

21. Paula Newton, "Child Bride Gets Divorced after Rape, Beatings," CNN, July 16, 2008, http://www.cnn.com/2008/WORLD/meast/07/15/yemen.childbride/index.html.

22. Borzou Daraghi, "Yemen Child Bride Nujood Ali Gets Divorce," *Los Angeles Times*, June 11, 2008, http://articles.latimes.com/2008/jun/11/world/fg-child-bride11?pg=1.

23. Paula Newton, "Child Bride's Nightmare After Divorce," CNN, August 26, 2009, http://www.cnn.com/2009/WORLD/meast/08/26/yemen.divorce/index.html.

24. Ibid.

25. Nicholas D. Kristoff, "Divorced Before Puberty," *New York Times*, March 3, 2010, http://www.nytimes.com/2010/03/04/opinion/04kristof.html.

26. Joshua Hersh, "A Ten-Year-Old's Divorce Lawyer," *New Yorker*, March 4, 2010, http://www.newyorker.com/online/blogs/newsdesk/2010/03/a-ten-year-olds-divorce-lawyer.html.

27. Ganny Hill, "Yemen Confronts Plight of Child Brides," *Christian Science Monitor*, August 22, 2008, http://www.csmonitor.com/World/Middle-East/2008/0822/p07s03-wome.html.

28. Ibid.

29. "Saudi Arabia: Young Girls Can Be Married," *Al-Bawaba*, January 14, 2009, http://www.albawaba.com/en/news/239350.

30. A. Faizur Rahman, "Justifying Child Abuse in the Name of Sharia," *Hindustan Times*, May 9, 2009, http://www.countercurrents.org/rahman110509.htm.

31. Ali, "Child Marriage in Islamic Law," p.122.

32. Mohammed Jamjoom, "Saudi Judge Refuses to Annul 8-Year-Old's Marriage," CNN, April 12, 2009, http://edition.cnn.com/2009/WORLD/meast/04/12/saudi.child.marriage/.

33. "Saudis 'to Regulate' Child Brides," BBC News, April 15, 2009, http://news.bbc.co.uk/2/hi/middle_east/7999777.stm.

34. "Saudi Arabia: Call for Legislation to Stop Saudi Child Marriages," Associated Press, August 7, 2008, http://www.wluml.org/node/4739.

35. "Saudi Studies Child Marriage Law: Report," Agence-France Press, April 22, 2009, http://www.google.com/hostednews/afp/article/ALeqM5gGshsijmNBBs-zvKr2zYlUXBwYcg.

36. Dennis Altman, *Global Sex* (Chicago: University of Chicago Press: 2001), p. 146.

37. Lindsay Goldwert, "Peru Lowers Age of Consent to Fourteen," Associated Press, June 22, 2007, http://www.cbsnews.com/stories/2007/06/22/world/main2970190.shtml.

5. PLEASURE ISLAND

1. Yaroslav Trofimov, "Upon Sober Reflection, Bahrain Reconsiders the Wages of Sin," *Wall Street Journal*, June 9, 2009, http://online.wsj.com/article/SB12445 0701841896319.html.

2. Mazen Mahdi, "Cars Torched as Manama Youth Riot Against Sale of Alcohol," *Arab News*, March 19, 2004, http://www.arabnews.com/?page=4&section=0& article=41500&d=19&m=3&y=2004; Sosebee, Stephen J.: "Arrests, Fatal Fire Bombing, Execution Raise the Stakes in Bahrain Unrest," *Washington Report on Middle East Affairs*, July 1996, http://www.wrmea.com/backissues/0796/96070 60.htm.

3. Trofimov, "Upon Sober Reflection, Bahrain Reconsiders the Wages of Sin."

4. Essam Al-Ghalib, "New U.S. Visa 'Prostitute' Query Shocks Saudis," *Arab News*, August 12, 2003, http://www.arabnews.com/?page=1&section=0&article=30191 &d=12&m=8&y=2003.

5. Ibid.

6. Ibid.

7. For example, see Zainy Abbas, "Makkah Police Raid Hide-Out of Prostitutes," *Arab News*, April 14, 2006; Badea Abu Al-Naja, "Prostitution Ring Busted," *Arab News*, June 25, 2007, http://www.arabnews.com/?page=1&section=0&article= 121003&d=31&m=3&y=2009.

8. Najah Alosaimi, "Web Newspaper Charged With Defamation," *Arab News*, May 2, 2009, http://arabnews.com/?page=1&section=0&article=122106&d=2&m=5 &y=2009.

9. Julanne McCarthy, "Bahrain," in Robert T. Francoeur and Raymond J. Noonan, eds., *Continuum Complete Encyclopedia on Sexuality* (New York: Continuum, 2004), p. 76.

10. John R. Bradley, *Saudi Arabia Exposed: Inside a Kingdom in Crisis* (New York: Palgrave Macmillan, 2005), pp. 6–10.

11. "One of Our Traditional Industries," *Babbling Bahrania*, January 25, 2005, http://bahraniat.blogspot.com/2005/01/one-of-our-traditional-industries .html.

12. Francoeur and Noonan, *Continuum Complete Encyclopedia on Sexuality*, p. 76.

13. Andrew Higgins, "Royal Flush: After High Hopes, Democracy Project in Bahrain Falters," *Wall Street Journal*, May 11, 2005, http://www.bahrainrights .org/en/node/270.

14. Ibid.

15. Wassayos Ngamkham, "Bangkok Post: Police Launch Bahrain Sex Probe," Bahrain Center for Human Rights, http://www.bahrainrights.org/en/node/872.

16. "Top 10: Sin Cities," AskMen.com, http://www.askmen.com/top_10/travel/top–10-sin-cities.html.

17. Mohammed Al-A'ali, "Police Reject 'Vice Mafia' Link Claims," *Gulf Daily News*, February 20, 2009, http://www.gulf-daily-news.com/NewsDetails.aspx?story id=243535.

18. Ibid.

19. Ibid.

20. Habib Toumi, "No Market for Prostitution in Bahrain, Official Says," *Gulf News*, February 16, 2009, http://gulfnews.com/news/gulf/bahrain/no-market-for-prostitution-in-bahrain-official-says–1.51838.

21. "Police in Bahrain Crack Down on Prostitutes," *Al-Arabiya*, April 4, 2009, http://www.alarabiya.net/articles/2009/04/04/69881.html.

22. Suad Hamada, "Involvement of Bahraini Girls in Prostitution Sparks Outrage," *Women Gateway*, February 2009, http://www.womengateway.com/enwg/News/2009/Feb/mainNews1en.htm.
23. Ibid.
24. Ibid.
25. Toumi, "No Market for Prostitution in Bahrain, Official Says."
26. Ibid.
27. Ibid.
28. Ibid.
29. http://www.byshr.org/.
30. See, for example, Rebecca Torr, "Cyber War on Sex Trafficking," *Gulf Daily News*, August 19, 2007, http://www.gulf-daily-news.com/NewsDetails.aspx?storyid=191055.
31. In late 2009, a Bahraini Islamist member of parliament essentially said the same thing: "Some hotels and furnished apartments are above the law as they are owned by VIPs, which means that they continue going on with their actions under the nose of police and tourism inspectors, without anything being done." See "Hotels Vice Probe Ordered by MPs," *Gulf Daily News*, December 23, 2009, http://www.tmcnet.com/usubmit/2009/12/23/4546958.htm.
32. "Present Strength, Future Directions," Bahraini TV, June 23, 2009, http://bahraini.tv/2009/06/23/present-strength-future-directions/.

6. MORAL PANIC

1. "Women of Southern Yemen Port Remember Better Times," Reuters, January 27, 2010, http://www.reuters.com/article/idUSTRE60L2ZD20100122.
2. Frederick Mercer Hunter, *An Account of the British Settlement of Aden in Arabia* (1877; London: Routledge, new ed. 1968), p. 146. See also Peter Pickering, "Prostitutes," Aden Airways website, August 28, 2008, http://www.adenairways.com/Prostitution.htm.
3. *An Account of the British Settlement of Aden in Arabia*, op. cit, p. 146.
4. Deniz Kandiyoti, *Women, Islam, and the State* (Philadelphia, Penn.: Temple University Press, 1991), p. 251.
5. I am grateful to Peter Pickering for providing me with this information by email, which he has gleaned from message boards on his website: www.AdenAirways.com.
6. Nefissa Naguib, *Interpreting Welfare and Relief in the Middle East* (Boston: Brill, 2007), p. 132.
7. For example, see John R. Bradley, "A Warning From Yemen, Cradle of the Arab World," *The Daily Star* (Lebanon), July 13, 2004, http://www.dailystar.com.lb/article.asp?edition_id=10&categ_id=5&article_id=6182.
8. John R. Bradley, "Saada Dispatch: Bad Fences," *New Republic*, February 19, 2004, http://www.selvesandothers.org/article6522.html.
9. "U.S. Kills Al-Qaeda Suspects in Yemen," Associated Press, May 11, 2002, http://www.usatoday.com/news/world/2002-11-04-yemen-explosion_x.htm; Frank Gardner, "Yemen's New Anti-Terror Strategy," BBC News, December 16, 2003, http://news.bbc.co.uk/2/hi/middle_east/3326121.stm; Damien McElroy, "U.S. Special Forces Train Yemen Army as Arab State Becomes Al-Qaeda 'Reserve Base'," *London Telegraph*, December 13, 2009, http://www.telegraph.co.uk/news/worldnews/middleeast/yemen/6803120/US-special-forces-train-Yemen-army-as-Arab-state-becomes-al-Qaeda-reserve-base.html.
10. "They Want Us Exterminated," Human Rights Watch, August 16, 2009, http://www.hrw.org/en/node/85049/section/5.

11. bin Sallam, Mohammed: "Preliminary Court Convicts 30 Suspects of Prostitution," *Yemen Times*, April 4, 2005, http://yementimes.com/article.shtml?i=830&p=local&a=5.
12. Ibid.
13. Alia Ishaq and Emad Al-Sakkaf, "Saudi-Style Volunteer Virtue Patrols Scour Hodeidah for 'Sinners,'" *Yemen Times*, August 12, 2009, http://www.yementimes.com/DefaultDET.aspx?i=1169&p=report&a=1.
14. Hakim Almasmari, "Gulf Tourists: Are They People of Lust and Corruption?" *Yemen Times*, August 29, 2005, http://yementimes.com/defaultdet.aspx?SUB_ID=21913.
15. "Sex Trade Fueled by Poverty, Study Finds," IRIN, November 17, 2005, http://www.irinnews.org/report.aspx?reportid=25703.
16. Ibid.
17. "Sex Trade Fueled by Poverty, Study Finds."
18. Jalal Al-Sharabi, "Yemen's Religious Police Target Massage Parlors," Al-Arabiya, July 15, 2009, http://www.alarabiya.net/articles/2009/07/15/78826.html.
19. Ibid.
20. "U.S. Imam Wanted in Yemen Over Al-Qaeda Suspicions," Associated Press, November 11, 2009, http://www.asharq-e.com/news.asp?section=1&id=18774.
21. Daniel Golden, "Western Scholars Play Key Role in Touting 'Science' of the Quran," *Wall Street Journal*, January 23, 2002, http://www.weatheranswer.com/public/wstjournal%20012302.txt.
22. Anita Singh, "Charles Darwin Film 'Too Controversial for Religious America,'" *The Daily Telegraph*, September 11, 2009, http://www.telegraph.co.uk/news/worldnews/northamerica/usa/6173399/Charles-Darwin-film-too-controversial-for-religious-America.html.
23. Ginny Hill, "Yemen Divided on Vice and Virtue," BBC News, August 11, 2008, http://news.bbc.co.uk/2/hi/7546907.stm.
24. Andrew McGregor, "Stand-Off in Yemen: The Al-Zindani Case," Jamestown Foundation, March 7, 2006, http://www.jamestown.org/single/?no_cache=1&tx_ttnews[tt_news]=692.
25. Al-Sharabi, "Yemen's Religious Police Target Massage Parlors."
26. Hill, "Yemen Divided on Vice and Virtue."
27. Al-Sharabi, "Yemen's Religious Police Target Massage Parlors."
28. Ishaq and Al-Sakkaf, "Saudi-Style Volunteer Virtue Patrols Scour Hodeidah for 'Sinners.'"
29. Ibid.
30. Hill, "Yemen Divided on Vice and Virtue."

7. VEILS AND VICES

1. The Moroccan press gave all of the women pseudonyms, and I am using them in this chapter.
2. Paul Belien, "Avenging Muslims Seek to Kill Belgian Journalist," *Brussels Journal*, July 13, 2005, http://www.brusselsjournal.com/node/66.
3. Ibid.
4. Anissa Herrou, "Secrets of Prostitution in an Islamic Kingdom," Afrik.com, November 18, 2008, http://en.afrik.com/article14904.html.
5. Belien, "Avenging Muslims Seek to Kill Belgian Journalist."
6. Ibid.
7. Ibid.

8. Laetitia Grotti, "Sexe, mensonges et CD à Agadir," *Jeune Afrique*, September 26, 2005, http://www.jeuneafrique.com/Article/LIN25105sexemridaga0/Sexe-mensonges-et-CD-a-Agadir.html.

9. Karim Bukhari, "Rumeurs. Peur sur la ville," *TelQuel*, June 26, 2005, http://www.telquel-online.com/177/couverture_177_1.shtml.

10. Karim Boukhari, "Scandale porno d'Agadir. Sur la piste du coupable," *TelQuel*, June 19, 2005, http://www.telquel-online.com/180/sujet1.shtml.

11. Belien, "Avenging Muslims Seek to Kill Belgian Journalist."

12. Karim Boukhari,: "Scandale porno d'Agadir. Les confessions de Servaty," *TelQuel*, July 2, 2005, http://www.telquel-online.com/183/actu_183.shtml.

13. "Philippe Servaty, le pornographe belge d'Agadir," *Infos du Maroc*, June 21, 2005, http://www.infosdumaroc.com/modules/news/article-print–139.html.

14. Marc Metdepenningen, "Agadir: les regrets du touriste belge," *Le Soir*, June 29, 2005, http://archives.lesoir.be/agadir-les-regrets-du-touriste-belge_t–20050629–000F4N.html.

15. Karim Boukhari, "Enquête. Pornographie et abus de confiance," *TelQuel*, July 9, 2005, http://www.telquel-online.com/177/couverture_177_1.shtml.

16. Marc Metdepenningen, "Justice Pornographe d'Agadir : la mémoire défaillante des députés bruxellois," *Le Soir*, March 14, 2007, http://archives.lesoir.be/justice-pornographe-d-agadir-la-memoire-defaillante_t–20070323–00A2H3.html?query=servaty&firstHit=0&by=10&sort=datedesc&when=–1&queryor=servaty&pos=3&all=2623&nav=1.

17. Boukhari, "Scandale porno d'Agadir. Sur la piste du coupable."

18. Boukhari, "Enquête. Pornographie et abus de confiance."

19. Ibid.

20. Belien, "Avenging Muslims Seek to Kill Belgian Journalist."

21. Bourhari, "Enquête. Pornographie et abus de confiance."

22. Belien, "Avenging Muslims Seek to Kill Belgian Journalist."

23. Ibid.

24. Ibid.

25. Boukhari, "Scandale porno d'Agadir. Sur la piste du coupable."

26. Ali Al-Ahmed and Logan Barclift, "After Sultan: Saudi Crown Prince Incapacitation Trigger Instability of Absolute Monarchy," *The Gulf Institute*, April 28, 2008, http://www.gulfinstitute.org/artman/publish/publications_policybriefs/After_Sultan_Saudi_Crown_Prince_Incapacitation_Tri_104.shtml.

27. See, for example, "Saudi King Abdullah Visits Crown Prince Sultan in Agadir," *Asharq Al-Awsat*, July 24, 2009, http://www.asharq-e.com/news.asp?section=1&id=17535.

28. "Morocco Clamps Down on Sex Tourism," *Morocco Times*, August 5, 2005, http://www.morocco.com/forums/open-board-forum-libre/22646-alert-will-moroccans-do-anything-better-life-europe-even-sell-themselves–6.html.

29. Boukhari, "Scandale porno d'Agadir. Les confessions de Servaty."

30. Intissar Fakir, "Make-Believe Reforms in Morocco," *The Guardian*, September 17, 2009, http://www.guardian.co.uk/commentisfree/2009/sep/17/morocco-monarchy-democracy-security.

31. In the 2008 Arab public opinion poll for the Anwar Sadat Chair for Peace and Development at the University of Maryland, conducted in conjunction with Zogby International, only 10 percent said they agreed with Al-Qaeda's "methods of operation," while 21 percent said they did "not sympathize at all" with the terror outfit. See: http://www.brookings.edu/topics/~/media/Files/events/2008/0414_middle_east/0414_middle_east_telhami.pdf.

32. Andrew Hussey, "Tipping Point of Terror," *The Observer*, April 2, 2004, http://www.guardian.co.uk/world/2004/apr/04/magazine.features7/print.

33. Blayne Slabbert, "Moroccan Opposition Fights Back," *The National*, August 24, 2008, http://www.thenational.ae/article/20080824/FOREIGN/511987762/1017/NEWS&Profile=1017.

34. Hussey, "Tipping Point of Terror."

35. Slabbert, "Moroccan Opposition Fights Back."

36. Tom Pfeiffer and Zakia Abdennebi, "Liberals and Islamists Clash Over Morocco 'Gay Wedding,'" Reuters, March 13, 2008, http://www.reuters.com/article/idUSL0581448520080313.

37. Daan Bauwens, "New Law, but the Same Old Men," Inter Press Service, June 30, 2009, ipsnews.net/news.asp?idnews=47895.

38. Zakia Abdennebi, "Threats Won't Stop Moroccan Aiding Unwed Mothers," Reuters, November 30, 2008, http://www.reuters.com/article/idUSGEE5AP2BJ.

39. Ibid.

40. Ibid.

41. Walter G. Andrews and Mehmet Kalpakh, *The Age of Beloveds* (Durham, N.C.: Duke University Press, 2005), p. 17.

42. Dror Ze'evi, *Producing Desire: Changing Sexual Discourse in the Ottoman Middle East, 1500–1900* (Berkeley: University of California Press, 2006), p. 87.

43. Murray, *Islamic Homosexualities*, p. 88.

44. Khaled El-Rouhayeb, *Before Homosexuality in the Arab-Islamic World, 1500–1800* (Chicago: University of Chicago Press, 2005), p. 133.

45. Ibid., p. 135.

46. Ibid., p.153.

47. Ze'evi, *Producing Desire*, p. 92.

48. Ibid., p. 93.

49. El-Rouhayeb, *Before Homosexuality*, p. 71.

50. See *Saudi Arabia Exposed* (New York: Palgrave Macmillan, 2005), pp. 153–63, and *Inside Egypt* (New York: Palgrave Macmillan, 2008), pp. 191–200.

51. John R. Bradley, "Saudi Gays Flaunt New Freedoms," *The Independent*, February 20, 2004, http://www.independent.co.uk/news/world/middle-east/saudi-gays-flaunt-new-freedoms-straights-cant-kiss-in-public-or-hold-hands-like-us-570584.html.

52. Abderrafii Aloumliki, "Réveillon pédophile à Marrakech," *Aujourd'hui Le Maroc*, February 19, 2002, http://www.aujourdhui.ma/societe-details9267.html.

53. "Acquittement d'un Irlandais poursuivi pour pédophilie," Bladi, November 30, 2007, http://www.bladi.net/acquitement-irlandais-pedophilie.html.

54. M'Hamed Hamrouch, "Marrakech: un réseau porno démantelé," *Aujourd'hui Le Maroc*, February 21, 2006, http://www.aujourdhui.ma/?mod=LireArticle&rub=societe&ref=43931.

55. "Sex Tourism on the Rise in Morocco," *Agoravox*, November 15, 2006, http://www.agoravox.com/news/society/article/sex-tourism-on-the-rise-in-morocco–4948.

56. "Moroccan 'Bride' Detained for Gay Wedding," Al-Arabiya, November 27, 2007, http://www.alarabiya.net/articles/2007/11/27/42200.html.

57. Murray, *Islamic Homosexualities*, pp. 37–41.

58. Tom Pfeiffer, "Liberals and Islamists Clash Over Morocco 'Gay Wedding," Reuters, March 13, 2008, http://www.reuters.com/article/idUSL0581448520080313.

59. Ibid.

60. Murray, *Islamic Homosexualities*, p. 28.

61. Ibid., p. 46.

62. Joseph A. Massad, *Desiring Arabs* (Chicago: University of Chicago Press, 2007), p. 53.

63. El-Rouhayeb, *Before Homosexuality*, p. 158.
64. Massad, *Desiring Arabs*, p. 172.
65. Ibid. p. 188.
66. Ibid., p. 184.
67. Boukhari, "Portrait. Homosexuel Envers en contre tous," *TelQuel*, June 18, 2007, http://www.telquel-online.com/277/couverture_277.shtml.
68. "Interview with Abdellah Taia," *Al-Bab*, January, 2009, http://www.al-bab.com/arab/articles/abdellah_taia_salvation_army.htm.
69. Jeremy Seabrook, Love in a Different Climate (London: Verso, 1999), p. 5.
70. "Gay Bullying in Schools 'Common'," BBC News, June 26, 2007, http://news.bbc.co.uk/2/hi/uk_news/education/6239098.stm; Wendy Berliner, "Gay in Silence," *The Guardian*, October 2, 2001, http://www.guardian.co.uk/education/2001/oct/02/schools.uk3.
71. Johann Hari, "Alan Bennett and the Question of Innocence," *The Independent*, November 27, 2009, http://www.independent.co.uk/opinion/commentators/johann-hari/johann-hari-alan-bennett-and-the-question-of-innocence-1828408.html.
72. Ibid.
73. "The Guide Interviews Camille Paglia," *The Guide*, January, 1999, http://www.ipce.info/library_2/files/paglia_guide.htm.

CONCLUSION

1. Chris Bull and John Gallagher, *Perfect Enemies: The Religious Right, the Gay Movement, and the Politics of the 1990s* (New York: Crown, 1996), p. 21.
2. Abdelwahab Bouhdiba, *Sexuality and Islam* (London: Saqi, 2001), p. 193.

INDEX